GETTING INTO
BUSINESS
SCHOOL

100 Proven Admissions Strategies
to Get You Accepted at the MBA
Program of Your Choice

3RD EDITION

BRANDON ROYAL

MAVEN

Maven Publishing

Published by:

Maven Publishing
4520 Manilla Road, Calgary, Alberta
Canada T2G 4B7
www.mavenpublishing.com

Library and Archives Canada Cataloguing in Publication:

Royal, Brandon, author
Getting into business school : 100 proven admissions strategies to get you accepted at the mba program of your choice / Brandon Royal.

Includes index. Issued in print and electronic formats.

ISBN 978-1-897393-80-2 (paperback)
ISBN 978-1-897393-82-6 (ebook)

1. Business schools--Admission.
2. Master of business administration degree.
3. Business education. I. Title.

HF1111.R69 2010   650.071'1   C2010-900320-9

Library of Congress Control Number: 2009909358

Technical Credits:

Cover Design: George Foster, Fairfield, Iowa, USA
Editing: Rosa Cays, Tempe, Arizona, USA

This book's cover text was set in Minion. The interior text was set in Scala and Scala Sans.

GMAT® is a registered trademark of the Graduate Management Admission Council, which neither sponsors nor endorses this product.

CONTENTS

Introduction

*If you don't know where you are going
you might wind up someplace else.*
—Yogi Berra

The MBA degree is the world's most versatile advanced education credential. With it you can rise in the ranks of the corporate world, start your own business, or go into government or not-for-profit work. An MBA is a highly transferable degree and, unlike law, medicine, accounting, or engineering, which may place quotas on the number of professionals that practice in a given region or country, there are no restrictions placed on the number of practicing businesspersons holding graduate business degrees.

The business school marketplace is both a buyer's market and a seller's market. With some 2,000 programs currently existing worldwide, and with more institutions offering an MBA degree every year, the good news is that if you just want to get an MBA you will have no problem doing so. However, for the majority of informed applicants reading this book who desire, and perhaps insist, on going to a top-tier, full-time MBA program, the equation is altered. Competition to get into the best full-time business schools is significant, with an acceptance rate hovering around 20 percent or less. You won't be alone in applying to the world's leading business programs and knowledge of as many proven strategies and tips will be essential to help successfully navigate the process.

Your Key to Applying to Business School

What would you pick as the *major* reason for rejection by a top business school?

A)   A candidate applies late rather than early.
B)   A candidate has minimal work experience.
C)   A candidate makes a number of grammatical errors in his or her application essays.
D)   A candidate has a poor admissions interview.
E)   A candidate has a "low" GMAT score.

This is a revealing question, but also a trick question. The answer is both all of the above and none of the above. It is all of the above in that the admissions process is holistic and it is difficult to isolate one particular factor as the key for rejection. It is also none of the above as none of the answers are likely correct in terms of the *major* reason for rejection. Each of these answer choices plays upon a common misconception about the admissions process. Students who assume choice A is correct make the assumption that their application is a "winner," but just late. This is a big assumption. Choice B might be true in some cases, but certainly not true in the majority of cases where applicants have sufficient work experience—usually two to five years—for the purpose of competing for a place in a full-time, one- or two-year program.

Candidates who choose choice C are likely confusing grammatical accuracy with the more important topic of essay content. Strategically correct writing combines what you write (content) and the order in which you write it (structure), which is more important than grammar, particularly for international candidates whose first language is not English. Choice D, a poor admissions interview, is also less likely to be *the* major reason. The trend in interviewing is to make cuts based on an initial review of business school applications, then offer interviews to a select number of applicants. Since most candidates will not make this cut, the interview will not be the major reason for rejection. Students choosing choice E probably underestimate the range of GMAT scores accepted at top schools. While it is true that the average GMAT score of successful candidates applying to top schools has increased significantly in the last decade, for an insight into the range of scores accepted, you may want to review the answer to question 13 in *Chapter 2*.

The answer to this question is none of the above as there is another choice not presented, which is more likely to be the major reason most individuals get rejected by top business schools. Approximately 50 percent of all candidates applying to top business schools fail because they cannot communicate concrete or well-defined career goals; in particular, as demanded by the "career goals" application essay. Business schools are impressed by candidates who know where they are going and have a clear idea of how they are going to get there. Consequently, this topic is of paramount importance and is addressed specifically in *Chapter 3*, under the topic of goal and vision statements.

A Word About Diversity

One of the biggest areas of interest for the international applicant is how to leverage international experience—professional and educational—in the application process. Business schools seek international applicants and prize applicants with international experience. Possessing geographically rich or unusual personal and professional experiences can be key to getting accepted by a top business school. This book provides many tips on how you can use your background to make yourself appear as a one-of-a-kind applicant.

Today's leading business schools make a real effort to support underrepresented groups in the admissions process. But rather than endorse specific strategies aimed at minority or international candidates, this book resolves to look at all candidates as unique in themselves and thus on equal footing. The words "international" or "minority" are slowly losing their significance because we live in a world that is increasingly multicultural. In the U.S., for example, international students comprise 30 percent of a typical high-profile business school class. That does not, however, imply that the other 70 percent of a typical U.S. business school class is homogeneous in makeup—regardless of how diversity is defined. Although 70 percent of an American business school class might be American, this could include Asian-Americans, African-Americans, Hispanic-Americans, native American Indians, or newly arrived U.S. immigrants from every conceivable geographical location. The same is true of international students, who although holding foreign passports, might represent a cross-section of different ethnic backgrounds.

The playing field for international applicants is being leveled. This means that it is mattering less, not more, where you come from. The days are disappearing when you could bet on an acceptance letter just because of your country of citizenship, your ethnic background, or your international travel experience. In years past, for example, if you were an applicant who had graduated from Moscow State University or Beijing University, you could count on being accepted by most top business schools. Nowadays, admissions officers are seeing many applicants from places considered unusual in the past. It is much harder to play the "take-me, I'm-from-a-strange-and-unusual-place" card. Every candidate should first think in terms of presenting him- or herself on the basis of his or her own merits, including intelligence, passion, personality, hard work, ingenuity, and dedication.

What Does This Book Cover?

MBA admissions is a process that covers the interplay of seven primary application components: (1) GMAT, (2) college transcripts, (3) résumé or employment record, (4) letters of recommendation, (5) interviews, (6) extracurricular activities, and (7) application essays. A common practice is to view the seven application components as divided between quantitative and qualitative elements. Whereas GPA (Grade Point Average) and GMAT are considered to be the "number side" of the admissions process, the résumé, letters of recommendation, interviews, essays, and extracurricular involvement are the qualitative side of the process. Although this book covers all of the seven application components, only light coverage is given to the "numbers" side of the admissions process. The GMAT is an intensive but completely separate undertaking. GPA, as reflected by college transcripts, is generally set before a person applies to business school and cannot be changed.

In short, MBA admissions strategies are focused on the "qualitative" aspects of the MBA admissions process—the ones over which you exercise significant control in terms of content and presentation. These strategies are aimed at helping each candidate write excellent application essays, present a strong employment record, get good letters of recommendation, embellish extracurricular involvement or community service, and prepare for interviews, when required.

The thrust of this book addresses the qualitative side of the MBA admissions process, with a focus on application essays. *Chapter 3* is an anchor chapter for addressing the four classic essays and highlighting common weaknesses and winning approaches for completing each of these four essay types. Sample essays are included to illustrate how these approaches are applied in practice. *Chapter 4* presents a discussion of the other commonly encountered MBA essay types and, again, includes sample essays for each type.

The ability to write optional essays, as covered in *Chapter 5,* could be a deciding factor in your being accepted by a business school. The answer to the question, "Is there anything else you would like the admissions committee to know?" lends itself to five separate uses. Very few prospective candidates are so stellar that they are without anticipated weaknesses. The secret here lies in both neutralizing any anticipated weakness and in emphasizing the strengths and diversity of your background. Writing optional essays can be a key step in doing both of these things. Finally, the employment record, letters of recommendation, interview, and extracurricular activities are each covered in separate chapters.

This book is a compilation of real-life experiences of students applying to top business schools. The road to building an exceptional business school application can be exhausting, but it can also be energizing. Once you master one application, it is easier to cut and paste your previous work to complete similar parts of other MBA applications. The time spent on applications will repay itself by getting you accepted by a "top" business school—the business school of your choice—and by taking you to the next stage of your career.

This is your workbook. Follow the practice of writing in this paperback book while you are making your review. Pencil your ideas and comments in the margins and you'll be less likely to forget them when sitting down to complete your essays and application package.

Chapter 1

What are Schools *Really* Looking For?

I would never join any club that
would have me as a member.
—Groucho Marx

Overview

The goal of the admissions committee (often times called "adcom") is to recruit the best students. Every school defines "best" a little differently, but in general, the following three things hold true. Business schools are looking for

1. Applicants with the best career potential and leadership ability;
2. Applicants with the best background and preparation, including academic, professional, and personal experience;
3. Applicants with the greatest need for getting an MBA, including the most compelling reasons for attending a particular school's graduate business program.

The admissions committee has an enormous responsibility with regard to selecting its students. Ideally, every school hopes to get students who are leadership minded and technically competent, focused and articulate yet personable and team oriented, and are able to contribute to their schools as students and alumni, and willing to give back something to their communities and societies.

To evaluate these things, admissions officers are said to summarize an applicant's candidacy by looking at "who you are" and "what you have done" and "where you are going" with your career, as well as why you want an MBA and why you want to attend a particular MBA program. Who you are likely translates to your being a person of good character with an interesting personality. What you have done translates to solid academic and professional achievements, including your accomplishments, awards, and recognition. Where you are going with your career translates into having reasonably clear career goals and, hopefully, the vision to articulate where your chosen industry is headed.

Another way to think about what schools are looking for is to view your background as a triumvirate of academic, professional, and personal experiences. Your academic background may be presented through your college transcripts, academic recommendation(s) (if applicable), and GMAT score. Your professional background may be presented through your résumé and professional letters of recommendation. Your personal qualities and background may be seen in all parts of the admissions process, but particularly through your interviews, extracurriculars, and application essays.

Although top schools are hoping to find ideal candidates, the perfect candidate does not really exist. Most candidates are weak in one or more areas. This is where the game of admissions begins—you will try to emphasize your strengths while minimizing your weaknesses. The admissions committee will try to pick the best candidates knowing it cannot find "perfect" candidates.

Obviously your primary goal as an applicant is to get accepted to the business school of your choice. To do this, you must show at a minimum that

1. You have a noble goal and a real need for an MBA;
2. You can explain in a reasonably clear way how you will accomplish your career goal and how your background and experiences act as stepping stones toward this goal;
3. You have sufficient experience, intellect, and passion to compete for your goal.

What is the ultimate goal for an applicant to achieve in the process of applying to a business school? Answer: To present an application that is so compelling that the admissions committee would believe that failure to accept you would cause the incoming class to be something less than what it would otherwise be. The good news is that most successful applicants cannot clear this threshold, so there no need to become preoccupied with meeting this criterion. In fact, most successful candidates are likely to have shown only that they are well prepared, sufficiency focused individuals with reasonably interesting backgrounds.

The first goal of the applicant: "To reveal a noble goal and a need for an MBA."

What is a "noble" goal? A noble goal is essentially any goal that you deem worthwhile to pursue and that will enable you to contribute to your future organization and society. Thus, the goal of becoming an investment banker is deemed to be equal to the goal of becoming a missionary doctor in Thailand who needs business skills to open a chain of clinics. What does it mean to have a need for an MBA? You must show that an MBA is a necessary stepping stone toward your future goal. Often an MBA degree can be viewed as a missing piece to your career puzzle. An otherwise well-focused and qualified applicant might get rejected if his or her goal is already included in his or her background, and an MBA would not be needed to reach it. For example, "I work as a stockbroker and want an MBA to continue to work as a stockbroker." The admissions committee will likely wonder how an MBA will help you or, more precisely, if you really need an MBA as much as other applicants do. The MBA must be perceived as having a value-added quality equal to or greater than that of other competing candidates.

The second goal of the applicant: "To explain how your background and experience act as stepping stones to your future career goals."

Although you may have an interesting background, it is best that your future outlook be a logical extension of your background. If a person's background and previous training differ greatly from his or her intended career goal, the impression will be that the future goal is not realistic. That is, the goal my not be deemed impossible but arguably implausible. Naturally, your goal should be "bigger" than your background, or else you would not have the need to go to a top business school to gain the elevated knowledge, credential, contacts, and confidence. The feeling that an admissions person should come away with after reviewing your application is that of transition. There should be a sense that the applicant is reaching, perhaps straining, but not unduly leaping toward his or her future goal.

Candidates sometimes reason that because studying for an MBA is supposed to be a transformational experience, so too must their reasons for wanting an MBA be transformational, especially in terms of their career outlook. Of course, studying for an MBA requires that one first be admitted to an MBA program. Once you're in, you can continue to refine or reformat your career goals. For the purpose of getting *into* business school, it's best to err on the side of showing clear progression to your career goals.

The third goal of the applicant: "To show sufficient experience, intellect, and passion to compete for your goal."

The committee is concerned with getting students who can do their best, contribute the most, and not unduly burden themselves, professors, or classmates while doing so. "Numbers" (GPA and GMAT) are important, but beyond given thresholds, numerical comparisons become fruitless. In general, business schools reject students not because they think students cannot do the work but because competition for admission forces business schools to make choices. In fact, most applicants applying to business school would make it through an MBA program, albeit not all with excellent records. One piece of evidence to support this fact is how few students actually flunk out of business school despite significant variations in GPA and GMAT scores among the entering students. Note that business schools also have a vested interest in helping students succeed and generally do everything in their power to help enrolled business school students pass and graduate.

On another level, admissions personnel want to attract those people who aim to be leaders in their chosen fields. This will likely require the skills and gravitas beyond those required to get through business school. Having sufficient experience and intellect to compete for your career goals involves not only getting through business school but also reaching your mid- to long-term career goals. The higher, more difficult your goal, the more experience and intellect you will require to reach it.

The Seven MBA Application Components

A common practice is to view the seven components as divided into quantitative ("numbers") and qualitative components (see *Exhibit 1.1*). The numbers side consists of GMAT score and GPA. Note that the numbers side is not called the numbers side because it represents only math skills as opposed to verbal or writing skills. It is called the numbers side because GMAT and GPA lends themselves to discrete measurement. The qualitative side does not lend itself to such discrete measurement.

The Order in Which Application Components are Reviewed

Application components are likely reviewed in the following order:

1. GMAT
2. College transcripts (GPA)
3. Résumé
4. Letters of recommendation
5. Interview results (if applicable)
6. Extracurricular activities
7. Application essays

Moving from quantitative to qualitative information is both simple and logical. First, your GMAT score and college transcripts are reviewed. Your GMAT score and GPA are easily quantifiable components that show up on the data input sheet, which is the first page or two of your application. Second, your résumé or employment record is reviewed. It is, after all, "business school." The reviewer will be curious to see where you have worked and the caliber of your work experience. Professional letters of recommendation will be perused after a review of your résumé because of the complementary nature of these two application components. Admissions officers will first seek to understand the nature of your work experience before going on to interpret what your recommenders have said about you and your experience. The same is true for academic letters of recommendation, when applicable, in which college transcripts are reviewed first before going on to interpret what your instructor or professor has written about you.

Interview results, if applicable, will be reviewed next. Interview appraisals are short documents, usually one page in length, and will be reviewed before your essays are read. Extracurriculars come next and essays are reviewed last. Essays are both longer and more subjective than other components, but will give the reviewer a more holistic picture of who you are as a person and where you are heading professionally. The following synopsis of the admissions process proves revealing: Unless your numbers are incredibly high or abysmally low, the committee must read your essays to decide whether to accept or reject you. Put another way, your offer of acceptance or notice of rejection will generally always come down to the reading of your application essays. This is precisely the reason that so much emphasis is given to essay writing in this book.

EXHIBIT 1.1   THE SEVEN MBA APPLICATION COMPONENTS

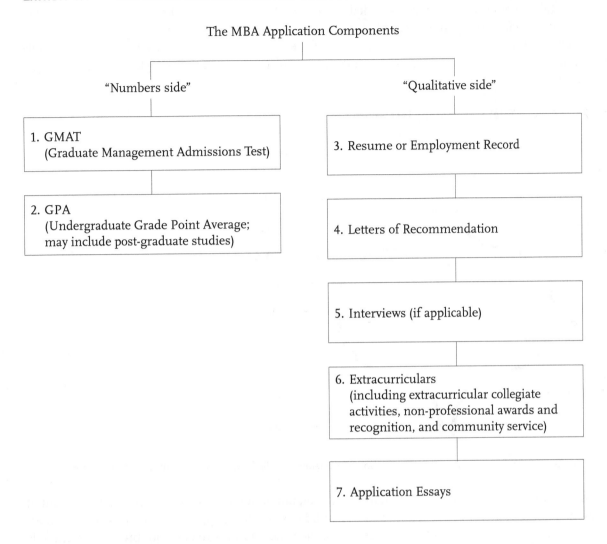

The MBA Application Components

"Numbers side"

1. GMAT
(Graduate Management Admissions Test)

2. GPA
(Undergraduate Grade Point Average;
may include post-graduate studies)

"Qualitative side"

3. Resume or Employment Record

4. Letters of Recommendation

5. Interviews (if applicable)

6. Extracurriculars
(including extracurricular collegiate
activities, non-professional awards and
recognition, and community service)

7. Application Essays

From the Number's Side—GMAT

The GMAT quantitative section contains two types of problems: Problem Solving and Data Sufficiency. Three types of problem make up the verbal side of the GMAT: Reading Comprehension, Critical Reasoning, and Sentence Correction. In addition, the GMAT contains a short writing exercise called the Analytical Writing Assessment (AWA) as well as a short section called Integrated Reasoning. Do not confuse the AWA essays that appear on the GMAT with your application (or admissions) essays required by each school, which are the focus of this book.

You actually receive five scores from taking the GMAT exam: (1) total (combined) score, (2) quantitative score, (3) verbal score, (4) AWA (Analytical Writing Assessment) score, and (5) Integrated Reasoning score. Your total score ranges from 200 to 800 and a corresponding percentile ranking on a scale of 0.0 percentile to the 99.9th percentile. Scores on individual quantitative and verbal sections range from 0 to 60 and are accompanied by a corresponding percentile rank. Your AWA score ranges from 0.0 to 6.0 while your Integrated Reasoning score ranges from 0 to 8. Both of these short sections are totally independent of your quantitative or verbal and/or total score.

Scores on the GMAT, like other standardized tests, increase geometrically as a test-taker scores better than the average test-taker. For example, it takes a scaled score of 620 to score in the 70th percentile and a scaled score of 700 to score in the 90th percentile. This means that an 80-point increase in scaled score moves you up by 20 percentile points. In layperson's terms, small differences in test performance can lead to relatively big increases in test scoring. This is one argument in favor of preparing for the test, including taking a GMAT test preparation course.

Exhibit 1.2   GMAT Total (Combined) Test Scores

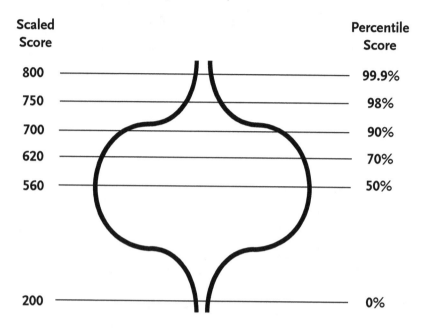

Source: GMAC.com – Percentages of examinees tested who scored below specified scores within a given period of time

Naturally, the higher your combined GMAT score the better, but generally, a scaled score of 700 (700 out of 800 corresponds to the 90th percentile) is what most candidates aim for if applying to top business schools. Although a high GMAT score does not guarantee acceptance and a low score does not preclude it, there is some credence given to the idea that everyone applying to a top business school is equal in the admissions process after scoring 700 or above. In other words, if you get rejected with a score of 700 or above, the problem lies not with your GMAT score but with another part of your application. In terms of applying to business school, particularly top business schools, admissions officers typically view GMAT combined scores as if divided into four arbitrary categories.

EXHIBIT 1.3   TRANSLATING YOUR GMAT SCORE

GMAT score	What this likely means
Less than 500	Not acceptable; take the test over again.
Between 500 to 600	Marginal; low for a top business school, although you could still get accepted.
Between 600 to 700	Below average/average; in the "ball park" for a top business school.
Greater than 700	Above average/excellent

From the Number's Side—GPA

GPA stands for Grade Point Average. Most U.S. schools grade on a 0.0 to 4.0 scale and will require the grades of students who have studied in international locations to be converted to a comparable scale. Academic transcripts are evaluated on three fronts:

- Reputation of your undergraduate institution
- Academic difficulty of your undergraduate major
- Actual Grade Point Average (GPA)

In other words, think of your academic transcripts as evaluated based on "where you studied," "what you took," and "what you got." Where you studied refers to the general strength and reputation of your undergraduate institution. What you took refers to the difficulty of the subject matter studied. Certain majors such as molecular biology are considered more academically rigorous than majors such as international relations. In addition to depth or intensity of your academic work, your breadth or variety of academic work (for example, dual majors, honors courses, special research) is taken into account. What you got refers to your overall GPA. Generally more emphasis is given to the GPA in your major, and/or your GPA trend (that is, it's better if third and fourth year GPA is higher than first and second year GPA).

In terms of applying to business school, admissions officers view GPAs as if divided into four arbitrary categories:

- Below 3.0—marginal
- Between 3.0 and 3.4—below average/average; in the running for top business schools
- 3.5 or higher—above average/excellent; includes honors standing, Phi Beta Kappa
- 3.8 to 4.0—highest standing (magna cum laude/summa cum laude)

For candidates whose undergraduate institutions do not have GPAs, some method of conversion must be done in order to express your GPA on a rough 0.0 to 4.0 scale. International applicants may want to contact the "academic transcript evaluator" at the school they are applying to. Basically, an A grade is considered 4.0, a B grade is considered 3.0, a C grade is considered 2.0. A potential problem may arise for international applicants who are applying to the U.S. with three-year undergraduate degrees rather than four-year degrees. You may want to cite an education report to substantiate your claim that a three-year degree is substitutable for a four-year degree. (Refer to the essay written by candidate Camilla in *Chapter 5*).

In both of the above-mentioned situations, you may need to contact the school you are applying to and determine what is needed to resolve the matter.

GMAT Scores vs. GPA

An apparent trade-off exists between GMAT scores and a candidate's GPA as obtained through undergraduate study. See *Exhibit 1.4* below. This analysis is hypothetical. In practice, admissions decisions are not based merely on comparing GMAT scores with GPA. But these two factors do give an indication of the strength of a candidate from the numbers side of the admissions process. The higher a candidate's GPA, the lower his or her GMAT score may be to still gain acceptance. Conversely, the higher a candidate's GMAT score, the lower his or her GPA may be to still gain acceptance. It is unclear whether business schools place more weight on the GMAT score relative to GPA or vice versa.

Exhibit 1.4   GMAT Scores vs. GPA at Top Business Schools

GMAT scores	GPA		
	Below 3.0 (marginal)	3.0 to 3.4 (average)	3.5 and above (above average)
500 to 590 (marginal)	No	No	Maybe
600 to 690 (below average/average)	No	Maybe	Yes
700 and above (above average/excellent)	Maybe	Yes	Yes

GMAT Scores vs. Quality of MBA Application Essays

A trade-off is also believed to exist between GMAT scores and the quality of MBA application essays. See *Exhibit 1.5* on the following page. In practice, essays cannot be contrasted merely with GMAT scores. GMAT scores are likely to be reviewed along with college transcripts for a "quantitative" measure of ability. Essays are likely to be reviewed along with employment record (résumé), letters of recommendation, extracurricular activities, and/or interviews for a "qualitative" measure of ability. There appears to be empirical evidence to support the idea that application essays carry more weight than the GMAT score in the admissions process. Assuming this to be true, an excellent set of essays with a low GMAT score (Maybe +) is closer to a yes than a high GMAT score with a mediocre set of application essays (Maybe –).

How Do Acceptance Rates Affect a Candidate's Admissions Chances?

Let's look at a few hypothetical scenarios in order to understand probable reasons why applicants get accepted and rejected by business schools as a function of falling acceptance rates. The summary contained in *Exhibit 1.6* is probably the closest we can come to applying analytics to the admissions process.

EXHIBIT 1.5   GMAT SCORES VS. QUALITY OF MBA APPLICATION ESSAYS

GMAT Scores	Application Essays		
	Marginal	Below average to average	Above average to excellent
500 to 590 (marginal)	No	No	Maybe (+)
600 to 690 (below average/average)	No	Maybe	Yes
700 and above (above average/excellent)	Maybe (−)	Yes	Yes

Ten Important Applications Tips

☞ *Tip #1:*   *Plan your attack and chart your progress.*

Applying to business school is not for the slothful; it takes a good deal of organization and perseverance. If you are applying to five or six schools, you will have many items to keep track of. It is recommended that you create a spreadsheet or label blank sheets accordingly. The formats depicted in *Exhibits 1.7–1.8* have been used by successful applicants. Duplicate forms are included for your convenience. See *Appendix VI: MBA Application Tracking Sheets.*

Exhibit 1.7 can help you keep track of the schools you are applying to and their pending application deadlines. The chart in *Exhibit 1.8* can be used to keep track of the items that go into the completing of your MBA application including college transcript requests, GMAT scores, letters of recommendation, interview dates, and application essays.

☞ *Tip #2:*   *Try to submit applications to all schools in a single round. If not, submit applications to "lesser" schools first.*

Try to first complete the applications for those schools that are not your very first choice. Candidates invariably improve on their ability to put together applications, including their ability to write effective essays, as the application process moves forward. You want to match your best applications with your most competitive schools. Too often, most candidates write and submit the essays of their first-choice schools right away, which often leaves the less competitive schools with a given candidate's best applications. Former applicants tell a similar story each year: "If I had to do it again, I would have applied to AAA school after first applying to BBB school…" This situation can be nullified if you start the application process early enough so that you finish all of your applications before sending off the first one, thus, ensuring that you have time to go back and incorporate changes into your previously completed applications. An alternative, more realistic approach is to send out your applications in batches of three. This way you can complete applications in "groups" and can incorporate positive changes in all applications before sending out any one of them.

EXHIBIT 1.6   REASONS FOR ACCEPTANCE OR REJECTION BY BUSINESS SCHOOLS

Acceptance rate	Reasons for acceptance or rejection
50% – One in two applicants gets accepted.	A candidate who fails to get accepted by a business school with a 50 percent acceptance rate generally has three or more weak areas in his or her application. For example, a low GPA and minimal work experience are further weakened by writing mediocre application essays. A likely reason that essays are mediocre commonly includes lack of a career focus or an inability on the part of the candidate to give adequate support using specific examples.
25% – One in four applicants gets accepted.	A candidate who succeeds in getting accepted by a business school with a 25 percent acceptance rate generally has two or fewer weak areas in his or her application. For example, a low GPA and weak letters of recommendation are nonetheless combined with a high GMAT score, a good résumé, a good interview record, as well as with well-written application essays, and evidence of extracurricular activities.
12% – One in eight applicants gets accepted.	A candidate who succeeds in getting accepted by a business school with a 12 percent acceptance rate generally has no more than one weak area in his or her application. For example, a low GPA is overshadowed by a high GMAT score, good résumé, strong letters of recommendation, a good interview, and solid application essays, including evidence of extracurricular activities and community service.
Less than 12% – Fewer than one in eight applicants gets accepted.	A candidate who succeeds in getting accepted by a business school with a less than 12 percent acceptance rate generally has no major application weak points and two or three outstanding application areas. For example, competitive GPA and GMAT scores are complemented by a particularly strong résumé and set of application essays. It is not necessarily correct to say, however, that the applicant is outstanding in all areas.

EXHIBIT 1.7   TRACKING SHEETS – APPLICATION DEADLINES

Universities	Berkeley	Chicago	Dartmouth	HBS	INSEAD	LBS	McGill
Rank (bw.com)	10	1	12	2	3	5	n/a
Application downloaded	✓	✓	✓	✓	✓	✓	✓
Fin. Aid. info.							
1st round	Nov 4	Oct 15	Oct 15	Oct 15	Oct 1	Oct 14	rolling
Reply	Jan 28	Dec 18	Dec 19	Jan 21	Dec 19	Dec 18	n/a
2nd round	Dec 9	Jan 7	Nov 12	Jan 6	Nov 26	Jan 6	n/a
Reply	Mar 18	Mar 25	Feb 6	Apr 2	Mar 6	Mar 31	May 1
Deposit req'd by							

EXHIBIT 1.8   TRACKING SHEETS – APPLICATION COMPONENTS

Universities	Berkeley	Chicago	Dartmouth	HBS	INSEAD	LBS	McGill
Transcripts sent	Nov 7	Nov 7	Nov 9	Nov 10	Nov 20	Nov 25	Nov 25
GMAT taken and scores sent	✓	✓	✓	✓	✓	✓	✓
1st recom.							
Rec'd. (or sent)							
2nd recom.							
Rec'd. (or sent)							
Essays okay							
Interviews scheduled							

🖝 *Tip #3:   Consider the need to retake the GMAT, but "protect" yourself against a lower score.*

Suppose you take the GMAT and achieve a score of 650. In one respect you're relieved because you know this is a decent score to use in applying to a top business school. On the other hand, based on scores you achieved on practice tests, you know you're capable of scoring 700. You have the time to take the test over and you want to, but you also would hate to score less than 650. What do you do? The strategy here is to first send your 650 score to all schools. It may be that you've already done so because, at the beginning of the actual GMAT exam, you're given the option of listing five recipient schools. Filling this information in means that the GMAC will automatically send your scores to any five schools free of charge (in addition to sending the score report directly to you).

You sign up to retake the test, but during the beginning of the exam, you do not list any recipient schools. At the end of that GMAT exam you'll see your unofficial score flashed on-screen at the end of the exam. If this score is equal to or greater than your new target score, have GMAC send these scores. If your score is not significantly greater than your target score, don't send the scores. Your score will now sit in the data bank of GMAC and not go anywhere. No one—no school—will ever know you took the test twice. Say you decide to take the test a third time (again don't list any recipient schools at the beginning of the exam). Voilà, you get the dream score you're looking for. Go ahead and get GMAC to send the score to all schools. It's true you'll have to pay US$28 per school to send these after the fact. It's also true that your final report will list all three scores, but at least the last score will appear. That's the important one for you, and schools, almost without exception, will take the highest score.

In short, GMAC will send all scores on file (actually your most recent five scores) whenever you request them to send the scores to any school. Whenever you take the GMAT for a second or third time, protect yourself against a lower score. Don't automatically get the score sent to the schools you are applying to if you risk scoring lower than your previous attempt and you don't want schools to be influenced by that score.

👉 *Tip #4:* *Decide on your career goal before asking any recommender for a recommendation and/or before undertaking any interview session.*

Resolve to complete your goal and vision statements before you write your essays or do anything else, including interviewing, given the option. You may want to refer to *Chapter 3* for clarification on the specifics of writing good goal statements and vision statements. Your goal and vision statements will directly affect the quality of your essays, and will indirectly affect all parts of your application, including your interviews and letters of recommendation. In short: A "goal statement" summarizes your career objectives; a "vision statement" summarizes where you think your chosen industry is headed and the special ideas you have on doing business in your chosen field. You may want to ask other people currently working in your company where they believe your chosen industry is headed. It never hurts to take a stroll past the magazine stand to see what trade magazines contain articles with information that sharpen your insights. Of course, on-line searches using Google, Bing, Yahoo, Ask, AOL, etc., will usually uncover up-to-date information about what is going on in your industry.

👉 *Tip #5:* *If you're undecided about your career direction, a good rule of thumb is to formulate a career goal that is primarily an extension of your current career path.*

If you're unable to support a career goal based on your current experience, consider applying to business school with the intention of continuing on with your current company or within your current industry. Say, for example, that you work for Citigroup as a customer relations officer. Your real reason for applying to business school has to do with wanting to try a career in investment banking. However, you know that based on your background, it's not easy to support the goal of investment banking, especially given the competition at the top business schools. Imagine seven other candidates with backgrounds similar to yours who are also applying to the same business schools. They state in the application that their goals are one of investment banking, venture capital, private equity, fund management, or management consulting. All things being equal, they'll get the spot because they'll come across as more focused; their positions in finance are more aligned to their chosen careers in high finance.

A better strategy for getting accepted would be to state that your goal is to become VP of Public Relations for Citigroup International. Now your goal is larger than your background, but also a logical extension of your background. You have shown both the need for an MBA, but also that your professional goal is believable. And make no mistake about it: It's often refreshing to see applicants who wish to do an MBA in order to reach higher levels within their current companies or industries. If in doubt, think about applying as a "bigger career version" of that which you already are.

☞ *Tip #6:*   *Write a response to the optional or "blank" question.*

Are you familiar with the question, "Is there anything else you would like the admissions committee to know?" Almost every business school has this question. Do not leave this area blank when given the choice to answer it. Plan to include one or two items in this section as extra material at the back of your application. The optional or "blank" question entry may be anything from the clarification of an anticipated weakness to a sample of your creative writing to a sample business document that you have worked on. Refer to *Chapter 5* for examples of the wide range of topics to write about.

☞ *Tip #7:*   *Build your application around a theme and think of yourself as a unique brand.*

Think of your application as tied to a theme. A theme may be used to link your work experience, as presented by your résumé or employment record, with your application essays and record of extracurricular activities. A theme is one way to express your uniqueness. It may assist the admissions committee in understanding why you are a person who is not only different, but who will make a difference. Building your application around a theme goes hand in hand with thinking of yourself as a unique brand. There are many clever ways to describe what exactly is a brand. Let's say that your personal brand is simply "how someone would describe you and, in terms of your application, what makes you distinctively different."

The most likely place to build a theme is around your chosen career path. Will you be an entrepreneur, consultant, banker, or marketer? Perhaps there is a general overall theme that characterizes your past, present, and future. A theme may tie to your background, skills, or talents. Are you also a star pianist, baseball aficionado, sports person, or fiction writer? Examine your background and find something that means a lot to you, perhaps a topic you're an expert on, around which you can build a theme. It is said that the admissions committees of major business schools enjoy being able to refer to a candidate in terms of a short, captivating phrase. For example: "That's the mathematics whiz who likes finance" ... "that's the female pianist turned management consultant" ... "that's the volunteer junkie who wants to do fashion merchandising." Think of yourself as a label or theme. For more on how to write your application essays around a theme, see Tip #12 in *Chapter 3*.

☞ *Tip #8:*   *Reality check—boil down the whole MBA process.*

The MBA admissions process may be thought of as boiling down to: (1) who you are, (2) what you have done, (3) where you are going, and (4) why a particular business program is right for you. Candidates sometimes get lost in the game of applying to business school. Certainly there are a number of valued tips of which you want to be aware and take advantage when putting together your application, but there is also a good deal of reality to the admissions process. The most important thing is to ask yourself, "Is the career goal I set for myself really true to me?" Say, for example, that you strive to be a venture capitalist. Stop and ask yourself, "Does my application feel like that of a venture capitalist? ... Is this goal coming like sweat out of my pores?" If not, then maybe you should choose another goal. In other words, often the problem with an individual's application is not with the writing of essays but rather with the person as he or she defines him- or herself. The sure-fire approach to setting up a winning application is for you to become one with the goal you seek. If you are not already like the person who would naturally succeed in a long-term career position, then start moving in this direction. Talk to people, join the clubs, read the magazines, and start thinking like the type of person who would be a leader in this field. Concentrate on *your* goal, not the one you think a business school would like to hear. Keep drawing a link between who you are, what you have done, and where you are going.

☞ *Tip #9:   Remember your target audience.*

Admissions staff members are the target audience and they are people persons. They are not necessarily businesspersons in the strict sense of the word. Besides being very good at the job they do, they look at things from a personal, human-interest perspective. They are especially moved by candidates whom they believe to be interesting and personable. Your ability to express the unique aspects of your candidacy will enhance your overall application.

☞ *Tip #10:   In a waitlist situation, write a strategic follow-up letter to support your candidacy.*

Imagine that you're a member of the admissions committee and you have two applicants on the waitlist with comparable backgrounds and experience. One candidate sends a short email, reiterating his or her interest in the school, and another writes a letter similar to the 1,200-word letter below. Anyone can appreciate the considerable effort required to draft a long, detailed letter. And this is precisely what moves that candidate closer to acceptance. The only thing that should be kept in mind is the letter should ideally present some new information and not simply rehash information already contained in your application file.

Dear Ms Taylor:

I am writing in response to your email dated March 15, 20xx. With respect to your recent waitlist decision, I would like to reiterate a few points that, unfortunately, may not have been fully articulated in my application or during the interview and which I feel could have proven critical to an initial, positive admissions decision.

My long-term career objective is to set up a continent wide-veterinary clinic system in Africa. In this respect I'll be assuming a role as leader, veterinary surgeon, entrepreneur, venture capitalist, and general manager employing thousands of people. In doing so, I need an MBA for a variety of reasons, one of the most important of which is to acquire the necessary specialist skills to identify the operational priorities, the organizational skills necessary for implementation, and the abilities to control financing structures necessary to sustain the program. I will need to engage individuals and seek funding from numerous sources for expansion purposes such as the IMF, World Bank, WTO, European Bank for Reconstruction and Development and various NGOs, and make speeches and presentations. Of crucial importance is the mobilization of a global network of expertise to participate in the project, including representations from scholars, UN agencies, other NGOs and the private sector.

Mobilizing science and technology, the backbone of the program, will require me to know how to involve partnerships of the public and private sector, both locally and globally. The Judge Business School has strong links with the science, technology and economics departments of Cambridge University. This will allow me to work with students, lecturers and researchers in these departments on incubating ideas for enterprise, new spin-outs and economic development. Finally, I will have to convince volatile governments to align national policies to give priority to animal health care as the engine of economic growth and I will have to develop local and export markets. These responsibilities require a solid grounding in business methods, a reasonable level of understanding of the global and national economies as well as the relationship between business and politics. The added confidence gained from increased knowledge and from possessing an important credential from such a renowned university will allow me to make long-term strategic goals and develop and set in motion a comprehensive plan that will have an extraordinary impact on this vast region.

Background to this goal: At the very heart of raising the socioeconomic status of Africans lies the critical importance of animal care and social engineering on the African continent. Amongst all the developing regions in the world, Africa alone did not benefit from the Green Revolution of the 70s and 80s. The important developments that allowed China, India and other parts of the developing world to escape the poverty, disease and famine did not occur in most of Africa. Today, as it has been for centuries, the vast majority of Africans rely on livestock not only as their main food source but also as an important source of revenue to buy the basic necessities such as clothing, nutrient for their land and medical services, if this is available and only if this can be afforded. An innovative and sustainable approach to systematic change is needed. Therefore, mobilizing serious efforts to design and put into action a sustainable food security system that stretches across country borders and projects over the entire continent is of the utmost importance.

Africa is a continent vulnerable to disease, instability and economic paralysis. With about 200 million malnourished people and millions more plagued by diseases such as AIDS, tuberculosis, malaria and other zoonotic diseases in Sub-Saharan Africa at present, the African continent is facing a human disaster of astronomical proportions. Hunger in Africa is still largely rural phenomenon with only 20% of the population concentrated in the large cities and 80% of the hungry people in rural areas. And 92% of the hungry are not victims of extreme events. They are not the dying Ethiopian children with flies in their eyes that we see on TV; they are chronically hungry. Poverty throughout the continent is a matter of life and death – indeed, mainly death. Diseases that plague the African nation and wars that are rampant in many parts of Africa are a direct result of the poor economic status of African citizens. The situation today in Sudan and the Kongo provide typical examples. While the average life expectancy in the United States is now 77 years, it is less than 50 years in most of Africa, and less than 40 years in some of the AIDS-ravaged African countries. Until the pandemics of AIDS, tuberculosis, malaria and other killer diseases are brought under control in Africa, and until people have the means to support themselves, economic development and political stability will remain crippled. These burdens can be overcome but will require the best science, the best technology, and the strongest global collaboration. A breakthrough on the economic status of the African people would help to unleash a virtuous circle of rising productivity, better education, lower fertility rates – and then lead to further increases in health and prosperity.

Why the Cambridge Judge Program? In one respect, it has always been my dream to attend Cambridge University. Notwithstanding the fame of the university itself, I view it as the home of great thinkers. I consider your program to be the ultimate platform for completing my formal education – a commercially focused graduate degree within a globally minded, entrepreneurially spirited curriculum.

The Drayton Centre at the Judge Business School aims to be the world's leading academic institution for social entrepreneurship. I believe that Cambridge's strength in entrepreneurship will add value in my endeavors in the social sector and help advance systemic change where existing economic and political structures have failed or are underdeveloped. Finally, because Judge also draws on the strength of the university's economics department, I would very much like to be given the opportunity, if possible, to do a small independent research study on the topic of the economic impact of community involvement on poverty reduction in Africa under the supervision of the world-renowned Professor William Warriner.

I firmly believe this is an unprecedented opportunity and would like to expand on my personal philosophy and motivation as is intimately tied to this aspiration. To make the greatest difference to my community, I need the best education available. As such, I have only applied to Cambridge.

One characteristic of Judge grads is their sense of appreciation and their lack of self-entitlement. Judge graduates are said to be "smart, industrious, loyal but not arrogant". The program, or more specifically, the students, professors, administrators, and facilities, will help me add additional tools, secure an understanding of how and when to use each of them, and ensure a balanced perspective.

While I understand that it is the policy of the Cambridge Judge Program not to give feedback regarding an applicant's application, I would greatly appreciate your considering me further for a waitlist spot for the class commencing September 12, 20xx. Although I would consider reapplying to your program, I feel there is urgency with respect to the need to pursue my current scholastic and professional objectives as soon as possible. Fortunately, in anticipation of attending business school, I have made plans to pass the reigns of my veterinarian business to one of my colleagues, and this will enable me to attend the university on the shortest of notice.

I thank you in advance for your additional consideration.

Sincerely,
Ebon Yomani

Chapter 2

20 Most Frequently Asked MBA Admissions Questions

My job is not to worry about insulting any of you. It is to worry about insulting each of you equally.
— The Socratic Mantra

(A comical reference to the need of teachers and professors to call on students at random for the purpose of answering in-class or case-study questions.)

1. Is it better to apply early rather than late?

As a rule, it is better to apply earlier rather than later. Applying earlier means that you gain some advantage over other candidates because a large number of applicants either procrastinate or underestimate the effort required to make the first round. Should you apply early and get accepted, there is one less spot for someone else. Most admissions officers recommend somewhat equally the first round or second round, but urge candidates to avoid the third round. In days gone by, as many applicants would apply in the third round as in rounds one and two combined. By admonishing applicants to apply earlier, schools (adcom members) have effectively moved the third round to the second round. That is, there are now as many applicants in the second round as in rounds one and three combined.

Let's review the theory behind the rounds and the potential advantages and disadvantages of applying in each. This helps explain why it is not categorically correct to say that it is always better to apply earlier.

Early. This theory is based on the simple idea of vacancy. In the beginning of the admissions process, there are more places available than at the end. There is also some truth to the idea that schools tend to over-accept in earlier rounds. Other reasons for applying early may include the advantage gained, if accepted, of having more time to arrange for finances, including applying for financial aid or scholarships. Furthermore, if accepted at the school of your choice, you may want to stop applying and save your time and energy in terms of application fees. The potential disadvantage of the first round is the idea that it has a disproportional number of "eager beavers" or overachievers. According to some, the toughest and most prepared candidates apply early, which makes the first round most competitive. There is also the belief that admissions officers take fewer chances in earlier rounds. Certainly this helps explain why first-round statistics such as average GMAT scores and GPA are usually slightly higher than they are for the second or third round.

Middle. There is a second theory that says that it is best to apply in the middle round (that is, middle-of-the-road is best). The rationale espoused here is that the first round has a disproportionate number of eager beavers or overachievers while the last round is too competitive because it has too few spots. Thus, middle is best.

Late. There is a third, much more unorthodox theory that favors the last round. It is grounded on the idea that if a candidate believes that the true strengths of his or her application is one of diversity, then he or she may be advantaged in applying late. It is at the end of the admissions process, more than at any other time, that the admissions committee looks for a well-rounded class. In looking for diverse candidates, admissions personnel may favor a unique last-round applicant more so than in earlier rounds. This may be particularly true if the "diverse" candidate has significant weaknesses in other areas of his or her application. The obvious disadvantage of this round is that most spots are gone. In a typical top-tier business school scenario, only ten percent of spots are available in the final round.

A candidate might avoid applying early should he or she feel that a significant future promotion or salary increase is probable. In practice, such a reason for applying late is unwarranted. If you feel that a significant promotion or salary increase is imminent, you may mention it in your application (and the basis for your assessment) and apply in an earlier round.

Realistically, there will always be some element of chance associated with the admissions process, regardless of whether one applies early or late. The admissions process is an imprecise science coupled with a human element. There is an ongoing mystery question: Would the same candidate with the same application get accepted or rejected at different times in the admissions process just because of vagaries, human or otherwise, inherent in the admissions process? The answer to this question is not known. That said, full-time admissions committee members at top schools are trained professionals who seek to reduce admission vagaries to a minimum.

2. Which of the seven application components is the most important? How is each of these weighted in the admissions process?

There are seven application components: (1) GMAT, (2) GPA, (3) employment record/résumé, (4) letters of recommendation, (5) interviews, (6) extracurriculars, and (7) application essays. Your essays are arguably the most important component. Whereas your GMAT score and GPA give an indication of your quantitative ability, the strength of your essays lie in their subjective, qualitative nature. With the possible exception of an interview, the essay is the closest the admissions committee will get to the "real" you. It is in your essays that you talk about yourself, your career goals, your accomplishments, your need for an MBA, and why a particular school is right for you. Essays include not only standard essays but also optional essays should you plan to include them.

The question of how application components are weighted is very difficult to answer because every school evaluates applicants a little differently and virtually no business school uses a simple weighted average system that assigns values to each application component, for example, 25 percent to GMAT, 25 percent to GPA, 50 percent to résumé, recommendation letters, essays, and/or interviews. In practice, it is extremely difficult to associate a percent or specific value with any individual application component. Not only does each school have its own admissions criteria, but, in general, the admissions process is holistic, not piecemeal.

3. Will the admissions committee start reviewing my application as soon as they receive it even if my application is not complete?

The admissions committee will not review an application until it is complete. In most cases, the admissions committee will not even see your application until the clerical assistants at each school check to verify that everything has been received and pass it to the committee members. The burden of making sure your application is complete rests with you. Schools follow the "whole app" rule. Make sure your official college/university transcripts and GMAT score have been sent, and recommendations have been submitted online.

4. Should I mention that I am applying to more than one school when asked in my application?

It makes little difference whether a candidate states that he or she is applying to just one school versus multiple schools. Some candidates believe that by stating that they are applying only to one particular business school, and putting all eggs in one basket, the admissions committee will favor their application. Committee members care about selecting the best candidates, regardless of how many schools that a candidate is applying to. Also, unless you have well-articulated, specific reasons for applying to just one school, committee members might be skeptical about why you cannot apply to a variety of top business schools and still gain much from these alternate programs. All in all, it makes little difference whether you mention that you are applying to one school or a number of top schools. It is just best to be honest and fill in this information exactly as it applies to you.

5. I've heard that business schools look for evidence of teamwork and leadership ability. How can I show this in my application?

There are a number of ways to show this. Firstly, the workplace is replete with opportunities for teamwork and leadership. Secondly, opportunities often stem from involvement in extracurricular collegiate activities, membership, or community service. Since many of these activities and organizations require working with people in groups, you will naturally have opportunities to mention teamwork or leadership. Rather than simply listing such activities or memberships and placing dates beside each of them, you need to elaborate a little and state what these activities mean to you. See *Chapter 8* for a discussion and illustrated examples on how to enhance this area of your application. Thirdly, interviews may also provide an opportunity for you to talk about evidence of teamwork and leadership ability. You can also mention some of these things when speaking face-to-face with alumni, admission committee members, or current students.

6. Is it necessary to write anything if asked in the application, "Is there anything else you would like to tell the admissions committee?"

Standard essay questions will likely not give you sufficient space to elaborate on all important aspects of your candidacy. In particular, you should anticipate weak points in your application that you need to address. Common examples of application weaknesses include low GPA or low GMAT scores. Clarification is needed if you have an undergraduate degree from an international location that you feel the admissions committee may have trouble recognizing in terms of its academic worthiness.

Not only is the optional question a chance to address your weaknesses, it is also an opportunity to celebrate your strengths, including portraying special aspects of your personal and professional background that ensure you come across as a unique candidate. For information on the uses of optional essays, as well as sample essays for each of these uses, refer to *Chapter 5*.

7. If I take the GMAT more than once, will schools recognize the higher score?

Rather than taking an average of GMAT scores, schools consistently claim to take your highest test score. You may, however, want to check the admissions office of your desired school for the official word. The reason that the highest score is almost always used has to do with a general philosophy in admissions of wanting candidates to present themselves in the best light possible. That is, admissions officers want candidates to look as good as they can before being judged. This may be contrary to what many prospective MBA students think—that admissions people are just looking to find flaws in their applications.

The GMAT is viewed as a representation of your academic potential. Here, there is a good argument behind the practice of looking to the highest score: It is hard to argue that a candidate got a higher score than he or she is ultimately capable of. It is, however, much easier to say that a candidate scored below his or her ability. Moreover, admissions officers prefer to look at the higher score in so far as the highest score is what schools will report for the purposes of business school rankings. It would not make a lot of sense for schools to evaluate you based on your lowest score, but upon acceptance, switch to reporting your highest score for ranking purposes.

8. What can I do to address application weaknesses?

First, think of doing something with the optional question, "Is there anything else you would like the admissions committee to know?" This is one place where weaknesses can be addressed. You may also mention a potential weakness during the interview, but it is generally best to do so through an essay question.

Specific explanations of weak points should not appear in your main essays, unless you are specifically talking about strengths and weaknesses, particularly as part of a "strengths and weaknesses" type essay question covered in *Chapter 4*. When addressing a weakness, try to do so in a positive, candid way, without glossing over it. Concentrate on seeing the seeds of greater benefit in your past failure or underachievement. When weaknesses are properly addressed, there is a feeling that they are strengths in disguise.

The most common anticipated weaknesses are low GMAT scores and low GPA. If you have a low GMAT or GPA, you need to communicate a sense of rigor to meet the academic challenge of business school. In looking at your GMAT score, determine whether one side (quantitative or verbal) is significantly lower than the other side. Next, analyze your college transcripts. Separating your undergraduate courses into technical and non-technical courses to analyze what course resulted in higher overall achievement.

Assuming that the problem lies with your GMAT score, start with the GMAT and work back toward your college transcripts. If, for example, your quantitative GMAT score is low, then search through your college courses and find examples of quantitative classes (for example, economics, accounting, statistics, computer science) in which you received above-average grades and make a case to off-set your weak math score on the GMAT exam. If your GMAT verbal score is low, then peruse your college courses for examples of liberal-art type courses (for example, English, speech, philosophy, law) in which you received decent grades to help offset your weak verbal score on the GMAT exam. Of course, if your college grades are shaky but your GMAT scores on both quantitative and verbal sections are strong, then this analysis works in reverse. The GMAT can serve as "proof" that your basic skills are strong.

Applicants generally think of weaknesses as being one of low GPA or low GMAT score because these are numerical in nature and less subjective. But weaknesses may also include having a weak résumé, weak recommendation letters, a mediocre interview, poorly constructed essays, or not having much in the way of extracurricular activities. Possible application weaknesses stemming from these latter qualitative application components are typically less able to be judged by the applicant as good or bad prior to actually applying to business school. Furthermore, in the case of recommendation letters and interview results, the candidate is unlikely to know what has been written by the recommender or posted by the interviewer. The most critical goal of this book is to proactively strengthen qualitative application areas.

If you do get rejected by a business school and plan to apply again, try to find out from the admissions office the possible reason(s) for your rejection. This will greatly help you plan a new strategy to strengthen the cited weakness, should you reapply the following year.

9. How do I highlight my diverse international study or work experience?

You will have a chance to mention your international experience when completing your résumé/ employment record, application essays, extracurricular activities, and/or when performing interviews. You may even highlight a diverse experience through use of an optional essay. You'll most likely make mention of your international work and study experience in your main application essays. In the "career goals" type essay, for example, you are likely to talk about aspects of your background and preparation leading up to your career goals. As discussed in *Chapter 3*, your background can be broken down into professional, educational, cultural/international, and personal components.

A time-tested MBA application principle involves showing the significance of any experience by stating why you feel it is important or relevant. The same is true with international experience. Do not merely mention in passing that you worked for a summer in the Middle East—state what you learned from this experience and why it is important to your future.

10. How do I handle a waiting list situation?

A waiting list is used by a business school to keep track of candidates who the admissions committee feels may be admitted in the near future pending availability of places. Some candidates on the waiting list get accepted; a number always get rejected. Rather than just wait it out, this is a chance to go the extra distance. It is important that you think about what additional pieces of information you may want to send to the school. A letter to the director of admissions expressing your continued interest in the school and/or current employment update are two such ideas. You want to give the impression that you are energetic and moving closer to your goals. Express your hunger—most candidates just sit back and wait for a decision.

Try to ascertain why you might be short-listed. Can you anticipate an obvious application weakness? If so, you might want to send a note to your interested school to specifically address this point. Addressing your anticipated weakness(es) may help to dispel possible doubts the committee has about your candidacy.

The trend among business schools is to waitlist more candidates, even though class size at most business school has remained roughly unchanged. In other words, a candidate is not as close to acceptance upon receiving notification of a waiting list, as he or she might have been in the past. One explanation for why schools place more candidates on the waiting list is to increase their "yields." From a candidate's standpoint, the most important number is "acceptance rate"—what percentage of the people who apply get accepted. But to a business school, the magic number is "yield." This is the number of people who accept the school's offer of admission. The higher the yield, the better.

Candidates placed on the waiting list must signal to the school that they are still interested, otherwise they will be dropped from consideration. This helps a school increase its yield, because it does not have to gamble as much with sending acceptance letters to candidates who might in turn "reject" the school.

11. If I get rejected one year, should I reapply the very next year? What are my chances as a re-applicant?

Generally, business schools welcome reapplications. But your chances as a re-applicant are better only if you submit an improved application. Your ability to reapply to business school the very next year following an unsuccessful first attempt is dependent in part on the reasons for initial rejection. If you can find out why, it will help you in forming a strategy for reapplication. For example, it is easier to reapply if your weakness was lack of work experience. An extra year of on-the-job work experience might spell the difference. Likewise, if you were rejected because you showed no evidence of extracurricular activities, you may get the hint that it is time to join a professional or service organization to bolster your application. On the other hand, if the reason for rejection was because you lacked a clear career focus, then this is arguably a harder deficiency to overcome (a discussion of goal statements is undertaken in *Chapter 3*). You must carefully map out a plan for why you are now choosing an alternative career path. Schools generally keep applications on file for two years before discarding/deleting them. If you plan on reapplying, you will want to update schools so that they will be sure to keep materials on file. On the other hand, if you want business schools to get rid of all the materials in your file, just wait a couple of years and come back with a brand-new application. But this means you will also have to get new recommendations because these will also be discarded.

12. How do I know if my application is good enough to send in?

Your application is ready when you have completed all information demanded in the application: sent in copies of your GMAT scores and academic transcripts, received confirmation that recommendation letters have been e-mailed, and written application essays. The last thing you will likely be working on are your application essays, and readying yourself for interviews. Your essays are finished when they "sit still" and no more major rewrites or changes are required. Ideally, this process requires letting your essays sit for a week or two before rereading them and making final changes.

Your application is good enough to send in whenever you figure you have a 50-50 shot at a top school. The rationale is that if you have a 50-50 shot and are applying to two top business schools, you are likely to be admitted to one of them. Think of tossing a coin. You may be thinking, "Wow, how can I apply with only a 50-percent chance of acceptance?" But the reality is that "good" candidates usually do not have better than a 50-percent chance of acceptance in applying to a top school. The acceptance rate at top schools is on average about 20 percent. When you have a 50-percent chance, you are saying that you have effectively two-and-a-half times the chance of the average applicant. The trick is knowing how to judge when you have a 50-50 shot. This unfortunately requires a good deal of knowledge about MBA admissions (and also current trends in MBA admissions), and is one reason for seeking MBA admissions help in applying to business schools.

13. Do business schools have GMAT or GPA cutoff points? Do schools use quotas to limit the number of applicants accepted from one region of the country or world?

There is no evidence to support the claim that cutoff points or quotas are used by today's leading business schools. The use of cutoff points would result in a rigid admissions criteria whereby the admissions committee would not even read an application unless a certain quantitative threshold were exceeded. For example, if a GPA cutoff point were set at 3.0, then no admissions person would read your application unless your GPA were 3.0 or above. Likewise, if a GMAT cutoff point were set at 600, then no one would even read your application unless your GMAT score were 600 or above. Not only do admissions personnel claim that cutoffs do not exist, but there is also concrete evidence which supports the complete absence of cutoff points. One piece of evidence that indicates the absence of cutoff points is the entering class profiles compiled and published by many leading business schools. Obviously, if cutoff points really existed, certain "lower" categories would not exist.

Exhibit 2.1 is a compilation of data that reflects the breakdown for a typical top-tier (full-time) MBA program.

The use of quotas would serve to limit the number of candidates that could apply from a given region, industry, or functional work area. Some observers conclude that because top MBA programs seem to have a particularly diverse makeup, this somehow implies quotas are in place. Admissions personnel simply point out that the diversity of an entering class (for example, geography, race, gender, age, academic, or work background) is largely a direct reflection of the diversity present in the applicant population as a whole. That is, in terms of geography, there are fewer people from say, Madrid, who apply each year to American business schools as compared with people from New York; hence there will be correspondingly fewer people accepted to American business schools from Madrid compared with New York. Likewise, because there are fewer people who apply to business school with majors in biological sciences as compared with engineering, there is a corresponding smaller representation of students accepted at business school who have majored in biological science.

EXHIBIT 2.1   PROFILE OF A TYPICAL, TOP-TIER (FULL-TIME) BUSINESS SCHOOL

GMAT distribution

500–590	5%
600–690	50%
Above 700	45%
Middle 80%	640–740
Mean	700

GPA distribution

Not calculated	20%
2.0–2.99	5%
3.0–3.49	40%
3.5–4.0	35%
Middle 80%	3.1–3.7
Mean	3.5

Demographics

Age of new entrants	27 years
Age range	21–42
Average years of work experience	5 years
Women	35%
Men	65%
International	35%
Married	15%
With graduate degrees	15%

Undergraduate Majors

Engineering (incl. Science & Math)	35%
Business/Commerce	30%
Economics	15%
Humanities/Social Science/Other	20%

14. What if I do not know what I want to do with my career, but I still want to apply to a good business school?

Arguably the most important thing to know in preparing for business school is knowing what you want to do with your MBA. Your career depends on it. And while in business school, your ability to know what you want to do after business school will also help you make better use of your time in terms of course selections, clubs, summer internships, etc. For the purpose of getting accepted to business school, it is paramount that you come across as a person who knows what you want to do with your career and are goal oriented. Admissions people want to be confident that you have a good idea of why you need an MBA. Business schools have a serious aversion toward people who have no idea of what they want to do with their careers. Generally speaking, the admissions committee will always be preferential toward a candidate who knows what he or she wants to do with an MBA as opposed to the person who is undecided or cannot articulate a reason.

If you do not know what you want to do and you still want to go to a good business school, you must above all else, concentrate on choosing a career focus. Any career focus is better than no career focus. In reality, many people go to business school uncertain of exactly what they want to do, but hopefully exit their programs with a sufficiently clear career direction. If you are still undecided about what you want to do with your career, the best advice is to pick a plausible goal based on your current background and experience and try to support that career goal or vision. Goals and vision are of paramount importance and are covered in *Chapter 3*.

15. Can I exceed the length limits of application essays and, if so, by how much?

Acceptably exceeding limits does sound like a paradox. But in the same way that a driver may marginally exceed the speed limit without fear of getting a ticket, an applicant can arguably exceed the word count limit without being penalized. Almost all business schools assign word limits to the writing of application essays. The rule of thumb is that you should go over by no more than ten percent. If the essay states 500 words, keep it to 550 words. Some schools ask you to put the number of words in brackets at the bottom of an essay to ensure that you have stayed within the prescribed limits. In this case, exceeding limits is a slightly trickier proposition.

Many candidates complain that business school essays with limits of 200 to 500 words are too short to use to adequately address points. However, consider two facts. First, if business schools didn't think it was possible to answer within such limits, then they wouldn't have set such limits. Second, any essay question can in theory be answered in a single sentence, so 200 to 500 hundred words provides a sufficient opportunity to answer the question and add relevant detail.

The vast majority of applicants claim to be better writers as a result of having gone through the application process. This is invariably the by-product of three processes gained from the application essay writing process. The first process is distillation. Relatively short essays require you to write in a forceful, straightforward way, culling out the unnecessary. The second process is resourcefulness. You will not always have the perfect answer (based on your background) to answer every essay question. This requires that you be creative and strategic. The third process is introspection. In thinking about your past experiences, you will be forced to glean meaning from them. Why were they important? What did you learn from them? How do they fit within the grand scheme of your life?

16. Is it a good strategy to limit the number of schools I'm applying to in order to concentrate effort and bolster the quality of my application?

Students who unduly limit the number of schools they choose to apply to may find they have zero acceptances at the end of the application process. Let's say that eight schools is the ideal number to apply to. With acceptance rates hovering around 20 percent at most top business schools, the average "informed" candidate would have to apply to five schools in order to be accepted at one. Even if you're an informed applicant, informally defined as one having twice the chance of acceptance as the average candidate, (that is, a 40-percent chance of acceptance to a top school), you would still need to apply to three schools to hold at one.

Once you've completed three or four applications, it's easy to replicate (cut and paste) various parts of your application, particularly the essays, from one school to another, because application essay responses generally contain overlap. So the idea that you need to conserve all your energy is unfounded. An applicant might take 40 hours to complete an application to the Harvard Business School, but need only one weekend to complete his or her fourth and fifth applications. Welcome to economies of scale.

It is human nature to pick "good" schools and overlook lesser ones. But rest assured if you are only accepted to a single school, this lesser school will look much better to you at the end of the process than it did at the beginning of the process. Some candidates start the process by saying, "If I don't get accepted at A, B, and C schools then I'm not going to business school." There's nothing wrong with this stance. But it assumes that you like your job, and business school isn't a priority. In truth, most candidates do not have this luxury. Their jobs are grueling or monotonous and they long for a life-style change; they want a break from the grind and the chance to finish their formal education.

17. Should I discuss the decision to go to business school with my family, friends, colleagues, and even my boss, given that their input will likely prove critical in my decision to apply for and attend business school?

In truth, discussing your decision with individuals in your immediate circle will generally not sway you in this important decision one way or the other. There are several reasons for this. First, bosses will too often advise you to delay or forego going to business school. They'll say, "Stay and work…it's not necessary…why leave to get the same job back in two years?" Such will be the advice, ironically, even if employers have MBA degrees themselves. Keep in mind that employers tend to judge the MBA in terms of what it means within their particular company and, moreover, they are not usually sympathetic to personal reasons for leaving one's job. Most young professionals choose to apply to school because they are looking for a personally enriching experience as well as a professional booster shot. Not surprisingly, friends will generally favor your decision to go to school because they view the idea of "returning to school" as an interesting or challenging personal endeavor.

In the end, the only persons other than yourself who will provide critical input in the decision to go to business school are those people who are directly affected by your decision. This usually means your spouse or significant other and/or your parents, especially if they are helping finance your education.

18. Given that business schools typically invite a candidate to interview only after an initial review of his or her application is complete, is the interview the deciding factor in the admissions decision?

Most schools follow the practice of interviewing. Very few top schools do not interview. Because most schools want to interview every applicant but don't have the resources to do so, they generally follow the policy of offering interviews only after making an initial review of applications. Schools will try to cut 50 percent (or more) of all applicants and offer interviews to those remaining candidates. In taking half of these remaining candidates, they get an acceptance percentage of around 25 percent (or less).

The interviewer, even if required to complete an interview form rating the candidate, will too often reach the consensus that the candidate is solid and would make a nice addition to the incoming class. The admissions committee will think: "Yes, we basically came to that conclusion by ourselves. That's why we gave the candidate an interview in the first place."

Unfortunately interviews frequently give no critical new information about candidates and thereby fail to be makers or breakers. Anecdotal information supports this. Students sometimes report, "I had the best interview with XYZ School, but I later got rejected." One explanation is that unless you're on one of the extreme ends of the interview process, the interview will not be the breaker. An example of an extremely positive statement made by an interviewer might be, "This is one of the most dynamic individuals I ever met, you must take them." An example of an extremely negative statement made by an interviewer might be, "This person is a scum bag; you must reject them."

Interviewing has gained in popularity among schools, partly as confirmation that personality is an important component of business school and on-the-job success. One problem has been the difficulty of comparing interview results, given that no two individuals see things in the same way. Why do school interviews then? One reason is that more information is better than less information. Schools may respond with something to the effect, "We want to avoid false positives and false negatives." False positives occur whenever a school accepts a candidate whom it should have rejected. For example, an accepted applicant writes smashing essays but arrives on the first day of classes with difficulty being able to speak English. False negatives occur whenever a school rejects a candidate it should have accepted. For example, a rejected applicant goes on to become businessman or businesswomen of the century.

As a sidebar, there are always rumors floating around regarding famous businesspersons who were rejected from famous business schools. Warren Buffet, reputed to be the world's greatest investor, was rejected from Harvard Business School. Perhaps the most famous rejection outside the business school arena is that of Steven Spielberg's rejection from the USC Film School. It is said that USC Film School is now more famous for rejecting Spielberg than it is for the film school itself (not good!).

19. Is there any truth to the idea that a high GMAT score can't make you, but a low score can break you?

There is a saying in the GMAT world: "The GMAT is not as important as candidates think it is, but it's more important than schools say it is." In the current hypersensitive GMAT arena, there is likely truth to the idea that a high GMAT score (significantly higher than the average expected scores at a given school) won't make you, while a low score (significantly lower than the average expected score at a given school) can indeed break you. There is credence given to the idea that everyone is equal in the admissions process after scoring 700 or higher (700 out of 800 is equivalent to the 90th percentile). That is, if you get rejected with a GMAT score of 700 or higher, the problem is not with your GMAT, but with another part of your application.

Every year, a number of students are accepted at various top business schools with low, even very low, GMAT scores. These are exceptions. Such candidates obviously have something else going for them. For example, they may have a great transcript, been a star athlete, or possess exceptional musical ability. Maybe they come from an unusual place in the world. But the point is they have that "something else" to prop up their application chances.

Admissions officers themselves are fond of saying, "A high GMAT score does not guarantee acceptance and a low score does not preclude it." This statement is hard to dispute, but it's a little deceptive. With reality factored in, the GMAT is more of a breaker, not a maker. Many times, applicants who score 700-plus on the GMAT think it's game over. Kudos, but be forewarned: This is not tantamount to acceptance. Remember that the average score at most top schools approximates 700. The smart applicant savors the accomplishment, but gets to work on his or her application without believing that acceptance is inevitable.

20. Is it a smart strategy to try to find out what each school wants and target them on these key points?

The answer to the question is both yes and no. Certain schools are known for their specialties. For example: Chicago and Wharton are renowned for their specialties in finance; Northwestern, for marketing; Harvard, for general management; Stanford, for entrepreneurship; and INSEAD, for international business. A common idea is that you should tailor your application to embellish those parts of your background that tie to a particular school's specialty.

Will targeting schools in this manner help? In one respect, yes it will. You will be signaling to a school that you fit in. There are two forces going on in the application process: Your ability to fit in and your ability to stand out. The advantage of appealing to a school's strength is that you will fit in. The disadvantage is that you won't stand out. For example, suppose a professional photographer applies to the Sloan School at MIT, a school known for its manufacturing and technology expertise. The photographer will certainly stand out because MIT Sloan likely sees very few applications from photography majors and/or professional photographers. Because the photographer is quite unusual, he or she stands out but hardly fits in. The school will wonder whether the candidate's experience is mainstream enough.

In theory, it is unclear whether a "target the school" strategy proves net positive. As one top admissions officer remarked, "What you think our school may want may not be what our school sees in you." Moreover, applicants concentrating on what a school is looking for are usually those applicants who end up second guessing everything they write by asking, "What does the school want to see in this essay question?" A time-honored piece of advice is to identify your individual strengths, develop a theme, and never try to outguess the committee members. Have the confidence to know that if you answer the questions honestly and present yourself memorably, and the school doesn't accept you, then it's not your school—period.

Chapter 3

Writing the Classic MBA Essays

Put it before them briefly so they will read it, clearly so they will appreciate it, picturesquely so they will remember it and, above all, accurately so they will be guided by its light.

—Joseph Pulitzer

Introduction

Application essays are arguably the most important of all admissions components. Essays are subjective in nature but it is this subjective element that gives them that extra weight in the admissions process. Here is your chance to tell your story and interpret events in your own way. Essays are sometimes referred to as interviews on paper. Regardless of whether or not this is true, with the possible exception of the interview, essays are the closest that the admissions committee can get to knowing the "real" you.

What Types of Essays are There?

Business school essays are subject to considerable variety. They may vary based on the number of required essays, the length of a given essay, and the type of essay question asked. The number of essays may range from two to eight depending on the school, while the length of essays may vary from a couple of paragraphs to three or more pages; in terms of word count, essays may vary from 100 words to 1,000 words. There are effectively ten different types of essays:

1. Who are you?
2. Career goals
3. Why an MBA?
4. Why XYZ school?
5. Background and diversity
6. Strengths and weaknesses
7. Greatest accomplishments, leadership, or team building
8. Overcoming difficult situations
9. Analyze a business situation
10. Wildcard questions

In short, there are two broad classifications of essay questions. The first is the "who are you?" type question, which seeks to pinpoint your personal character, motivations, and diversity. Often other essay types are used that mimic the "who are you?" type essay and these include: "background and diversity," "strengths and weaknesses," "greatest accomplishments, leadership, or team building," "overcoming difficult situations," and "wildcard" essay questions.

The second major essay type is the "career goals" essay. The "career goals" essay is ubiquitous and found in every business school application. The primary purpose in asking this type of question is to find out what you plan to do with your future and to capture important elements of your professional background. Often the "career goals" essay question is combined, for practical reasons, with the third and/or fourth essay questions, "why an MBA?" and "why XYZ school?"

Although there are ten different application essay types, the first four may be considered classic essays: "who are you?," "career goals," "why an MBA?," and "why XYZ school?"

Business schools change their essays from year to year, but invariably incorporate one or more of the classic essay types within each application. The purpose of these four essays is to find out what kind of person you are, where your career is headed, why you want an MBA, and why a particular business school is the right choice for you. There is no better place to begin a discussion of essay writing than with a review of the best approaches on how to write the classic MBA application essays.

Important note: Candidate names, corporate names, and any dates appearing throughout the sample essays and documents in this book may have been changed to protect the confidentiality of the persons or organizations involved. In some cases, essay content may have been modified for presentational purposes. The current trend in MBA admissions essays is for shorter essays of approximately 400 to 1,000 words.

Essay questions asked by business school are subject to change. As one business school drops one or more questions and replaces them with new questions, another business school will choose to add a question similar to the one dropped by another school. Broadly speaking, the kinds of essay questions asked by a business school has not changed substantially during the past ten years. The overriding goal in choosing essays for this chapter (and chapters 4 and 5) entails choosing essays that are recurring in nature. Essays written in response to typical questions provide the best learning tools.

The sample essays included in this book provide candidates with examples of essay writing principles in practice. The actual business school essays that each candidate writes should contain his or her ideas and words, but any candidate is welcome to follow the approaches contained in these sample essays.

Snapshot for Writing the "Who Are You?" Essay

The "who are you?" essay is one of the most difficult essay types both in terms of content and structure.

Sample essay questions

➤ "Please tell us about yourself and about those key influences that have shaped who you are today."

➤ "Tell us about those personal or professional characteristics that distinguish your candidacy."

➤ "Describe yourself to your classmates."

Common mistakes

Three common mistakes made when writing a "who are you?" essay include

- Not using a clear and simple structure to help organize and signpost your discussion of who you are;

- Not supplying specific concrete examples to support what is said;

- Not describing who you are, but rather what you have done.

Another common mistake is to take on too many topics. For example, don't use using a shopping list of traits to describe yourself. One actual candidate put the following sentence in her essay: "I am an energetic, loyal, creative, diligent, honest, strict, humorous, responsible, flexible, and ambitious person." Giving adequate support for all of these traits is practically impossible. A better approach is to choose two or three of these traits and develop each in more detail.

Winning approaches

The following is a summary of three winning approaches for writing a "who are you?" essay.

- Use a clear structure to organize your essay. One way of looking at a "who are you?" essay is to consider breaking it down into one or more of these categories: people who have influenced you; places you have visited or lived in; events or situations that have influenced you; key turning points; personal traits you possess; personal strengths and weaknesses; other relevant categories, including hobbies and interests that have had an impact on you.

  Once you have decided which categories you want to include in your discussion, create an outline. Consider using a lead or summary sentence to break your essay into its major parts. A lead sentence is like a topic sentence, but whereas a topic sentence summarizes the contents of a single paragraph within an essay or report, a lead sentence is used to summarize the contents of an entire essay or report or its major sections. Each topic mentioned in the lead sentence should be developed into a separate paragraph in the body of the essay. For example, when introducing personal traits, you may use the following summary or lead sentence: "Who I am as a person can be seen in the three personal traits that best describe me, namely my courage, empathy, and practicality. In terms of courage (one paragraph) ... In terms of empathy (one paragraph) ... In terms of practicality (another paragraph)."

- Supply specific, concrete examples to support what you say. If you are writing about your personal traits and you say that you have an analytical mindset and work with numbers, you must give examples to support the idea that you really do have an analytical mindset and have a facility with numbers. You must clarify these statements. Show the reader exactly what is significant about working with numbers and the benefits of having an analytical mind. You cannot assume that the reader knows.

- Talk about the kind of person you are, not just about what you have done. Say you are writing about your personal traits and you state that you ran a marathon. This is an example of something you have done, not necessarily who you are. The following is more effective: "I am a person of great perseverance and generally finish the things that I start. Running a marathon in under three hours is one example of my ability to..." In this latter example, you are strategically mentioning the kind of person you are (that is, a persevering person) and using your accomplishments (that is, running a marathon) as examples to support the kind of person you are.

Seven Tips for Writing the "Who are You?" Essay

☞ *Tip #11: Make an outline for your "who are you?" essay.*

The first challenge you are likely to face when writing a "who are you?" essay is deciding what to include in your essay. This is a content issue. The second challenge is how to organize your essay. This is a structure issue. Incidentally, readability (in addition to grammar, diction, and spelling) is the only other major issue, and this entails making your writing look presentable. This latter concern is the focus of *Chapter 10*.

The ability to write an outline for your essay and reduce it to point form greatly increases the odds of writing an effective essay. The easiest and most efficient way to proceed with writing a "who are you?" essay (or any longer, formal essay for that matter) is to prepare an outline and begin filling in information. Try to envision what you want to put in your essay and then break your essay down into paragraphs. Dedicate one paragraph to each of the points you will cover. *Exhibit 3.1* provides an example of a generic outline for the "who are you?" essay.

EXHIBIT 3.1   GENERIC OUTLINE FOR THE "WHO ARE YOU?" ESSAY

I.   Introduction

II. Discussion (choose one or more of the following topics to
     write about)
     a.   Three people who have most influenced you
     b.   Three places you have visited or lived
     c.   Three events or situations that have influenced you
     d.   Three key turning points
     d.   Three descriptive traits that best describe you
     e.   Three personal strengths and weaknesses
     f.   Three hobbies or interests
     g.   Other relevant categories

III. Conclusion (optional)

Note that "three" is an arbitrary number, but it is recommended that you cite no more than four items to be covered under each specific category—people, places, events or situations, turning points, traits, strengths and weaknesses, hobbies or interests, etc.

Exhibit 3.2 presents a sample outline for a "who are you?" essay. While the subject of beer is a bit outrageous, this is an example of how to build your essay around a theme and still break your discussion into manageable parts—in this case, three people and three events.

☞ *Tip #12:   Decide on the best writing approach for your "who are you?" essay.*

There are two basic approaches to use in writing your "who are you?" essay. The first may be called the straightforward approach while the second may be called the creative approach. The straightforward approach entails first finding a one sentence answer to the question "who are you?" For example, "I am a proactive person who likes to see the commercial impact of ideas." Once you have summarized things in a single sentence, the next step is to break up your writing into, say, three subtopics and explain those subtopics in more detail. Tip #14 covers a few ways of how to go about breaking down the body of your writing.

Creative approaches, on the other hand, are less straightforward but potentially more interesting. In her sample "who are you?" essay, Audrey (pages 47–49) writes her essay using the Chinese elements of fire, metal, water, wood, and earth. Each of these elements is used as a metaphor to represent aspects of her life. Fire represents the unpredictable events in her life, like the burning down of her home in California; metal is a fundamental building material that represents her chosen career in architecture; water separates her ancestral China from her home in America; wood represents her creative abilities; and earth stands for her well-grounded belief systems.

Shannon (pages 50–53) builds her essay around the parts of a wristwatch, her product specialty area at Walt Disney. The headings within the essay include the dial of creativity, the gears of teamwork, the strap of humanity, the hands of direction, the case of leadership, and the complete watch. Each topic describes her individual characteristics in a complete and multifaceted manner. Her final sentence serves as a summary: "Creativity, cooperation, humanity, career focus, and leadership are all components in my life, which must balance and work together to make sure that I stay 'on time'."

EXHIBIT 3.2   SAMPLE OUTLINE FOR A "WHO ARE YOU?" ESSAY

I.   **Introduction (para 1)**

I like beer. Beer explains more about me than anything in the world. Who am I? I am the beer man – at least that is what many of my close friends call me. To understand why this gold-colored substance tells so much about me, I must mention two things. The first concerns the most important people who have influenced me. The second centers on those truly unique events that have shaped me at critical times in my life.

II.   **Discussion (para 2–7)**

a.   There are three people I have known in my life whose influences have been monumental. Their names are Ms. Teacher Go, Businessman Mo, and Aunt Sally, the fortune teller. All three tie into beer...
...Ms. Teacher Go (para 2)
...Businessman Mo (para 3)
...Fortune telling with Aunt Sally (para 4)

b.   There are three events in my life that have had a major impact on my love of beer. These include my coming to America, my role in the armed forces, and my experience as a captive in an African jail.
...Coming to America (para 5)
...Joining the armed forces (para 6)
...In an African jail for 10 days with just water (no beer!) (para 7)

III. **Conclusion (para 8)**

Three important people and three important events have come together to make me the kind of person who will always be interested in beer. I believe that if any of the above individuals or events had not played the role they did, my life and personal and professional focus would be less than what it is. What I do know for sure is that this beverage of golden color will continue to play a role in my future. It is a future that will use my past influences and focus them on marketing in the beer industry.

A candidate might want to pick one subject that he or she knows very well and build the whole essay around this one subject. This is especially true with respect to hobbies and interests. A superb pianist might choose to make the piano the focal point of his or her essay. A superb tennis player could break the game of tennis down into three parts, namely training, match play, and mental outlook. Using the game of tennis as a metaphor, these three aspects could be used to describe that person's life. Training could represent the person's background and preparation (in tennis and other endeavors), match play could represent the person's achievements, and mental outlook could stand for those additional things that the person finds important in his or her life.

Regardless of whether you choose to use a straightforward approach or a creative approach for writing your "who are you?" essay, it is always best to think about building your essay (and your application for that matter) around a theme. What are the most common themes that show up in business school essays or applications? The following are eight classic themes:

- ❧ Entrepreneur/Innovator
- ❧ Team Player/Bridge Builder
- ❧ Leader/Motivator
- ❧ Problem Solver/Pragmatist
- ❧ Technical/Specialist
- ❧ Creative/Individualist
- ❧ Internationalist/Culturalist
- ❧ Social Activist/Volunteerist

Obviously, these categories are not mutually exclusive and overlap with one another. As such, many business school candidates could describe themselves as fitting into two or more of these categories.

☞ *Tip #13:* *Choose between two time-tested ways to begin a "who are you?" essay—write a short introduction that engenders interest or, alternatively, begin with a summary or lead sentence.*

Introductions serve to catch the reader's attention. In short, introductions should be brief, relevant, and memorable. Your introduction could be an excerpt from your actual essay, where you choose to highlight an aspect of your background. It might even be a quote that is relevant to your life. In the following sample excerpt, the applicant describes where he is from which provides a glimpse into his family background and helps ground the essay for the reviewer.

> I was born and raised in Eastern Canada in the city of Mont-Laurier. In terms of preparing me as an individual and businessperson, I see my youth as helping me develop an interest in business and sports. My father worked as a general manager of a hotel chain and his involvement helped foster in me a sense of initiative, salesmanship, and mutual cooperation. I was also encouraged to play sports from an early age. I played hockey nearly every weekend from the age of five before switching to skiing at the age of thirteen. Four years later I had qualified for the National Junior Downhill Ski Team and was invited to tour and compete in Europe.

If you choose not to write an introduction, a second, more direct approach comes into play. Start your essay using a summary or lead sentence. As already mentioned, a summary or lead sentence is a very useful tool for use in writing your essay. A lead sentence foreshadows what is to come; it highlights what items you will discuss and, most probably, the order in which they will be discussed. Each item in the lead sentence should be developed into at least one separate paragraph within the body of the essay. The candidate cited above could have omitted an introduction and opened his essay using the first sentence of his second paragraph as follows:

> I would like to show who I am through a discussion of three special turning points in my personal and career development, through an assessment of my personal strengths and weaknesses, through a selection of the three traits that best describe me, and through a look at what motivates me in my work.

☞ *Tip #14:* *Break your discussion into three or four major parts.*

Applicants frequently have problems structuring their essays, no matter what the length and no matter what the essay type. How will you divide up major sections of your essay? What is the best way to group things? Think in terms of threes; break your essay into three parts. Of course, three is an arbitrary number, but it's a good starting point. With reference to *Exhibit 3.1,* the following provides more detail about how to structure your "who are you essay?" as well as find appropriate content.

Writing about people, places, events, situations, or turning points. Perhaps the easiest way to write a "who are you?" essay is to start with three people who have influenced you. Think of your mother and father. You have some of the traits of your father, some of your mother and, of course, you have your own individual traits. This could be a three-part structure. You may choose to view three people as mentors and write about them each contributing a guiding insight. Another easy method is to write about three geographical places. Say that you have lived in England, the U.S., and India. You could spend about a third of your essay covering each area geographically, relating how each has influenced who you are as a person. Another category is events and situations. Certain events and situations can influence us in "geometric" ways—they may last a few seconds, but stay with us our whole lives. For example, people who are battle worn, have been in an accident, or even won the lottery, can testify to this truth. On the other hand, some events or situations are more gradual in their effect. These include going away to college, getting married, getting a promotion, buying a car, making your first investment, etc. Think of the people, events, and situations in your life as representing distinct turning points.

Writing your essay around personal traits. One way for you to approach the "who are you?" type essay is to build your essay around three or four different personal traits. One thing worth mentioning at the outset is that it is not the traits themselves that are most important, but rather the support given to the traits. The examples and the specifics are what will determine whether the writing is both distinctive and believable. When using traits to describe yourself, keep in mind that the reader should be convinced from your writing that you do possess such traits. If you say that you are imaginative, philosophical and industrious, then the reader expects that you will tacitly prove your case.

In writing your essay around traits, you may want to think of your life in reverse chronological order. That is, you are a certain kind of person today, so how did you get this way. You will want to show how a number of different factors—people, places, events or situations, or things—have influenced you and how each plays a role in helping you develop the traits posited.

Writing about strengths and weaknesses. Strengths can be a powerful way to tell someone about who you are. Strengths may represent positive traits possessed that are either inborn or developed as a result of opportunities and personal initiatives. For example, you may be personable, and this is a positive trait. You may want to write about the events in your background that have helped you become personable, including the many opportunities you have had to meet people and the role your family background plays. How did you and/or other family members become gregarious people?

Weaknesses should ideally be viewed as strengths in disguise. What have you learned from your weaknesses? If you have struggled to overcome them, they may indicate proactivity and tenacity of character. Always express how your weaknesses contain the seeds of greater benefits. For example, for the candidate who was too focused on sports to the detriment of more serious academic achievement, he or she might cite participation in sports as the catalyst to becoming a more well-rounded person.

☞ *Tip #15:   Choose specific, concrete examples to support what you say.*

As a generalization, the difference between a really good essay and a mediocre one is that a really good essay uses specific examples while a mediocre one does not. This could not be more true than in the case of the "who are you?" essay. To be sure, "average Joe" applicant will not use many examples at all. When you write your drafts, you may want to try to emphasize points by placing "for example" immediately after what you write. That is, if you say you worked for Mercer Consulting and you have analytical skills, put a "for example" after this and cite some evidence. Do not assume that the reader will believe that just because you worked for Mercer Consulting that this automatically implies, and therefore guarantees, that you possess good analytical skills. There must be support in terms of specific and concrete examples. If you concentrate on using examples to support what you say in your essay, you are well on your way. See Tip #99 (page 199).

☞ *Tip #16: Consider the use of quotes and anecdotes.*

Quotes. To make your essays more interesting, it is probably a good idea to consider including some quotes throughout your essay. What other people say helps make you seem more real. Quotes from famous and familiar people may be used to support a particular philosophy you live by in conducting your personal or professional affairs. In bygone days, candidates would often place random quotes of famous people on the top of each page of their essays in order to impress the reader. Nowadays, reviewers have become more discerning and expect an applicant to explain the meaning behind a quote and why it is relevant to him or her.

Anecdotes. Anecdotes are little stories used to embellish a point made by a writer. The following anecdote might be useful in describing how an entrepreneur can succeed despite what the others believe are realities to the contrary.

> My uncle was an entrepreneur who inspired me. He had a little story comparing entrepreneurs to bumblebees. According to my uncle, NASA has done extensive studies on the bumblebee's flight capabilities, and aeronautically speaking, the bee's wings are too short to support his body weight in flight. Scientists desperately want to communicate to Mr. Bee to tell him that he is in imminent danger of crashing. But scientists do not know "bumblebee language," and so in the absence of any direct communication, Mr. Bee continues to do what he does best—fly.

☞ *Tip #17: Consider the appropriate use of readability tools to ensure reader friendliness.*

Keep track of your readability factor, also known as reader friendliness. In the case of the sample essays written by candidates that follow in this chapter, a number of stylistic and readability tools are employed, including bolds, italics, indentations, enumerations, dashes, and some very short sentences. These all help make the essays more readable, but hopefully not too "busy." Bolds and italics may be used to emphasize keywords or divide the essay into sections; italics may also be used to draw occasional attention to small but important words such as *not, don't, no,* and *first.* Headings and headlines, along with other stylistic and readability tools, are covered under Tip #93, in *Chapter 10.* Note that you may not have some of these stylistic options at your disposal with online applications, although the trend is in favor of giving applicants more online functionality.

Sample "Who are You?" Essays

Candidate: **Audrey from the U.S.**
Target school: **Stanford**

> Throughout history, mankind has tried to explain the events and situations encountered in life through philosophical and mystical means. The Chinese have a unique way to explain their lives and their world through an understanding of the five elements which comprise all matter: metal, wood, water, earth, and fire. In the same way that these elements can characterize all matter, they can metaphorically characterize each of our lives, our health, and destiny, not to mention how we interact in Society, how we affect others and our immediate surroundings and vice-versa, and ultimately, how we affect the world. These elements, collectively, produce both a creative and a destructive cycle, eventually bringing balance and harmony in our lives. Through a review of the

symbolism of each of these elements, I would like to explain the influences of how the people, events, and situations in my life have shaped who I am today.

Metal symbolizes my chosen profession in the field of architecture. Architecture has been influential in my life as an art form that integrates multiple disciplines in both its academic approach as well as professional application. Through my undergraduate studies and working career, I have infused the disciplines of analytical skills, scientific knowledge of physics, environmental science, geology, mathematics, and art for the constant experimentation of architectural forms, into daily use in the form of critical analysis, strategic thinking, and creative problem solving.

Wood is symbolic of my artistic and creative abilities. As the source material for all paper products, wood symbolizes a relevant point in my childhood. At age eight, I was the youngest person at that time to have exhibited a piece of artwork at the Oakland Museum. In my third grade class, I had produced entirely from mental images and my hands, a papier-mache Thai elephant which, was so realistic in its effect that my teacher, Mrs. O'Neill, presented it to the school principal. The school principal arranged for it to be exhibited at the Oakland Museum to encourage program support for art studies at the elementary school level. After the exhibition was over, my father proudly featured my elephant on his desk in his private den. Throughout my life, it proved as a constant reminder to me that I had creative skills which set me apart from most other people and encouraged the artistic development of my young mind. The elephant papier-mache project saw the beginning of my artistic and creative aspiration, which has been a common thread in my life, whether this talent is applied toward my work, my hobbies, or my perceptions and appreciation for aesthetic values in life.

The element *water* is representative of my Chinese cultural and international background. The Pacific Ocean is the body of water that connects East to West, or my ancestral home of China with my physical home in the U.S. This waterway has had a profound influence on my life in many ways, including insight and admiration for other cultures in the world and the ability to learn multiple languages. From the time I was an infant, I had traveled back and forth from Asia to the States, first as a necessity while my father was serving in the U.S. Army as a medical officer, then later to visit my grandparents and other family members who live in China and Hong Kong, and recently as I have been working in Hong Kong. The travel experienced when I was younger most profoundly influenced me in my language abilities. As a four-year-old going to kindergarten in Hong Kong, I was compelled to speak, read, and write Chinese, although I only knew how to speak English at the time. By the time I had begun to learn and understand some Chinese, my family moved to Seoul, Korea where my father served in the U.S. Army as a medical officer. There, at the International School, I was taught in English but also was exposed to the Korean language. A year later, we moved again, this time back to the States to Monterey, California. My struggles with languages and as a result, identity, had initially provided me with challenges as a child but subsequently, with strength in knowing I can accomplish whatever goals I set.

In its elemental form, *earth* symbolizes my well-grounded belief systems. As an earthquake tests the stability of the ground, so have my belief systems been tested by the professional endeavors I have undertaken. Last year, I reported a case of bribery arising from one of our business dealings to my manager who in turn reported it to the director of our client company. Subsequent to this situation being remedied, I have not again personally encountered a similar situation since. However, I find myself in touch with peers and other members of my industry who are confronted with such decisions with increasing frequency. My advice to them is to do their best to discourage the development of such behavior and to uphold the principles by which our industry has traditionally thrived.

Fire represents the most devastating event of our lives, and for me it resulted in the loss of our family home of 20 years. The Oakland and Berkeley Hills fire burned down thousands of homes, destroying a once-beautiful tree-nestled hillside community in the East Bay. I was home that morning of the fire and was the first in my family to notice the dark gray clouds of smoke amidst the clear blue skies of the Indian summer's day in northern California. My mother, my youngest brother, and I were the only ones home that Sunday morning as my father was on-call at the hospital and my sister was still away at law school. We were given 15 minutes to evacuate our home and in the hustle of packing two cars with our life's possessions, we had forgotten our family photographs. To this day and forever forward, we will only cherish those images in our minds as those precious photos are gone forever. I will never forget the sight of the charred and smoldering land where our family home once stood when, two days after the fire, my mother and I were finally allowed to view the damages in person. Chinese TV Channel 26 apparently was in the area filming some of the damage and caught on film my mother and I as we collapsed at the brick footsteps of our previous home which had become a mountain of hot ashes. I learned a valuable lesson from the whole experience. I learned that nothing is more important to me than the safety and togetherness of my family. We had survived the drastic event together and it no longer mattered to me that I lost forever all my yearbooks, family heirlooms and valuables, mementos from our past, and even the papier-mache elephant which made my father so proud.

♦ ♦ ♦

Candidate: **Fritz from Germany**
Target school: **London Business School**

My life is intertwined with four different cultures – German, Russian, Swedish, and Belgian. I am German by birth, educated in Germany and Belgium, started my first two companies in East Germany, and have plans to expand to Russia, in addition to Western Europe. At the age of 26, I started my two companies: Spatuck Limited and Rusk (Germany-Russia) Co. Ltd. Spatuck Limited is engaged in the marketing of diversified consumer products. Rusk (Germany-Russia) Co. Ltd. is engaged in the manufacturing of hair wigs and related products. These two companies are an extension of my father's field of business. Rusk (Germany-Russia) Co. Ltd. is the major supplier of products and sells products through Spatuck Limited. Through these two companies, I manage about 200 people with annual sales of US$9.5 million. As discussed in the next essay, my goal includes taking my companies public in five years' time while concurrently helping my Swedish father-in-law enter the Russian market.

I see myself as a new breed of German entrepreneur, defined as one who is internationally educated, linguistically adept, sales-oriented and technically competent, culturally rounded, and focused on more than just money.

My father told me that when he was five years old, he was so poor that he had to earn money by guarding cows on a farm in order to have a meal. If he did not work that very day he would starve. I was influenced by my father a lot. Education and family are two of the most important values that I inherited. My mother and father emigrated from East Germany to West Germany in 1967 as a result of a rare scientific and technical exchange between the two countries. Although my father's family was very established in East Germany before the war, after the war during the time my grandfather died, my father's family lost everything and became very poor. Neither my father nor my mother could afford to have higher education after graduating from high school in East Germany. As a result, both of my parents especially my father, always wanted us to have as much education as possible. In terms of family, my father never really had a family. My grandfather died when my father was born and my grandmother died when my father was only four months old. So my father always stresses the importance of family to my two sisters and myself. As the oldest and the only son in a German family, I inherit a lot of expectations from my father.

My Swedish father-in-law's company, Rohan, is among the top 20 largest conglomerates in Sweden. His business interests are very diverse in many different industries – chemical, textile, insurance, finance, computer networking, telecommunication, etc. When I first met my father-in-law in his office in Stockholm, I was very impressed by his plain but powerful looking office. There was nothing on his desk except a few pictures – one of a chemical plant and the others of him standing with some important people such as the prime minister of Turkey. My father-in-law is a Christian. He always says that if God gives you abilities, you should not waste them and use them as much as you can. At the age of 63, I do not think he feels he should slow down, rather he is expanding his company at speed. He told me once he likes to see that he is creating jobs for other people. He likes to help others. As a tradition, every Christmas Eve he will go to one of the most remote villages in Sweden to distribute presents to those old people. He has been doing this for 25 years. He too is interested in more than just money.

I see myself in the new age of European entrepreneurship. Even though I was born a German, I have never really thought of myself as purely German. A former prime minister of Germany once described Germany as "Capitalism with a socialist hat and a feudal belt." I think of myself as a West German with an East European heart. My life experience so far has equipped me with crossover characteristics of German, Russian, French, and Swedish. I have a disciplined mind like that of a German person, yet I have a flexible demeanor like a French person. My French education taught me to see things with an open mind and be direct. I am somewhat strong-minded like a Russian. Continuous perfection becomes part of my attitude toward whatever I do. My exposure to Scandinavian culture affects me so much that family and stability are always two very important aspects of my life. My background helps me to act properly when I deal with different cultures in business. I feel like I am a bridge connecting the gap between Western and Eastern Europe. I am carrying on the traditions of an old generation to meet the demands of a new global generation.

❧ ❧ ❧

Candidate: **Shannon from the U.S.**
Target school: **Dartmouth**

Is your watch accurate?
Like the components of the Disney watches which I develop every day, my individual characteristics must function together to truly represent who I am.

The dial of creativity
The dial or face of a watch can often show its personality. Printing a character on the face can bring the watch to life and set it apart from other watches. Often when I am working on a project, especially for Disney, I create many options for our product assortments. Although I am not, nor ever will be, a professional artist, I often generate rough concepts for product or dig through hundreds of artworks to find just the right one to support our brand. In doing this, I focus on the target customer, the retail market, and the technical limitations of the product whether it be watches, clocks, mugs, pewter, or stationery.

Likewise, I find creativity is often needed when solving challenging problems. During my undergraduate studies, I spent my junior year abroad at Stirling University in Scotland where I volunteered to help teach mentally-impaired adults at a local day-care center. One lovely elderly lady I was teaching found it extremely difficult to understand the abstract concepts of money and coins. After two sessions on this topic, we were both quite frustrated. I decided to show her monetary value on a more practical level, so I brought some basic supermarket products from home and we played shop. Although it was a bit juvenile, she began to grasp the use and value of the different British coins in making her daily "purchases" and was soon adding them up to "buy" the items she desired.

The gears of teamwork

The gears inside of a watch movement work together to achieve their shared goal of accurate time. I believe that cooperation, similar to that in a watch movement, is vital to the success of any organization.

After seven years of debate competition I have learned the value of teamwork. The enormous amount of research necessary to be competitive in policy and parliamentary debate could never be accomplished by a single individual. Over the years, I have researched a tremendous number of topics on everything from acid rain to third world nuclear proliferation to world hunger. Throughout my debate career, I made a point of sharing new and important findings with my other team members so that we could all be more competitive. I continuously helped to coach younger debaters by giving them both my research and time. Through cooperation with my team, I was able to qualify for finals in multiple debate tournaments, win the highly competitive AAA Georgia State Debate Championship in high school, and break the Guinness Book World Record for the longest debate as a freshman in college.

The strap of humanity

When an individual wears a watch, the strap holds the watch in place on the individual's wrist. On many watches, there is a soft, pseudo suede material that provides comfort to the skin beneath the strap, no matter what type of material may be on the outside. As my organization faces different external pressures, I believe it is imperative to maintain certain core values which are always "strapped" in place beneath our group (that is, social, ethical, and community responsibilities) that will not waiver under any circumstances.

At Disney, we often develop watches that could potentially have fantastic monetary results in the retail market. However, if the product is not completely safe for children due to small parts, sharp edges, or other potential safety issues, my decision to forego the style is unquestionable, irrelevant of the potential sales generated from the product. The safety of children comes first.

Whether as a leader or member of an organization, I believe it is my duty to be a role model for ethical and responsible behavior. As a manager, I hold myself and my team at Disney accountable to a high ethical standard. Certain business practices make working in a purchasing organization quite difficult at times due to "entertainment" invitations and "gifts" from suppliers. By politely turning down these offers and returning personal gifts, I try to show my staff that the acceptance of this type of "compensation" is not acceptable in our organization.

Commitment to the needs of others is also quite an important aspect of my personality. Working with a group called Hospice of Scotland County in North Carolina, for example, was emotionally the most difficult endeavor I have ever undertaken. Hospice is an organization that takes care of terminally-ill individuals who have stopped receiving treatment for their illnesses. I was a volunteer caregiver in this group and had several patients that I would visit weekly. Developing a relationship with them, while knowing they will soon die, can be a heart-wrenching experience. However, the knowledge of how much you can help a family or an individual far outweighs the emotional strain.

The hands of direction

The hands of a watch must be set, and re-set as needed, to consistently point to the accurate time. My professional goals are the same. Without direction in my career, I would find it difficult to continuously decide the life choices I need to make or to dedicate myself to performing at my full potential. From my initial decision to double major in International Business and International Politics at St. Andrews College in North Carolina to my decision to leave a good job at Silicon Watch Company to join Walt Disney, I have always had a vision. Although re-adjusted and fine-tuned, my goal to work in international business dealing with consumer products has remained constant. It was commitment to these career ambitions that actually led me to Geneva four-and-a-half years ago.

While finishing my Bachelor of Arts degree in North Carolina, I spoke with several consumer product companies who indicated that only senior level employees could work in their international areas. With encouragement from my dean, I decided to move to Geneva to gain international work experience in the area of fast-moving consumer goods. Geneva was the perfect choice as Geneva and Zurich collectively manufacture over 50 percent of the world's watches along with a vast majority of other related products. Thankfully, I had already spent one year studying in Scotland, so leaving the U.S. to live in a country I had never visited was not a difficult concept. Therefore, after graduation from college, I moved to Geneva, résumé in hand, to find a job in consumer products. Thankfully, my plan worked. Three weeks after arriving in Geneva, I was hired by Silicon Watch Company for its marketing department. Although I was the youngest employee in the company when I started, I was assistant manager of the watch division by the time I left to join Disney in Geneva two years later.

I have always held the basic tenet that most goals worth achieving require a great deal of hard work. My career goals are no exception. In preparing myself academically to work in the international arena, I spent many hours developing my knowledge base, researching and writing papers as well as interacting with professors and classmates. As a result, I not only graduated Magna Cum Laude, but I was better equipped to handle many business and political issues which have presented themselves to me here in Europe such as analyzing my division sales and costs as well as better understanding the cultural barriers when manufacturing and distributing in Europe.

While developing my experience in consumer goods here in Geneva, I have worked hard to learn many of the production processes we use in order to fully understand how items are made and the limitations for their development. I have visited dozens of factories in smaller locales and asked so many technical questions that I am positive some of the plant managers were ready to strangle me by the end of the tour. Furthermore, in creating growth for my divisions at Silicon and Walt Disney, I spent many hours sourcing new suppliers, evaluating our business needs, and developing my teams. Only through hard work combined with cooperation and creativity were we able to create a level of customer satisfaction that has kept our business on a continual increase.

The case of leadership

The case, or housing, of a watch is actually one of its most important aspects. The case holds all of the other components together so that they can work in unison. The face, hands, and movement are contained inside the case while the strap is attached externally. As both a leader and a manager, my role mirrors that of a watch case. I bring together the different individuals in my organizations, whether professionally or personally, so that we can work to meet our goals.

Initially, I refined some of my leadership skills as elected President of the St. Andrews College Model United Nations Delegation in North Carolina. In order to attend the National Conference at the real United Nations in New York, we had to raise several thousand dollars and comprehensively prepare all issues to represent our country properly. I divided the responsibilities amongst my officers and created individual task force teams to accomplish our goals. The reason I decided to take this approach, as opposed to having everyone work on all aspects needed to attend the conference, was to empower my officers and to give everyone specific responsibilities. By asking each member of the team to take partial "ownership" of his/her task force, the work necessary to meet our goals was more evenly balanced and several creative ideas for problem solving were actually generated.

As a manager or leader in any organization, I have always considered my role to be the stimulus for creating teamwork and to make sure that everyone is properly motivated to do their individual tasks so that we can achieve our goals together. At Disney, I try to provide continual support for my team in helping them to solve problems with product, suppliers, or customers and to give them guidance as needed. I do not believe that being a good leader means coming up with every idea or giving directions consistently from the top downward. I believe in listening to my team members and empowering them to make decisions, assuming it is within their capability and responsibility. In my group at Disney, we share in both the problems and the achievements of our area. Only by supporting those under my supervision can I help the members of my team to grow and learn, making them more valuable to our organization and to themselves.

The complete watch

The dial, movement, strap, hands, and case of a Mickey Mouse watch form a complete timepiece. Individually, the components have little value. However, when combined, they create substantial worth. Such is the same for my individual characteristics. My leadership abilities and career focus mean little without the necessary creativity and cooperation. Moreover, my core values and compassion are ingrained within all aspects of my personality. Creativity, cooperation, humanity, career focus, and leadership are all components in my life which must balance and work together to make sure that I stay "on time."

❧ ❧ ❧

Candidate: **Gary from the U.K.**
Target school: **New York University (Stern)**

I am a British citizen of Jamaican ancestry living in Hong Kong. Walking down Market Street in Manchester, England, I wonder how I am viewed by the onlookers. To the British person I would probably be viewed as second-generation West Indian, and they'd be right. Short-cropped, neat hair. Head upright, with a straight-backed gait. An Englishman may take it as a strut. There is a lilt to my English accent that marks me a Jamaican. Folks assume I am loaded with street smarts. At the pub I drink Guinness and thump to the sounds of Britain's best rappers.

On High Street in Kingston, Jamaica, how do Jamaicans see me? My cousins tell me I "WALK like an Englishman." Folks mark me as British from a hundred metres away. And my Jamaican Patois, so cool back at home, sounds contrived around the boys on the beach. "It is the Queen's English," they tell me. They think I must have money. Anyone who comes from England must have money! They think I am soft, not really street tough. I try to stroll barefoot along a stony beach in Montego Bay. Oh, how I wince. My younger cousin laughs and shakes his head. At the dance hall we drink Kingfisher beer and groove to the heavy reggae bassline.

On Hsin Hai road in Taipei, Taiwan, I accidentally bump into an elderly gentleman and apologize to him in Chinese. He smiles and asks me where I am from. I tell him I am from England. "You're joking! You have black people in England?" he asks. He (he has watched a lot of NBA) and knows I am not dark enough to be African! And how in the world can I speak Chinese? My head is bopping. At the Hard Rock Cafe, I sip a bottle of Tsing Dao beer and bop to Chinese rock-pop divas.

On three different continents I am viewed quite differently. And on three different continents I can adapt to each environment. My experiences across the globe have enabled me to appreciate the differences amongst people and to utilize the similarities we have to flow between different cultures. I have adopted some of the traits of my various "hometown" locals: the hardworking nature of the Chinese, the perseverance of the West Indians, and the dry wit and humor of the British. I am a music lover – a jazz freak, because it transcends language to unite all cultures. You do not have to be from South Asia to move to a higher plane listening to a 15-minute live recording of John Coltrane's India.

My sights are now on a U.S. education. Where will I fit in? Will I join Stern's Black Business Students Association, the Asian Business Students Association, or the International Business

Club? Maybe I will join all three. Maybe more. The point is, I could feel comfortable with each group. I look forward to sharing my quirky diversity with my fellow classmates. And I look forward to learning from theirs. At Stern, with its healthy cultural and ethnic mix, I expect to fit right in.

❧ ❧ ❧

Snapshot for Writing the "Career Goals" Essay

The "career goals" essay is the most pervasive and arguably the most important of the business school essay types. The purpose of this question is to get you to explain what you want to do in your future work and how your background plays a role. As noted earlier, the "career goals" essay is often combined with the "why an MBA?" and "why XYZ school?" essay questions. Thus, the purpose of the essay is to find out what you want to do with your career, why you want an MBA, and why you want to attend a particular business school. For example: What are your career goals and how do you see your career developing? Why do you wish to pursue an MBA and what attracts you to our school?

Sample essay questions

➢ "How do you see your career developing, how will an MBA further that development, and what attracts you to our program?"

➢ "Briefly access your career progress to date and elaborate on your future career plans."

Common mistakes

Three common mistakes made in writing a "career goals" essay include

- Not mentioning what your career goal(s) are or, when doing so, not having reasonably specific career goals;

- Not showing an effective or plausible transition to your future goals, particularly with respect to linking your background—work, educational, cultural/international, personal—to future goals;

- Not using a clear and simple structure to help organize and signpost your discussion.

Winning approaches

Here are three winning approaches for writing a "career goals" essay.

- Clearly state your short- and long-term career goals early in your essay. You may even want to begin your essay with a statement of your goals, which explicitly defines your career objective in terms of an industry, area, and functional focus.

- Write about your background and experiences in the body of your essay and remember to include all relevant aspects of your background including professional, educational, cultural/international, and personal experiences.

- Draw an outline and use a summary or lead sentence to signpost what you will talk about in the body of your essay. Allocate at least one paragraph to each of the topics mentioned in the lead sentence.

Seven Tips for Writing the "Career Goals" Essay

EXHIBIT 3.3   GENERIC OUTLINE FOR THE "CAREER GOALS" ESSAY

I.   Introduction (brief)

II. Goals (+ vision)

III. Background
   a. Professional experience – work experience (both full-time and part-time); may also include professional credentials
   b. Educational experience – undergraduate majors, research projects; academic awards; may also include extracurricular collegiate activities
   c. International/cultural experience – travel, language, family, country, culture
   d. Personal experience – hobbies and interests; relevant traits, insights, philosophies, mentors, career or personal turning points or setbacks; may also include community service

IV. Why an MBA?

V.   Why XYZ school?

VI. Conclusion (optional)

 Tip #18:   Make an outline for your "career goals" essay.

Exhibit 3.3 provides an example of a general outline for a "career goals" essay. The easiest way to proceed with writing your "career goals" essay is to prepare an outline and begin filling in information. The "why an MBA?" and "why XYZ school?" essay questions are technically separate essays, but are frequently combined with the "career goals" essay to form a single essay. In short, the two biggest questions you are likely to have in terms of writing this essay type is what to write and how to divide up the essay. In a combined "career goals" and "why an MBA?" and "why XYZ school?" type essay question, there are essentially four component parts: (1) your goals (and vision), (2) your background, (3) why you want an MBA, and (4) why you want to attend XYZ school. *Exhibit 3.4* provides a sample outline for a candidate whose goal is to work in investment banking.

Tip #19:   Ensure that this essay contains a clear statement of your career goals and make mention of your goals in the first paragraph of your essay or, alternatively, in the first sentence of the second paragraph.

Do not spend more than one short paragraph on the introduction, because the longer you take before you state your goals and address relevant aspects of your background, the greater the chance that your essay will get sidetracked. An even more direct approach is to just start off your essay with a succinct statement of your career objective. An applicant's career goals are arguably the most important sentences in the entire application package. Placing your goal statements in the opening sentences of your essay is consistent with their overall importance.

EXHIBIT 3.4   SAMPLE OUTLINE FOR A "CAREER GOALS" ESSAY

I.   **Introduction (para 1)**

II. **Goals (para 2)**

   a.   Long-term goal – Investment banker doing IPO (initial public offering) work in Argentina
   b.   Short-term goal – get an MBA, join investment bank in New York, transfer from New York to Argentina

III. **Background and experience (para 3–7)**

   For the past five years, I have been building a specialty in finance and real estate.

   a.   Professional experience (para 3)
        1.   began work in "ABC" real estate firm
        2.   currently working for "XYZ" bank

   b.   Educational background (para 4)
        1.   obtained bachelor's degree in finance with minor in real estate
        2.   took part in extracurricular activities

   c.   Cultural/international experience (para 5)
        1.   traveled and worked in Mexico and Spain
        2.   speak Spanish and English; have working knowledge of Portuguese and French

   In addition to solid work experience, I possess some valuable personal traits and have gained some insights that will be invaluable to my future work in investment banking.

   d.   Personal insights and business vision (para 6–7)
        1.   my sharp people skills
        2.   my great persistence
        3.   why technology holds the key to the future of this industry

IV. **Why an MBA? (para 8)**

   a.   Cross-functional skills
   b.   Recognized for advancement purposes

V.   **Why XYZ school? (para 9)**

   a.   Academic specialties and course offerings
   b.   Students, faculty, and facilities
   c.   Geographic location and employment opportunities

☞ *Tip #20:   Create goal statements.*

The "career goals" essay requires that you make mention of your career objective. You want to make mention of your short-and long-term goals in such a way that the reader can easily figure out what you want to do with your career. How specific should your career goal statements be? The test of specificity is the following: The combination of both your short- and long-term career goals should spell out what you want to do in terms of an industry, area, and functional work focus. The following provide two examples of career goal statements.

Poor: My goal is to work for a multinational company and obtain an international position.

Better: My long-term career goal is to be a top marketing executive in the fast-moving consumer goods industry in Asia. My short- to mid-term career goal is to pursue work with an international consulting firm and gain a specialty in consumer goods marketing.

The better long-term goal statement us in just one sentence that the candidate plans to work in marketing (functional specialization), to work in the fast-moving consumer goods field (industry specialization), and to work in Asia (area specialization). Your two career goal statements are the most important sentences in this essay and are the key to showing career focus. Because of the importance of the career goal statements, you may choose to simply start your essay with your goal statements.

The opening paragraph of your essay will follow the first two statements:

First sentence: "My long-term career goal is to ..."

Second sentence: "My short- to mid-term career goal is to ..."

The following are some examples of different functional, industry, and area specializations:

- Functional specialization (e.g., accounting, finance, marketing, manufacturing, personnel, general management, consulting, sales, trading, research)

- Industry specialization (e.g., investment banking, consulting, real estate, marketing, fashion, food and beverage, oil and gas, chemicals, entertainment, pharmaceuticals, communications, hi-tech, Internet)

- Area specialization (e.g., Asia, North America, Europe, Russia, the Middle East, China, South America, Africa)

Some candidates have a company focus within an industry focus. For example, "I have worked five years for General Electric (GE) and I will return to GE after business school." It is by no means necessary to be so specific as to have a company focus—just an industry focus. Likewise, a number of candidates may have a country focus within a continental bloc. For example, a number of applicants from Asia may be specific in citing China, Japan, or India as the place they want to work after business school. Again, it is by no means necessary to have a country focus, but it is recommended that you have an area specialization in terms of continents.

☞ *Tip #21:   Create vision statements.*

Vision may be thought of as your personal idea(s) or insight(s) about where your chosen industry is heading. Vision is a kind of intangible factor that acts like glue to hold your background and previous experiences to your short- and long-term goals.

Top business schools try to attract people who are not just going to survive in their chosen field but, instead, who will become leaders in their respective fields. In order to make a case for your leadership potential, you should indicate why you are likely to become a leader in your future industry. As a future leader, you will be at the cutting edge of your industry. Are you the kind of person who actually thinks and acts ahead of industry trends? It is helpful to write a little about the thoughts and insights that you may now have that will signal how you will move your career forward.

Vision may be stated in either a few sentences or a single paragraph. In a combined "career goals" and "why an MBA?" and "why XYZ school?" essay question, you will probably want to talk about your vision near the beginning of your essay after mentioning short- and long-term goals. An alternative is to wait and include it in the body of your essay during your discussion of your relevant professional background and personal experience. Note that in the sample outline per *Exhibit 3.4*, the vision statements occur in paragraphs 6–7.

The following are examples of vision statements.

Retail banker: Reveals how technology and brand marketing are the key to future banking, but how each is not always a complementary force. Technology helps banks increase product offerings and services to customers. However, such technological products end up becoming commodity offerings as other banks inevitably follow up with similar competing products. Branding, including astute marketing and advertising, is needed to help banks differentiate themselves, so customers will not think all banks are fungible or substitutable entities.

Public affairs consultant: Writes about how public affairs is different from public relations and how public affairs is an underutilized strategic business tool. Whereas executives of multinational companies traditionally budget for accounting, legal, and other professional services, they do not typically think about public affairs, or how they can proactively lobby governments on macroeconomic and political issues (for example, tax laws, import quotas, regulations) that could affect their companies or industries.

Some tips to help you find vision in your chosen field:

- Peruse the newsstand of a large bookstore or look online for magazines containing articles of interest about the people or companies operating in your current or future industry.

- Ask your boss or other knowledgeable persons where they think your chosen industry is headed and reconcile these ideas with your own.

- Use an online search system, such as Google, Bing, Yahoo, Ask, AOL, etc. and search for current newspaper and magazine articles that will supply you with insights and ideas on the market dynamics and direction of your chosen industry.

A short case study

Goals and vision work best in tandem. Rarely does a candidate have a significant business vision without first having a well-defined career objective. The following are all excerpts taken from business school essays. The first example below is written by a candidate who is eager, but lacks a developed idea of how he will become a fund manager:

> Having majored in Statistics, I have a solid foundation in quantitative training. In addition, minoring in Computer Science gives me a strong background in information technology. I have always had a keen eye for financial news and still do analysis using computer on stocks and options at home after work. It is necessary for me to acquire a business degree in investment management to broaden my vision in investment and risk management, and the use of information technology in a career in the financial markets. My immediate goal is to become a financial analyst with the eventual goal of becoming a fund manager.

Compare the candidate above with the candidate below who shares the identical goal of becoming a fund manager. The latter has a much more developed idea about why she wants to work in the fund management area and the abilities it will take to succeed:

> I view money managing as an ultimate form of art in the financial industry. In order to become a successful money manager, one must be very well acquainted, not only with the whole spectrum within the financial industry including stocks, bonds, interest rates, and foreign exchange rates, but also a diverse number of industries. My past experience is limited to the equity market. I feel I need more exposure to the other financial areas in order to become a successful money manager in Korea. Korean financial markets are still in their developmental stages and companies and retail investors in Korea are accustomed to earning 15-20 percent return on their investment due to the high market interest rate. With Korea joining the OECD, all this is going to change in the near future. The interest rates are going to adjust to the levels of the more developed countries and making money is going to become more and more complex with the introduction of futures and derivatives. Currently there exists only eight national and regional investment trust companies, with the three largest ones taking up almost 80 percent of the whole industry. Because of their size, they are slow to change, adapt new ideas, and too conservative in their approach. I expect to see many small sized boutiques booming and I plan to work for one of them.
>
> The characteristics that are necessary to become a successful money manager include a calm demeanor, perseverance, confidence, and of course, strong analytical abilities. All these qualities must be developed through proper education and experience. Only a solid combination of knowledge and experience can guide you through the good as well as the hard times. To gain the knowledge and insight and learn how to link this knowledge with the real world, I have chosen to apply to XYZ business school. Your outstanding reputation in marketing and finance together with the international independent study courses will allow me a chance to apply the knowledge to real world situations. Becoming a bond trader after obtaining my MBA will help me to gain exposure in the bond market which, in Korea, will develop astonishingly over the next ten years.

Vision means having some idea of how and where your future business will come from. The following excerpt is taken from an essay used in applying for the joint Lauder-Wharton MBA program. The candidate clearly highlights how China is important to her future with her family-owned shipping company. Most candidates in talking about China cite generalities such as China is a big country and there will be big growth in the future. Anyone who is not living in a submarine knows this. You must specifically relate the growth in China with the growth in a specific aspect of the China business you are interested in:

At Lauder, I intend to concentrate on China. China's relevance to our business is evidenced by the remarkable growth of its liquefied petroleum gas (LPG) sector during this decade. In 20xx, for example, LPG imports to China totaled 3.4 million tons, an increase of 92 percent from the previous year. That same year, one-third of this import demand was supplied from a large breakbulk terminal in the Philippines. As volumes into China increase through the next millennium, so will the demand on shipowners to provide value-added services for this trade. Philippines-based vessels are logistically well-suited for this supply route. However, the ability to form close business relationships with Chinese companies will give our company a formidable advantage in the race to expand and develop ventures in this booming market.

In contrast, the essay below could be said to represent the quintessential "career goals" essay of the "average" MBA candidate. The essay is good but not great. The point being made here is that simply wanting to go to business school is not enough of a reason to be accepted by a top business school. Consider the phrases used: "…transition into a new field and gain some corporate experience…now I want something more… remain open to entrepreneurial possibilities." The critical reviewer will expect a more specific idea about where the candidate is going and a better idea that the candidate is driving his or her career as opposed to merely bumping along. In summary, this essay might be fine for many business schools, but for the top schools, competition will force reviewers to up the ante and expect the candidate to have a clearer, more defined direction.

After graduating from Occidental College in 20xx, I established my own restaurant business in Pasadena California. Managing my own restaurant operations over the last seven years has given me well-rounded business experience in that it required me to perform multiple functions and constantly learn new roles in order to become successful. Actively involved in all aspects of operations in my restaurants, I have proven experience as a leader and manager of people and practical hands-on experience in management, accounting, consulting, marketing, business development, and human resources. I believe the skills to effectively and efficiently handle numerous activities simultaneously will translate effectively to any post-MBA career I undertake.

Upon making the decision to close my company's main restaurant operation at the beginning of summer, I faced a significant setback in my career. I decided it was time to reassess my career goals and analyze my career options. I realized that this was the perfect opportunity to develop myself further by building on my strong hands-on entrepreneurial experience by undertaking a comprehensive MBA program. Completing a rigorous MBA program would provide me the appropriate foundation to make the transition into a new field and gain some corporate experience.

Considering my background as an entrepreneur and undergraduate liberal arts education, I strongly believe that an MBA is essential to achieve my career goals, through expanding on the skills and practical knowledge I have acquired through operating my own businesses. I feel I have achieved a lot but now I want something more. Business school will help me to round out my practical experience and provide me the opportunity to learn new analytical and quantitative skills. My short-term career goal upon completion of my graduate studies is to return to the Food and Beverage Industry and work for a multinational corporation. I believe I can achieve this goal through utilizing the practical knowledge I have gained from my professional and life experiences and combining it with the fundamental business foundation my MBA will give me. Over the longer term, I remain open to entrepreneurial possibilities, whether they are an opportunity of my own making or the chance to focus on establishing or expanding a business overseas.

I am interested in pursuing a graduate degree at Kellogg based on the quality of the school and its MBA program. Of special interest to me is the International Business & Markets major, which is compatible with understanding business in a global context. This would allow me the opportunity to take part in the Global Initiatives in Management, and receive a strong foundation in international business strategy, accounting, and marketing. I am also interested in taking electives offered by the Entrepreneurship & Innovation major to build on my past entrepreneurial experience. In addition, I am impressed with Kellogg's emphasis on working in teams and the level of communication and partnership between the faculty and students, which clearly distinguishes Kellogg from other graduate programs. The innovative curriculum development process, in which students have direct input in creating new classes, represents a learning environment that I would like to be a part of.

☞ *Tip #22: Clarify your career path.*

One thing that so often characterizes superior business school applicants is not only their clear sense of focus (and vision) but also their ability to articulate how they will get there. Here is an example of an individual who wants to use his MBA for work in the public sector. The theme is centered around China, but by analogy, the principles used in writing this essay are relevant to candidates with experience in other domestic or international settings. The last paragraph makes it very clear what his career path is. This lends credence to his career goals:

My career goal is an ambitious one – to obtain a senior position in the Ministry of Foreign Economic Relations and Trade (Mofert) of the People's Republic of China. This goal ties my previous ten years of work experience in the pharmaceutical industry in China and Asia with my aspiration to enter top level government work in China. Mofert directly oversees and establishes the policies of foreign joint ventures in the PRC including the Sino-American joint venture of "ABC" company under which I currently hold the title of Manager, China. Mofert also governs all foreign trading activities.

   For the past year, my extensive dealings with Mofert have helped me realize the urgent need for effective leadership at the senior level of the ministry. The upper ranks of the ministry are occupied by a much older group of "communists" who are familiar with the domestic situation in China but who are ignorant of modern business practices. In short, China needs individuals to design its economic future.

   My greatest asset lies in the fact that I can deal with both sides of China's domestic business equation – private and public – as well as with both sides of the international equation – Eastern and Western culture and business practices. An MBA would give me advanced business skills which, when coupled with my in-depth work experience and significant PRC contacts, would ensure my goal of reaching a top position in Mofert.

   After graduation from XYZ business school, I plan to join Mofert and work with foreign joint ventures. I will help design policies ensuring the future success of foreign joint ventures. After two years, I would like to transfer to work aimed at attracting foreign capital to invest in modernizing infrastructures such as power plants, telecommunication, and transportation. Also, I would like to work in a trade department position with hopes of being stationed in the U.S. to promote trade between the U.S. and China. After working in several critical departments in Mofert, and having proven myself with significant achievements, I expect to be promoted to a Vice-Minister position.

☞ *Tip #23: Summarize key elements of your background—professional, educational, cultural/international, and personal experience—in the body of your "career goals" essay.*

As highlighted in *Exhibits 3.3–3.4*, a person's background may be broken down into four major "experience" categories: professional, educational, cultural/international, and personal. The main takeaway is that your background includes more than just your work experience. Many candidates forget to mention their relevant educational, international, and cultural backgrounds. In addition, your background includes your personal beliefs, values, insights, and philosophies, both of a professional and personal nature. A distinction can be drawn between "business vision" and "personal insights." Business vision is used to describe where your company or industry is headed; personal insights are used primarily in a non-business sense to refer to the ideas you have about how to work or live successfully.

The following is an example of how you can summarize your background information and make it easy for the reviewer to read. The preferred approach uses a "top-down" style, placing the summary first.

Poor: I graduated from college…My first job out of college was with MoeMoe Bank and I worked there for three years…Next, I worked for JoeJoe Securities…Finally, I found work with my recent employer, ABC company…

Better: For the past five years, I have been involved in developing a banking specialty. This has been accomplished in four important ways. I have obtained solid work experience, pursued relevant undergraduate education, honed my language skills, and gained a few personal insights about living and doing business in the Middle East.

☞ *Tip #24: Choose examples that are both specific and relevant.*

Above all else, examples must be both specific and relevant. Examples must be specific in that they must be detailed enough to support what you say. Examples from your background must also be relevant in order to best support your long-term goal. You cannot include all of your background and experiences—only those aspects that are relevant and which you choose to highlight.

For example, the fact that a person stops on the way to work every morning to get a coffee from the local boutique coffee shop is likely irrelevant, at least for 99 percent of applicants. However, for the applicant whose future goal is to work in the coffee business, this fact may well be relevant. Stopping for coffee every morning might serve the added purpose of keeping abreast of consumer trends in coffee.

Not only must you choose relevant examples to support the things you write, you must also use specific, concrete examples. As previously mentioned, when writing business school application essays, candidates often write in generalities such as "I have good people skills…communication skills… analytical skills." There must be support. The following examples also serve to give you some idea of how to use standard and personal support points. The basic difference between them is that personal support points give the reader an idea of what the writer personally came away with as a result of such-and-such experience. Comments of a personal nature stand out in the reader's mind. The following examples are used to give you some idea of how to use standard and personal support points. You will want to review the sample essays that follow in the next chapter to note which examples in these essays stick out in your mind.

Example 1: PricewaterhouseCoopers (PWC) Consulting

Statement: I have analytical skills.

Standard support:

❧ Analytical skills help me work with numbers to both read and interpret financial statements.
❧ Analytical skills serve as objective measures for the basis of good decision-making.

Detailed support:

My time spent working at PWC Consulting helped me develop an analytical mindset. I learned to relate what is said verbally with its financial reality. When a client says his or her problem is high costs, I systematically break down total costs into their individual components. Once I know where the numbers point, I look for the stories behind these numbers. Sometimes the problem is not with high costs as the client may have thought but with another factor in the overall system.

Example 2: Korean Language

Statement: I speak Korean.

Standard support:

- Speaking Korean helps me do business efficiently.
- Speaking Korean helps me understand Korean culture.

Detailed support:

Speaking Korean, however, is only the tip of the iceberg. Direct communication is important, but the ability to understand what Korean people think is more critical. In becoming fluent in Korean, I started to gain a sixth sense about what Korean people were thinking, and this became my secret weapon in business negotiations.

Viewing the "Career Goals" Essay as an Argument

☞ *Tip #25:   Test your "career goals" essay by viewing it as an argument in disguise.*

The ability to look at essay writing as an argument can be useful in order to test its persuasiveness. After all, much of expository writing is an "argument in disguise." An argument, as referred to in formal logic, is a claim or statement that is made supported by some evidence. The reason that it is worthwhile to stop and analyze our writing as an argument is that our writing, like any argument, has assumptions. It is primarily by strengthening these assumptions that we, in turn, strengthen the arguments we make. There are three parts to any argument: conclusion, evidence, and assumption.

- The conclusion is the claim or point that the writer (author) is making.

- The evidence is the facts, examples, information, or data that the author uses in support of his or her conclusion.

- The assumption is the author's unstated belief (unstated evidence) about why his or her claim is merited. An assumption is that part of the argument that the author takes for granted or assumed to be correct without stating so. It is sometimes said to be the glue that holds the conclusion and evidence together.

Argument:	Because Dorothy achieved a high score on her GMAT, she is guaranteed success in business school.
Conclusion:	Dorothy is guaranteed success in business school.
Evidence:	High GMAT score.
Assumption:	Success in business school requires the same set of skills as does performing well on the GMAT.

Exhibit 3.5 provides an outline of a sample "career goals" essay and serves to show how the "career goals" essay can be understood in terms of a classic argument structure. As previously mentioned, this analysis shows the importance of personal traits and skills, which become assumptions in disguise.

Take the case of someone applying to graduate school such as business school, law school, or medical school. Admissions committee members do not make decisions based solely on quantitative measures, most notably candidates' college transcripts and test scores. Instead, they try to also evaluate those intangible factors that will not only help the candidate succeed in graduate school, but also help the candidate succeed in his or her professional career. After completing graduate school, these factors often determine who will become a leader in a given field. Any applicant who takes the opportunity to mention intangible factors, such as positive personal traits, insights, and career vision, is helping the admissions committee decide why he or she is the right candidate to be admitted. The point of this is to say that intangible factors in these situations very much form the basis of assumptions.

A classic example is seen in the business school application process when responding to the question, "Why are you applying to business school and what do you want to do with your career?" A candidate applying to business school is essentially saying, "I'll succeed at XYZ school and in my chosen profession as evidenced by my background." The statement becomes an argument—a claim supported by some evidence.

The "career goals" essay is like an argument that contains a conclusion, some evidence, and one or more assumptions. Your conclusion is embodied by your goals; that is, you will reach your goals. Your evidence is embodied by your background and experience to date. What is your assumption and what will strengthen it? Your assumption is embodied by those traits, personal qualities, and business vision that will ensure your reaching your future goal(s). Mentioning these kinds of qualitative things help you build up more evidence, thereby strengthening your assumption and, in turn, your argument.

Question: What is the conclusion part of your "career goals" essay?

Answer: Your conclusion is that you will reach your short-term and long-term goals. Note that you address your conclusion explicitly if you use goal statements: "My long-term career goal is to...My short- to mid-term career goal is to..."

Question: What is the evidence part of your argument?

Answer: Your evidence consists of those relevant aspects of your background and experience. Anything that is historical information about yourself can be cited as evidence, but it must be relevant. Again, your background typically consists of a combination of your professional, educational, cultural/international, and personal experience.

Question: What is the assumption?

Answer: The assumption is said to be the glue that holds the evidence to the conclusion. Here, it is the belief that you can bridge the gap between your background (evidence) and your future short- and long-term goals (conclusion). Your assumption is simply that your background is sufficient preparation to enable you to reach your goals.

EXHIBIT 3.5   VIEWING THE "CAREER GOALS" ESSAY AS AN ARGUMENT

I. Introduction
 	
II. Goals
   a. My long-term goal – Investment banker doing IPO (initial public offering) work in Argentina.
   b. My short-term goal – get an MBA, join an investment bank in New York, transfer from New York to Argentina.
	Conclusion:
	"My future business goals are such and such, and I will attain them."

III. Background and experience
 	
For the past five years, I have been building a specialty in finance and real estate:
   a. Professional experience
      1. began work in "ABC" real estate firm
      2. currently working for "XYZ" bank
   b. Educational background
      1. obtained bachelor's degree in finance with minor in real estate
      2. took part in extracurricular activities
   c. Cultural/international experience
      1. traveled and worked in Mexico and Spain
      2. languages: speak Spanish and English; have working knowledge of Portuguese and French
	Evidence:
	"My relevant background and experience are such and such."

In addition to solid work experience, I possess some valuable personal traits and have gained some insights that will be invaluable to my future work in investment banking.
   d. Personal insights and business vision
      1. my sharp people skills
      2. my great persistence
      3. why technology holds the key to the future of this industry
	Assumption:
	"Sharp people skills and great persistence, in addition to my background, are compelling reasons to believe that I will achieve my goals."

IV. Why an MBA?
   a. Cross-functional skills
   b. Recognized for advancement purposes	

V. Why XYZ school?
   a. Academic specialties and course offerings
   b. Students, faculty, and facilities
   c. Geographic location and employment opportunities
 	
VI. Conclusion	

Sample "Career Goals" Essays

Candidate: John from the U.S.
Target school: Columbia

My six years of work experience has taken place in two of the premier organizations in the world: The United States Marine Corps and The Coca-Cola Company. The Marines taught me to lead and Coke taught me to market. Both organizations provide practical, hands-on experience in the fundamentals of management in the international arena. I want to pursue an international general management career after obtaining the professional qualifications provided by an MBA from Columbia Business School. My long-term goal is to become an International Group President for Coca-Cola. My short- to mid-term goal is to obtain a masters in business administration from CBS and return to The Coca-Cola Company to run a small international unit.

Thorough preparation, self-confidence, and credibility are all traits of a leader and my four-year block in the Marine Corps is testimony to this. Leadership in the Marines is unique in that it comes with great responsibility and commitment to personal safety. As Infantry Company Commander Captain, I managed and led 250 Marines including 5 officers. Some of my responsibilities included setting mission objectives, establishing training goals, writing performance evaluations, conducting career counseling, disciplining Marines, and managing the Company's fuel and ammunition assets. I also conducted numerous live fire evolutions that involved over 300 Marines. One Division operation required conducting a live fire company attack at night and also performing in a simulated chemical environment. Before I left the Marine Corps, I was ranked #1 out of 12 Captains in the Battalion by the Commanding Officer and awarded the prestigious Navy/Marine Corps Commendation Medal for my service.

The flow of illegal drugs through the border between New Mexico and Mexico has long been a serious problem. As a 1st Lieutenant in the United States Marine Corps, I was the mission commander for a Joint Task Force operation along the border. In this real-world mission my unit worked alongside the U.S. Border Patrol. To highlight the seriousness of this mission, the unit that replaced mine, had an altercation with a Mexican teenager that resulted in his death. For this operation, I independently planned, organized, budgeted, and executed the mission that was successful in preventing $1,000,000 worth of illegal drugs from entering the U.S. An equally important success of the mission was the fact that no Marines were injured, no equipment was lost or damaged, and all 45 Marines involved conducted themselves in a highly professional manner. The reason for our success was due to the amount of planning, intense training and preparation that we undertook before we ever arrived on the border. I have learned from this experience that success stems from well-thought-out and organized planning.

It was also in the Marines that I developed a real international focus. I spent one year in Okinawa, Japan, during which we trained alongside military units throughout Asia. This military experience has been invaluable in the formation of my leadership and international philosophy. Believing that I had accomplished my military goals, I turned my attention to a career in business.

Working for Coca-Cola in the Atlanta Headquarters has allowed me to understand the company's progressive international distribution network. Working in the International Bottling Division, I support the needs of bottlers worldwide and work with the Bottler Annual Plan to outline and monitor specific performance targets. I spearheaded a Parallel Product Tracking System that resulted in a 45% drop in illegally transshipped products to overseas markets.

Although Coca-Cola is an enormously large company, it has recently taken steps to undergo a significant change in business practice and philosophy including aggressive plans to double shareholder value within five years. First, the company has redefined its market: Traditionally it has been a Carbonated Soft Drink Company with 85% of the world's market. Now it is a Ready-to-Drink

Beverage Company with only 25% share of the market. This has posed challenges to the marketing team! Second, the company is no longer solely a "carbonated beverage company" receiving orders from Atlanta, but has become a total beverage company requiring small unit leadership, product innovation and local marketing expertise. In the midst of a significant structural change, I have gained substantial exposure in innovative marketing concepts and mediums that include the Internet and cashless vending.

◆ ◆ ◆

Candidate: **Vivian from the U.S.**
Target school: **HBS**

Extreme self-motivation, diligence, and a talent for leadership characterize the diversity and scope of my personal and professional accomplishments. My global work experience in Hungary, Hong Kong, and the U.S. and my educational background in communication and business have given me a broad perspective on the commercial world. These accomplishments have instilled in me a unique and formidable blend of skills and competencies. When looking into the future, my real aspiration is to become a leading female executive at General Electric (GE) International.

Graduate of General Electric's prestigious Financial Management Program. Upon graduating from GE's two-and-a-half-year Financial Management Program (FMP), I joined the alumnae of GE's top finance managers and CFOs. I view this as my most substantial accomplishment because graduating from GE's FMP demonstrated my self-discipline, intellectual stamina, and strength in applied quantitative skills. FMP honed and sharpened my skills and gave me a firm foundation in finance and business.

One of corporate America's most prestigious and most competitive financial training programs, FMP is an intensive and grueling combination of a full-time on-the-job finance experience and formal educational training. Concurrent to taking five graduate level finance courses such as Financial Reporting, Financial Accounting, and Auditing, trainees or "FMPs" rotate through five six-month assignments in all functional finance departments, from General Accounting, Investment Finance, Sales and Marketing to Manufacturing Finance.

Key positions with General Electric in Eastern Europe, Western Europe, and Asia. For the past six years, I have held a series of intensive and challenging managerial positions in Eastern and Western Europe and Asia with General Electric. Achieving the responsible and visible level of these assignments demanded extremely hard work, excellent analytical and quantitative skills, and top management approval and support. I regard the attainment of these positions as significant work accomplishments. It took enormous diligence and dedication not only to be chosen for each position, but also to move quickly through the ranks at the relatively young age of 26.

From my leading role as manager of the Western European Internal Audit Department for GE Lighting in Europe (GELE) to my present position as finance manager of the CNBC Channel for NBC Asia in Hong Kong, I delivered results and success. At NBC I created my position from scratch and provided financial counsel to management as the first financial manager of the channel. At GELE, I created all audit plans and led all business reviews throughout the Western European affiliates. I demonstrated not only my financial and business acumen through these varied roles, but also great adaptability, stamina, and a large threshold for hard work and rigor.

I took advantage of all avenues and opportunities to learn and grow professionally at General Electric Lighting Europe. Even during my first year of work, I requested and received additional assignments. One of my first assignments was to implement GELE's first investment tracking system for over US$44 million worth of capital investments. After successful completion, I went on to help spearhead the company's first ever detailed analysis of product pricing and profitability by lighting product line. I received a management award for my recommendations which generated US$5 million in incremental margin during its first year of implementation.

Above all, however, I value my work because I achieved success in vastly different and enormously complex environments. Environments that spanned different continents, cultures, and industries – from Eastern Europe to Asia and from manufacturing to broadcasting. I lived in foreign countries far from home for over six years and worked in new and often struggling corporate divisions.

• • •

Candidate: **Kenji from Japan**
Target school: **Northwestern (Kellogg)**

Career objectives and professional outlook

The Industrial Bank of Osaka was founded by my great-grandfather and has been run by my family since 1907. From modest beginnings, the Bank is now a highly recognized independent local Japanese bank in Japan with total assets of nearly US$30 billion. Apart from having nearly 100 branches in the country, it has established its presence not only in many Asian countries, but also in England, Canada, the U.S., and the Caribbean. At present, the Bank ranks 147th in the world, based on asset size.

Just as my father is committed to building the Bank as a member of the third generation of the Kamimura family, it is my aspiration as a fourth-generation Kamimura to build further on our banking traditions and to lead the Bank in new directions. After completing my Master of Management, I hope to gain two years' working experience in an American financial institution, particularly to learn more about their approach to modern technology. My longer-term aim is to work in the Industrial Bank of Osaka as a managing director for foreign operations and ultimately, if I demonstrate the requisite talent, to become the CEO.

Banking is one of the most fundamental businesses in any economy. In the context of a developing Asia, the term "developing economy" presupposes that an efficient banking system exists to fuel growth and development. In one respect, financial institutions are the central element in the growth equation. Without the ability to access capital, individuals and their businesses would cease to function.

In my view, the future of banking involves a marriage of technology with branding which can be both complementary and divisive forces. Technology is the driving force behind banks' increasing product offerings and services to customers. For example, "smart cards" are set to revolutionize our payment systems. Smart cards will soon be the medium of money, replacing notes and coins. However, such technological products and services could end up becoming commodity offerings as other banks inevitably follow up with similar offerings. Branding is needed if banks expect people to associate financial services with a particular bank. It is clearly not in the interest of banks to be seen as a group of fungible or substitutable monetary institutions which consumers cannot tell apart. Thus, while technology is needed to provide better service to customers and therefore attract more clients, it also has the means to erode close customer relationships. Astute marketing and advertising on the part of the banks will be required to build brand image.

Development to date

While my long-term objective is to pursue a career in finance, I entered the legal profession to gain an understanding of the framework that governs all business activities. The training that I received from Maples, a leading international financial law firm based in New York has provided me with broad experience in today's fast-moving business world. Thus far, I have participated in transactional management and documentation of transactions of a wide-ranging nature. Apart from transactional work, I have advised on regulatory as well as procedural frameworks for financing structures, and have been involved in a number of contentious matters, such as international fraud cases and minority shareholder disputes.

I believe that my legal experience has greatly benefited me. When a good lawyer comes to draft an agreement, he or she seeks to protect the client against all potential risks that could arise during the life of the contract. Thus, I am now used to stretching my imagination to contemplate not only the foreseeable risks, but also the unforeseeable ones, and to address them at the outset. During the last two years, I am delighted to have had the opportunity to work in both London and Tokyo. I believe this has given me the chance to learn about European and Asian styles of business dealings as well as to understand internal workings of corporations of different geographical origin.

For example, whereas Europeans see a contract as a "clear set of rules," Asians tend to look past the details and to view the contract as merely a document to "start a business relationship." From their point of view, details are meant to be worked out on a daily or ongoing basis. Thus, there exists a significant margin for potential conflict, since Europeans will demand strict adherence to contractual terms from the outset and Asians will want to alter terms as business progresses. As a young lawyer, I have tried to admonish Asian clients to think more in depth about the actual terms of a contract prior to entering an agreement in order to avoid future conflicts. The internal workings of European and Asian corporations also vary because of cultural and organizational differences. The European system is much more organized and structured than the Asian system. This means that, in the Asian context, the person you are dealing with has more influence over a business transaction, and you must be more aware of how personality will affect a business outcome. On the other hand, the European system is less subject to the vagaries of the individuals concerned.

My academic and practical legal training thus far has helped me to solve problems by thinking primarily in an inductive manner. Legal work requires one to combine the details of relevant laws with authoritative decisions in order to form a conclusion for clients on their proposed course of action. Although this type of thinking process will be relevant to doing future business, I hope to be able to perfect my ability to think deductively as well. I believe a Masters of Management degree will assist me in this respect, as case studies develop one's ability not only to use the details of a specific case to draw an overall conclusion but to think deductively by bringing related business themes to bear on the situation at hand.

Snapshot for Writing the "Why an MBA?" Essay

Sample essay question

➢ "How will an MBA help you achieve your personal and professional goals?"

Common mistakes

A couple of common mistakes made in writing a "why an MBA?" essay include

- Not showing why an MBA is needed to you get from where you are now to your future goals ("missing concept" idea);

- Not showing a sincere motivation for wanting to get an MBA (implying, for instance, that you want an MBA primarily because you need the "piece of paper" rather than for the knowledge or skill to be gained from obtaining the degree).

Winning approaches

Here are two winning approaches to use when tackling a "why an MBA?" essay.

- Show a real need for an MBA. You will want to evaluate your reasons for getting an MBA and you may want to review one or more of the following:

Functional diversification—"your desire to acquire skills." An MBA can help you acquire different skills through exposure to different courses, such as finance, marketing, operations, human resources, strategic planning.

Career advancement—"your desire to move up in an organization." An MBA can help you advance from an analyst to associate, clerk to manager, manager to executive, etc.

Switch industries—"your desire to switch industries." An MBA can help you move from banking to brand management, accounting to marketing, advertising to accounting, etc.

International placement—"your desire to move into global markets." An MBA can help you switch from being a regional employee to a national employee, or national employee to an international employee.

- Show a sincere desire for an MBA. Concentrate on writing about what you want to do with an MBA as opposed to what an MBA can do for you.

Five Tips for Writing the "Why an MBA?" Essay

☞ *Tip #26:* *Reflect upon those classic traits that define a businessperson: purposefulness, practicality, resourcefulness, and the desire to see the commercial impact of plans and ideas.*

☞ *Tip #27:* *Mention (or imply) that an MBA is the missing link between where you are now and where you will be in the near future. You may choose to mention your proposed MBA major, in addition to your career goals, as a way to draw a link.*

☞ *Tip #28:* *Discuss academic reasons for wanting to do an MBA, including the need to gain additional knowledge and business theory en route to securing greater professional opportunities.*

☞ *Tip #29:* *Cite the need to obtain cross-functional skills. A common example is a person who has expertise in finance and who wants to study marketing (or vice versa).*

☞ *Tip #30:* *Evaluate other reasons for wanting an MBA, including but not limited to the following: switching industries, signaling that you are ready for career-advancement opportunities, pursuing work in a different geographic region, securing a hedge against job uncertainty, obtaining an important credential, gaining future contacts, and making new friends.*

Sample "Why an MBA?" Essay Excerpts

The two most common reasons why people seek an MBA degree include a need to acquire cross-functional skills and the desire to be considered for advancement purposes. These reasons are supported by a goal to move both "across" and "up" an organization or industry. Moving "across" usually means wanting to acquire a variety of different skills, while moving "up" means wanting to be considered for advancement purposes.

Here is the sample response citing the need to acquire cross-functional skills as well as the need for acquiring international managerial skills for the purpose of being considered for promotion:

Essay excerpt #1, "Why an MBA?"
Why an MBA? Whereas all my experiences to date have given me a good understanding of basic business practices, and to some extent a specialty in finance and accounting, I must develop a far greater strategic marketing and selling component to use in my future career. Specifically, I will need to be able to select, package, and promote our company's hotel, travel, and cruise-related services across Europe. This requires an understanding of all major business disciplines: marketing and brand management, strategic planning, economics, quantitative methods, production, operations, and relationship management. It also requires excellent international managerial skills. Thus, I view MBA training not only as a way to increase my cross-functional skill level but also as a means of ensuring that I am recognized for advancement purposes en route to becoming a distinguished international executive.

In the sample essay excerpt that follows, the candidate mentions her need for acquiring elements of a traditional business background, learning how to evaluate projects from a financial perspective, and being able to speak to high-level businesspersons in a business vernacular.

Essay excerpt #2, "Why an MBA?"
As I do not have a traditional business background from an educational or professional standpoint, an MBA would provide me with the essential skills and knowledge to be effective as a global corporate facilities management professional in the business world. One critical area of knowledge that I currently lack in an industry that is extremely cost-sensitive is the skills and understanding to evaluate the financial aspects involved in facilities management. In a recent article about career strategies in Facilities Design & Management Journal, leading corporate real estate and facilities management executives state that up-and-coming management individuals must have a firm grasp of financial tools and investment management skills. These requirements allow a real estate or facilities executive to be cross-functional, allowing one to be able to speak about finance to a CFO in a language mutually understandable. I need to be able to understand the corporate side of the picture as well as the assets themselves, real estate or corporate facilities. Collectively, I am in search of an MBA program that is strong in the fundamentals of business, including finance and economics, has a renowned international business and management perspective, a celebrated entrepreneurial program, and is located geographically in proximity to high-technology and telecommunications corporations.

In the following sample essay excerpt, the candidate is focused on working internationally:

Essay excerpt #3, "Why an MBA?"
To accomplish my career objectives it is vital that I obtain the necessary formal training from a top business school. I see myself going back to work for Coca-Cola in a business planning and

development role for an international division. In this role, I will be responsible for business development in emerging markets to include innovative marketing concepts, financial structures and investments, distribution methods and operating efficiencies. Following this role I would become the country manager of a medium-sized county. It is in this role that my concentration in general management and consumer marketing from Columbia Business School would be of most value.

Even though my experiences to date have provided me with a good understanding of basic international business practices, I am aware of my need for more formal training in finance, consumer marketing, and business planning in order to be a cross functional general manager. I plan to focus on General Management while selecting electives from the international business and marketing departments. I am particularly interested in the International Marketing and High Performance Leadership Courses. I feel that my varied background will be a contribution to the class, which employs the teaching method of lectures, case studies, guest speakers and breakout time.

Snapshot for Writing the "Why XYZ School?" Essay

Sample essay question

➢ "Why have you chosen to apply to XYZ business school?"

Common mistake

One pivotal mistake made in writing this essay type includes

■ Not showing clear and specific reasons for why your goals are necessarily tied to a particular school's business program.

Winning approaches

There are three general areas you may want to cover in addressing why you want to go to a given MBA school and how a school's specific strengths and offerings tie to your plans. Review the following outline when writing this essay type.

Academic

- Academic specialties, course offerings, teaching method, and class size
- Courses: accounting, economics, entrepreneurship, finance, general management, human resources, international business, management information services (MIS), manufacturing, marketing, new venture management, nonprofit, organizational behavior, strategy, etc.
- Teaching methods: lecture, case, or combination
- Class size: large class vs. small class size
- Joint-degree programs including MA, law, medicine, and engineering
- Library and research opportunities; independent study courses
- Overseas educational exchange programs
- Special leadership programs, new product labs and work exchanges

People

- Faculty, facilities, and student body
- Renowned professors, diverse student body
- Alumni and social/professional networks

Geography

- Location and living environment
- Personal development and diversification: East Coast vs. West Coast; big city vs. small town; weather; linguistic challenges
- Professional development and diversification: internship opportunities and post graduation work opportunities
- Ask: What major companies are located near your prospective business schools that might provide internship/full-time work opportunities?

Ten Tips for Writing the "Why XYZ School?" Essay

The "why XYZ's school?" question is an important essay (or interview) question, and candidate's can blow it. Most applicants do not get enough detail into this question. First, a lot of information is right in school brochures or on the Web. Schools put in a great deal of their effort into producing MBA brochures, and admissions officers are understandably perturbed when candidates appear not to have taken the time to read the brochure. Second, writing a good response to this question not only shows you have done your homework, but it also shows good salesmanship. It sells the admissions committee on their own school. Candidates generally think in terms of convincing a business school on why an MBA is right for them. Actually schools are much more interested in why their particular business school is one of your top choices. It is simply a matter of branding. Deans and admissions directors think constantly about how their schools are perceived alongside other competing business school programs. The following are ten tips for writing a "why XYZ school?" essay.

☞ *Tip #31:* *Mention that a school has a talented, diverse student body, high-caliber faculty, and/or top-notch facilities, and/or strong alumni networks.*

☞ *Tip #32:* *Cite positive comments made by current students, alumni, or industry experts that you believe capture the essence of what attracts you to a given school.*

☞ *Tip #33:* *Cite specific courses that you would like to take and/or mention the names of one or two professors whose courses you would like to enroll in.*

☞ *Tip #34:* *Mention wanting to do some independent research and cite a proposed research topic.*

☞ *Tip #35:* *Evaluate other reasons for wanting to attend a particular school, including academic specialties, joint degree programs, exchange programs, special leadership programs, teaching methods, class size, and geographic location.*

☞ *Tip #36:* *If enrolled in a two-year program, mention what you would like to do with your summer internship opportunity.*

☞ *Tip #37:* *Cite extracurricular organizations you may want to join while attending a given business school.*

☞ *Tip #38:* *Think in terms of how you might contribute to the school as an alumnus or alumna.*

☞ *Tip #39:* *Find out as much first-hand knowledge as you can about the school. For example, visit the campus, sit in on a class, talk to alumni, contact student group leaders, or engage social media.*

☞ *Tip #40:* *Research your prospective school. Use various search engines—Google, Bing, Yahoo, Ask, AOL, etc.—to obtain relevant and current information. Even travel guidebooks—Lonely Planet, Fodor's, Frommer's, Insight Guides, etc.—can be useful to glean information about the city in which your chosen business school is located. Also, refer to Appendix II: GMAT & MBA Informational Websites for a list of dedicated websites, including chat rooms and MBA podcasts.*

Sample "Why XYZ School?" Essay Excerpts

The following essay excerpt highlights a reasonably detailed response to the "why XYZ school?" question. Various specifics—characteristics of the school and program, courses of interest, names of professors, extracurricular organizations—all help to show that the candidate has done his homework and has thought through his decision to apply to Stanford.

Sample essay excerpt #1, "Why XYZ School?"

Why Stanford? As a new breed of German entrepreneur, I would like an MBA education to help grow my current and future businesses. I have chosen the Stanford program as a result of the following: (1) student body and small class size, (2) faculty and academic reputation, and (3) location and employment contacts and opportunities. Stanford's diverse student body and the small class size would enable me to learn as much as I can from the school as well as from other students in a cooperative environment. The outstanding faculty would give me the advance insight and ideas of many business aspects. Stanford University is located in the heart of Silicon Valley. There are many high-tech startups and venture capital firms which can give me a lot of opportunities to talk to them and exchange ideas of manufacturing as manufacturing is part of my background.

The renowned faculty members in Stanford University such as Nobel laureates Professor William F. Sharpe attract me. I would like to learn about Capital Asset Pricing Model from Professor William F. Sharpe, Auction System from Professor Robert Wilson and Professor Paul Milgrom, and New Growth Theory of Economics from Professor Paul Romer. Courses such as Strategy and Action in the Information Processing Industry would give me the chance to talk to prominent business leaders such as Mr. Andrew Grove, the President and CEO of Intel Corporation.

Stanford Business School's course flexibility and emphasis on the development of ideas will be essential to achieving my career goals. I am particularly interested in entrepreneurship and am also applying to the Global Management program. I would like to take as many elective courses as I can. Courses such as M356 – Global and International Marketing; E302 – International Development Management; S354 – Entrepreneurship and Venture Capital; S356 – High-technology Entrepreneurship; E323 – International Financial Management; and R393 – Cultural Diversity and Organizations all looked very interesting and challenging to me.

I would also like to participate in a few extracurricular organizations while at Stanford University. I would like to be active in the Stanford Venture Forum, the New Enterprise Forum, and the Entrepreneurship Conference. I also would like to take the opportunities to join as many student organizations as I can such as Multimedia Club, Manufacturing Club, Telecommunications Club, Venture Capital Club, Entrepreneur Club, Outdoor Adventure Club, Golf Club and Wine Circle.

I have a unique perspective from dealing every day with German and European culture. I believe I could be forthright in presenting my opinions in class and would welcome the opportunity to assist in developing case studies with an in-depth cultural component. Perhaps in the years to come, I could serve as an alumni representative to help individuals in finding appropriate employment opportunities in Europe.

Sample essay excerpt #2, "Why XYZ School?"

My long-term goals in ethics and corporate citizenship represent a shift in my present career in finance. My four years' international finance experience and my work in ethics consulting have exposed me to my intended field of study and provided me with an invaluable foundation, but the route to leadership in this new field will be through research, study, and advanced education. A top MBA program would provide me with the education, resources, and time to further my business ideas. An MBA would expose me to distinguished professors, experiences of my peers, and both independent and related summer study. I would be able to pursue my goals full time with all my energy and commitment.

The school's course flexibility and emphasis on the development of ideas will be essential to achieving my career goals. Very few graduate programs today offer the immense selection of wide-ranging elective courses and the opportunity to organize independent study with distinguished professors. Along with the business school's entrepreneurial focus, all these factors will be critical to hone and organize my ideas into a road map. Courses such as Ethical Dilemmas in Management and Corporate Governance, Power, and Responsibility will combine ethics on an individual level with corporate governorship on a corporate level.

As an HBS student, one of my goals will be to develop case studies in ethics and corporate citizenship consulting. I want to couple my practical and anecdotal international work experience in business ethics at a major general management dynasty – Proctor & Gamble – with research currently undertaken at Stanford Business School. I want to offer my experience in the most recent Proctor & Gamble corporate ethics initiatives and programs. According to Larry Ponemon, National Director of Business Ethics Consulting at KPMG, P&G now has one of the best ethics compliance programs in existence.

I have been following a series of seminars given by the American Chamber of Commerce in New York relating to the topics of ethics and corporate citizenship. I want to work with other students at Stanford to present a series of seminars on ethics for first-year students. By referring to ethics and compliance cases I worked on at P&G, I can contribute real-life examples arising from different geographical and cultural settings as well as different industries and functions.

Sample essay excerpt #3, "Why XYZ School?"

Having acquired full qualifications to practice law in both the English and Japan jurisdictions, I feel I have come to an important turn in my life, namely to divert my focus away from the legal field toward the finance industry. Thus, I am attracted to the Kellogg Graduate School of Management, which is widely acknowledged to be at the pinnacle of academic institutions for business management and marketing. I believe the Kellogg MM program will provide me with essential skills and knowledge to be effective as an international financier with a marketing outlook. This can be seen in the broad core subjects that are compulsory for all first-year students. As I feel that a sound understanding in finance, marketing, and information systems will be very useful for my career, I would find the following courses most beneficial: Complex Financial Structures and Global Risk Management; International Technology Management; Competitive Intelligence, Strategies, and Structures; International Marketing Channels, and Managing Strategic Alliances. In addition, I am delighted to learn that students have the opportunity to do a research paper during the second-year term of the MM program at Kellogg. If I am admitted, I hope to have the opportunity to work with the school's renowned professors on the essential microeconomic reforms that Japan will have to undergo early in the next millennium.

Since I have lived all my life in an environment with either strong British or Japanese traditions, I would like to experience another way of life. I am most eager to acquire a flavor for life in America's Midwest; I have been told that Chicago has more aspects of America than any other American city. My reasons for wanting to attend Kellogg are fourfold: first, many of the brightest students are at Kellogg; second, interdisciplinary learning is emphasized; and third, the Kellogg School attracts top business leaders, such as Bill Gates, Howard Martin, Robert Crandell, and Marlene Johnson, to share their views in their areas of expertise. Fourthly, for my summer internship during the first year, I hope to work at the World Bank to gain some exposure to global banking and to learn how the IMF deals with debt in emerging countries.

Chapter 4

Writing the *Other* MBA Essays

The applications that I think are the most disappointing are those that talk about only one dimension. All four or five essays will talk about an element of their job, or their personal life, or a particular aspect of their professional accomplishments. This inability or unwillingness to capture the variety of life contrasts greatly with the multi-thematic flavor we see in the applications of successful candidates.

—Jon Megibow, former Director of Admissions, Darden Business School, University of Virginia

Writing the "Background and Diversity" Essay

"Background and diversity" essays are used by business schools to get an idea of who you are. In other words, these essays are often used as shorter substitutes for traditional "who are you?" essays.

Sample Essay Question

➢ "How will your background and diversity contribute to the incoming class?"

Common mistakes

Common mistakes made when writing a "background and diversity" essay include

- Not using the full-range of personal background and experience as is often the case when talking only about professional experience;

- Not using specific examples and/or tying them to a common theme to advance your discussion;

- Not using a clear structure to advance a discussion of your background and diversity essay.

Winning approaches

Bear in mind the following three tips when writing a "background and diversity" essay.

☛ *Tip #41:*   *Do not define your background too narrowly. Your background envelops professional and personal experiences and educational and cultural backgrounds.*

You may break down your background into: (a) professional experience—work experience, both full-time and part-time employment, including professional credentials, (b) educational experience—undergraduate major(s), research projects, which may also include extracurricular collegiate activities, (c) cultural backgrounds and international experience—travel, language, family, country, and culture, and (d) personal experience—hobbies and interests, relevant traits, insights, philosophies, career or personal turning points or setbacks; this may also include community service.

☛ *Tip #42:*   *Find your "diversity trigger."*

Analyze your background and ask yourself: "What one thing represents my greatest diversity? ... What one thing can I count on to stand out?" Generally, "diversity triggers" center on one of three areas: culture, geography, or employment. Perhaps your ethnic background is really different. Perhaps you are from an unusual place (or your parents or grandparents are from an unusual place). If, for example, you have lived on three different continents, then you must tell why this is important. This may signal a better understanding of doing business in these geographical areas, or perhaps you have a superior understanding of the culture and language of these areas.

Perhaps neither your culture nor your geography defines you, but the nature of your employment does. Perhaps your true diversity is a personal hardship, unusual childhood experience, or exceptional achievement. The sample essays in this chapter and in *Chapter 5* provide numerous examples to celebrate diversity.

☞ *Tip #43: Use a workable structure and signpost your discussion.*

As mentioned, a summary or lead sentence can be a useful tool. For example, "My potential contributions to the entering class in terms of my diversity of background and character can be seen in my work, education, culture, and personal outlook." In this example, the reader will expect at least one paragraph to cover each of work, education, culture, and personal outlook.

Sample "Background and Diversity" Essays

Candidate: John from the U.S.
Essay topic: How will your background and diversity contribute to the incoming class?
Target school: Columbia

The Secret Formula
Comparing two bottles of Coca-Cola one would likely, and hopefully, find a very homogeneous product. However, the process behind Coca-Cola's homogeneous product quality is very much heterogeneous, bringing together people of diverse cultural and technical ingredients. Similarly, my unique leadership and international experiences will contribute like a "Secret Formula" to enhance the community of Columbia Business School.

For over 100 years the beverage industry has attempted to identify and mimic the Coca-Cola secret formula. My own secret formula consists of quite varied and distinctive real world leadership experiences. I have led by example, as wrestling team captain in high school, running the extra mile and staying late after practice. I have led by command as Company Commander in the United States Marine Corps, directing the attack and disciplining the unruly Marine. I have led by supervision in Coca-Cola, managing market development projects and writing performance evaluations for my team. I have led by persuasion, working daily with the bottling partner in Macau and Mongolia, providing the profit story and selling successful worldwide practices. Each of these varied leadership experiences has helped to hone my own unique leadership style that will contribute to the class.

"I would like to buy the world a Coke"
No other company in the world can match the international distribution capability of Coca-Cola. Company Management has learned over the years, and continues to learn, the best and most efficient means to provide a cold Coke to the farthest stretches of the world. I have learned from my varied international experiences – as a tourist viewing the Soviet Union behind the iron curtain; as a peacekeeper in the Marine Corps sitting off the coast of Jakarta, Indonesia; and as a business manager living and working in Hong Kong – to adapt to the best local practices. In the same way that I use my experiences everyday to help form decisions, these international experiences will also contribute to the incoming class.

Marketing is the key in making Coke the most recognized brand in the world. The T.V. commercials, the radio jingles, the neon lights, all work together with the great taste to spark spontaneous purchase. Combining my varied leadership experiences and vast international exposure, I too have a heterogeneous product that will spark conversation, while providing valued insights and real world examples to my classmates.

❧ ❧ ❧

Candidate: Priyanka from India
Essay topic: Please provide us with a summary of your personal and family background, and perhaps special memory of your youth.
Target school: UCLA

Gandhi once said, "Any generalization about India is likely to be wrong." India is indeed a big country with immense diversity. In India, a person will hear a new language, see different clothing, and get different food to eat after every five kilometers of travel. India is a home to so many different cultures and religions; a person can find people of each and every religion, including Hindus, Buddhists, Jains, Parsees, Muslims, or Christians. In spite of our differences and diversity, we are still one and united. Indians are peace loving and take pride in their "unity in diversity."

In terms of my personal and family background, I see a combination of both traditionalism and progressiveness. My father served in the Indian Army for 25 years and is currently working as Hospital Administrator with The Heart and Vascular Institute and Research Center. He was a valiant soldier and earned a lot of respect during his career. He was decorated in the 1971 Indo-Pak war, at a time when he was a mere 19 years of age. He was also deputed (posted) in Sri Lanka during the IPKF Operations. The Army provided us with an excellent quality of life and its influence gave me and my brother a disciplined upbringing. Because of my father's job we got to see almost all of India. I have inherited the joy of traveling from my dad. I have seen the Thar deserts in the west of India and the beautiful sand dunes of Jaiselmer. I have toured the whole of southern India and seen the beautiful beaches and backwaters of Kerala, the famous temples in Tamil Nadu, and the awesome Menakshi temple, whose shadow does not fall on the ground at any time of the day. I have also been to the beautiful tea gardens and mountains in Eastern India. My father was posted in Darjeeling for two years and from there we got a chance to visit the Natula Pass, which towers at the height of 14,000 feet. As a result of my father serving in the Indian Army for 25 years, it gave us an opportunity to learn in depth about my rich Indian heritage and different cultures.

My father never let us get used to the comforts provided by the Army and made sure we earned everything we acquired. As a result, I can manage anywhere and everything on my own. He always encouraged me to do different things and supported me in whatever I chose to do. What inspires me most about him is his sincerity and honesty. Like my dad, I am a very straightforward person, and he has taught me to stand up for what I believe in. For example, in India, people have a very bad habit of throwing litter on the ground instead of using a bin. This is a sensitive issue for me and whenever I see people throw litter around I often approach them and ask them to acknowledge the bin.

My mother is an extremely talented person and a perfectionist. She loves to learn new things and does not leave anything incomplete. She is an excellent cook, painter, and, believe it or not, an astrologer! She does wonderful embroidery, knitting, and tailoring. I have inherited her creativity and her passion for painting. She had started learning to paint from a very early age and eventually shared her knowledge of painting with me. She learnt it from 'guru' Satyanad, who was a very renowned painter and tutor of his times. My mother paints on almost anything and everything – canvass, tiles, ceramic pots, and glass and on earthen pots as well. All the paintings in our house and my grandmother's house have been made by her. My mother has a very pleasant and calm nature. I have never seen her unnecessarily worried and bothered. Her presence is very comforting in difficult times. She is my best friend and we share a good relationship with each other and we have always done things together such as shopping, going to a movie, and cooking dinner. I know I can call her up anytime with any problem and she will always have a solution. This "sisterhood" that my mother and I have developed is responsible for my sensitive nature and my willingness to help my friends and sit with them for hours to help solve their problems. My younger brother, too, is a very helpful, kind, supportive, and intelligent. Though at times he tends to be a more easy going person and I hope he becomes more aggressive with his opportunities. In spite of this difference and the fact that we fight a lot, we share a good relationship too.

In terms of a special memory, when I was in third standard (eight years of age) my father was posted in Wellington, a small hill station in South India. The accommodations on Gorkha Hill housed the officer's families and there were many children around. It was a beautiful and a peaceful place and we could see the beautiful valley with a stream running through it and on the hill facing our houses was the college and the main market area of the small town. Adjoining to Gorkha Hill was another hill that had patches of terrace farming interspersed with jungles, and there was a big cross with the statue of Christ on the top of that hill, which had intrigued us children very much. One day we could not hold our curiosity and we decided to go climbing on the hill to find out what was there on the top of the hill. We took permission from our parents and packed our picnic bags. Excited to explore the unknown, we were also a little scared. First, we crossed the terrace farms annoying the farmers as we trampled their crops. Then came the jungles, which were thick and spooky, and as soon it started raining, we all stuck together. But our curiosity to see what was at the top overpowered our fear. We kept on climbing and soon the jungle gave way to tall grass and beautiful flowers. With the sun shining again, we were all exhilarated and overwhelmed at the beauty of the nature. There was the big cross standing at least ten feet high. And from on high we could see the whole city below. This small experience has stayed embedded in my memory, as it has become symbolic of the small struggles still faced on daily basis and the importance that the role of determination, courage and hope plays on the path to victory.

❧ ❧ ❧

Candidate: **Karen from Canada**
Essay topic: **How will your background and diversity contribute to the incoming class?**
Target school: Columbia

My Western education and Chinese heritage will certainly enhance the diverse community of Columbia Business School. Having lived and studied in Hong Kong, England, and Canada, I feel that I am in a position to share with my potential colleagues the different experiences that I have encountered in these places. During my five years at boarding schools, I have learned to be independent and considerate of those who are around me. Moreover, my multi-lingual skills (Cantonese, English, Mandarin, and rudimentary knowledge of French) enable me to communicate effectively with people from different places and adapt to new environments quickly and easily.

Joining AIESEC is one experience that I will never forget. AIESEC is the French abbreviation for the International Association of Students in Economics and Commerce. It was a valuable opportunity to make friends and exchange ideas with students from all over the world. I held many different positions during my two-year involvement at the University of Toronto. I joined as an office manager, where I maintained regular office hours every week. My duties included recruiting new members and answering questions about AIESEC on the phone and from walk-ins. Later, I joined the marketing team. We would set up appointments with recruiting managers of various corporations in Toronto and try to help arrange traineeships for those students who lived abroad but wanted to work in Toronto. We also organized many fund-raising activities to support the programs that AIESEC had to offer. For example, we called up many companies and corporations to solicit sponsorships to support the University's Career Day and various seminars. As the culmination of my involvement in AIESEC, I was chosen as one of six delegates from AIESEC Toronto to attend the National Congress in Fredericton, New Brunswick on the east coast of Canada.

I consider myself fortunate to have traveled extensively over the years. My international network of friends has proved to be valuable time and again and during the first two years of my career. Exchanging ideas and information on a constant basis allows us to stay at the forefront of the business world. Since graduation, I have worked in a listed public corporation with over

150 employees and a small Hong Kong company of eight persons. Both companies taught me how close-knit teamwork among employees is essential for a company's expansion. I also had the chance to meet people of all levels during business trips to many Asian cities. Currently, I am working on a US$2 billion theme park project with the Mainland Chinese and Japanese. Being part of the team, I am exposed to the new generation of Chinese businessmen and the dynamics of Japan's advanced technology. I could not have dreamt of this opportunity several years ago. If I am admitted to the Columbia Business School, it will be my pleasure to share my unique background and international experiences with my colleagues.

Writing the "Strengths and Weaknesses" Essay

"Strengths and weaknesses" essay questions are also used by business schools to get an idea of who you are. In other words, these essays are often used as shorter substitutes for the traditional "who are you?" essay.

Sample Essay Question

➢ "What are you professional or personal strengths and weaknesses?"

Common mistakes

Common mistakes made when tackling this type of essay include

- Not being honest about your weaknesses; stating fake weaknesses;

- Not using specific examples and details in support of your strengths and weaknesses;

- Not showing how your strengths have helped you become a better person; not showing how your weaknesses can be overcome;

- Not using a clear structure to develop a discussion of your strengths or weaknesses.

Winning approaches

Keep the following three tips in mind when writing the "strengths and weaknesses" essay.

☞ *Tip #44:   Be honest. Don't try to outguess the admissions committee.*

If one of your strengths is that you are an "information sponge," say so. If your weakness is procrastination, say so. Keep it nice and simple. Be candid. If you really have problems trying to evaluate yourself, then ask a close friend what he or she thinks. Friends are usually right on the mark. Too often, candidates try to "figure out" what weaknesses are acceptable based on what they think the admissions committee wants to hear.

Be careful not to mention "fake weaknesses" such as "I'm too hardworking" or "I'm too generous." The reviewer will likely not believe you. After all, what should you do to become less hardworking or less generous?

One thing that can help you narrow down your list of strengths and weaknesses is to view them as being either professional or personal in nature. Professional strengths and weaknesses are usually skill-based while personal strengths and weaknesses are typically trait-based. Regarding weaknesses, it is generally better to have professional (skill-based) weaknesses than it is to have personal (trait-based) weaknesses. It is easier to change professional or skill-based weaknesses. Say, for example, you have two weaknesses: (1) you are bored easily, and (2) you have a fear of speaking to large groups of people. The latter is an easier weakness to tackle because it is more skill-based and easier overcome. In short, if given a choice of writing about a professional or personal weakness, it is better to stick to discussing a professional weakness.

☞ *Tip #45:* *Summarize any discussion of personal or professional weaknesses by showing how each is a strength in disguise or, at least, what you have learned as a result of struggling with your weaknesses.*

There is a saying that "every cloud has a silver lining." This means that every diversity carries with it the seed of greater benefit. In a similar way, every weakness may be viewed as a strength in disguise. For example, you say that you are a slow decision-maker. However, your slowness might nevertheless result in a fair degree of thoroughness when making significant decisions. Perhaps you are a slow adopter of new technologies, but this has allowed you to remain a traditionalist and not be easily swayed by gimmicks. If your weakness is "detail," you nonetheless may be good at the "big picture," and it is your big-picture view that enables you to hire "good" people who are themselves able to attend to important details.

The easiest structure proceeds as follows: "My strengths are A, B, and C and my weaknesses are D and E. In terms of strengths, I would like to talk about A (mention this trait and give it one paragraph). Next there is B (mention one trait, one paragraph). Lastly there is C (mention one trait, one more paragraph). In terms of weaknesses, I would like to talk about D (mention one trait, one paragraph). Next there is E (mention one trait, one paragraph)."

Sometimes another structure will work better for you. For example, "My strengths and weaknesses can be seen through my work on two different projects with ABC Company. First, my work on project A shows my ... (mention one positive and one negative trait). My work on project B shows my ... (mention one positive and one negative trait)."

☞ *Tip #46:* *Consider a "creative" approach in describing your strengths and weaknesses.*

The creative approach has already been discussed under Tip #12. Whereas the following essay written by Sameer illustrates a direct, straightforward approach per Tip #45, the succeeding essays written by Cedric, Alfred and Elena exemplify creative approaches per Tip #46. Cedric models his strengths and weaknesses around skiing, Alfred relates his personal strengths and weaknesses in terms of the geography of Innsbruck, and Elena cleverly depicts her strengths and weaknesses in terms of Russian Matryoshka dolls.

Sample "Strengths and Weaknesses" Essays

Candidate: Sameer from India
Essay topic: What are your personal or professional strengths and weaknesses?
Target school: London Business School

I made a decision nine years ago, when I completed my B.Eng. to go into the field of construction chemicals, in a sales/marketing position, which was perceived as highly unconventional in civil engineering. The field of construction chemicals was in its infant stage, but I could see that organizations dealing in construction chemicals were growing beyond the US$20 million/year marker.

Since then my work has taken me to various countries and three continents. During that experience, I have worked with different nationalities (35) and at different levels of construction industry, that is, from on-site workers to functional managers, like site supervisors/QAQC managers, to decision-makers like project directors/project managers.

As my employment history will testify, I am a self-motivated and proactive person, who has achieved goals consistently throughout my career due to perseverance. This is demonstrated by the fact that I have never obtained a position in my present field of the construction industry by responding to advertisement. I have always gone job searching in India and the Far East at my own expense and secured employment from the organizations concerned. My passion and will to succeed which have helped me all along in my career have enabled me to take innumerable challenges and risks. They are my biggest strengths, and what I am today, is a product of those two qualities.

Working in Dubai over the last four years, I came across a number of unforeseen work situations and problems. These resulted in the need to build the city's new airport (due to political situations) faster. I had to provide solutions, using my products to solve various problems. Providing a solution to a problem is one of my assets and I have the vision to see ahead and beyond the problem. This experience will be of significant importance in my MBA classes to me and to my fellow students.

Dubai, being a cosmopolitan city, and a melting pot of diverse people, culture, and language, provides an insight into the effects on people caused by social, technological, and political changes around the world. My intense personality and ability to thrive in diverse environments have enabled me to understand the psychological makeup of the markets (people) of many countries and their implications in the future. This skill has helped me and will help me in cross-cultural negotiations which will be a key element to do business in world business of the 21st century.

I am very ambitious and a natural leader through my ability to express myself and organize people and things. I like to make decisions quickly which sometimes has created problems with my administrative staff. I set a very high standard for myself, which I also expect from my staff. This creates problems because the desire need to quickly find solutions unnerves some people. However, I do not do this intentionally.

My weaknesses are largely connected to my strengths and one of my most glaring weaknesses is my impatience. I am a person who does not like to waste time, nor do I like to wait. I find because of my impulsiveness, sometimes, I come across as abrasive and overbearing. Over-enthusiasm sometimes puts pressure on my colleagues. However, because of my impulsiveness and enthusiasm, I do not lack decisiveness. Another weakness which I have observed over the last few years is a lack of good business report writing skills, and a knowledge to use the latest information technology tools. While my communication skills and vocabulary have continued to increase through reading and speaking, I recognize the ability to put ideas in a systematic written form as vital; I definitely see the above skills as really important in business.

♦ ♦ ♦

Candidate: **Cedric from France**
Essay topic: **Give a candid description of yourself in light of those personal characteristics you feel to be your strengths and weaknesses.**
Target school: **INSEAD**

I am a natural team-player with strong negotiation and communication abilities and solid analytical skills. However, I tend to procrastinate when I am not under pressure. During my second year of engineering school (ENST), I was the president of the ski club. My passion for this sport very much parallels my strengths and weaknesses.

While president of the ski club, I co-organized with peers from two other "Grandes Ecoles" the "3's Cup." Working with a strong teamwork spirit was the only way to successfully set up the event, a 3-day ski trip and competition in the French Alps for 300 students. In addition, I was able to share my passion for skiing with fellow students and recruit more competitors to double our ski team size. During my numerous experiences around the world, being a team-player and one who shares my interests and perspective have enabled me to better communicate with people from different nationalities and diverse backgrounds.

Skiing in powder parallels my strong negotiation and communication abilities. In powder, you must gain speed, make smooth turns and control your rhythm while enjoying yourself. While talking with potential customers or negotiating contracts, I analyze issues precisely, answer them with finesse and creativity, and still enjoy these relationships and learn through them. At 9TELECOM, I successfully led negotiations with France Telecom, because I could listen well to and understand others' points of views, articulate my opinion properly, and argue persuasively.

I use my strong analytical skills in ski races to judge the level of risk I will need to take. I match my strengths and weaknesses with those of fellow competitors, as well as those of the natural elements around me. My math-intensive education and my logical mind enable me to tackle complex problems and handle multiple tasks at once. These analytical abilities proved beneficial during my internship at Divicom. I developed pre-processing algorithms to improve the encoding of digital video, which were later patented.

Skiing can also parallel my strongest weakness. Since I perform at my full potential under pressure, I tend to procrastinate and get bored when I am not under pressure. In much the same way, when skiing through big moguls, you have to go straight through them keeping the pressure, or else a fall is certain. A tool I use to fight this tendency is task managing software, listing all the tasks I have to perform with associated deadlines and urgency levels. Moreover, I believe the intense MBA experience at INSEAD will help me further refine my time and task management skills.

♦ ♦ ♦

Candidate: **Alfred from Austria**
Essay topic: **Provide a candid assessment of your strengths and weaknesses.**
Target school: **Harvard**

In giving an assessment of myself, I would like to introduce the city of Innsbruck, where I grew up and spent 20 years of my life. The 800-year-old town, with 130,000 inhabitants, is the fifth largest city and situated in the western part of Austria. Innsbruck has gained prominence from its beautiful landscape and the Alpine mountain ridge that surrounds the city.

Though a small town, Innsbruck has hosted the Olympic Winter Games twice and is today a Mecca for hiking and skiing tourists from all over world, giving the city an international flair. Assisting my parents in their restaurant, I was exposed to guests from different nationalities, enabling me to early acquire global perspectives. Through my summer jobs working for Swarovski selling crystals to French, Italian and Chinese tourists, my university studies in Holland, Belgium and the Far East and my current position as a management consultant, I have not only constantly refined my competence in working with people from different backgrounds and origins, but have also achieved fluency in some of the world's preeminent languages (English, French, German and Mandarin).

Innsbruck citizens are characterized by their genuine character and straightforwardness. People say that the mountainous terrain and rough weather conditions have shaped people to be direct and open. Having adopted these traits, I consider it one of my strengths to be candid and not to be afraid to speak out, especially in uncomfortable situations. This has sometimes brought me criticism, but in the end people value my honesty. Today my senior staff members appreciate my sincerity and integrity and often ask for my opinion, especially with regard to clarifying tensions within the project team or issues with the clients.

Innsbruck lies in a valley (580 meters above sea level) and is enclosed by mountains. Due to its unfavorable and isolated location, historically, people always had to endure much physical hardship to cross the mountain pass to get to the other communities. This gave them a perseverant and enduring character, which is still present today. I am not afraid to overcome difficulties and challenges in the pursuit of my goal. For example, despite having asthma, I mastered the rescue swimmer's rigorous training module and became a certified rescue swimmer eligible to practice in pools and also the open sea.

Growing up in a small and remote town with little of the fast-paced cosmopolitan atmosphere of large cities, I see myself as less aggressive in behavior and more individualistic than many people from big cities. This can be considered a weakness; however, I feel that without this character I would not have achieved what I have today. I believe in a supportive and collegiate team culture and I look forward to contributing my strengths to the HBS student community as well as learning from my fellow classmates.

❧ ❧ ❧

Candidate:	Elena from Russia
Essay topic:	Give a candid description of yourself in light of those personal characteristics you feel to be your strengths and weaknesses.
Target school:	INSEAD

"Matryoshka" is a special word in Russian. This traditional Russian souvenir, consisting of a series of painted wooden dolls which fit one inside the other, is a symbol of Russia and Russian folk art.

Playing with Matryoshka, one cannot see what each inner doll looks like until the outer one is first removed. Because one big doll holds many small dolls inside, it is quite irresistible to want to open each up to see what's inside. "M-Dolls" force me to be inquisitive. Looking back at my pre-school and school years, I remember myself tormenting parents and teachers with questions. My strong desire to learn more about a subject forced me to prepare reports containing material one couldn't find in a textbook at school. I even read encyclopedias and dictionaries without any special purpose, just for enjoyment. I spent a lot of time traveling during my university vacation time. I have been almost everywhere in China, have traveled across India, enjoyed Australia, traveled from North to South Vietnam, and crossed the Cambodian border and seen the famous Angkor Wat. In my professional life a good doctor must be inquisitive, as medicine is both an art and a science. Even the intuition that I discovered during childhood in Russia is now stronger as a result of my years of living in China and the Far East.

Originally considered as a toy, Matryoshka is as much a puzzle, and can represent an analytical way of thinking, progressing from big to small, and from small to big. My analytical skills serve as objective measures and the basis of good decision-making in both work and life. The progression of going from bigger to smaller leads to cures in medicine. It starts with the "big" patient and then progresses to smaller and smaller clues as to what the cure is. My country and family background and creativity equally help me to find solutions to confusing situations in my everyday life.

Each of the dolls is made individually, and they differ not only in terms of size but in styles and colors. They are made by hand, so the decoration is original. Typically, each doll is smiling, colorful and friendly. The creative process of making the dolls involves no measurements, relies on intuition and requires skill and patience. Referring to my strengths, I would add that I am a friendly and approachable person and one with whom people feel comfortable. In a doctor's practice, one of the crucial elements of success is to find rapport with a patient. A doctor must be open-hearted and friendly to be able to listen to a person in need. This trait helps me in my professional and personal life. While studying and traveling, I interact with people from different countries to find out the details of their lives. There always exist distinct differences with respect to inter-relations, gift giving, face, humor, and food. It is these details which are very important for getting along with people. The fact that Matryoshkas are made of soft woods (lime and birch), reminds me of how people are all impressionable (one can leave a dint on the dolls), but the dolls are also firm enough in makeup (wood is pretty solid), so one must be able to adapt to another person's personality, peculiarities and disposition, without demanding that they be different.

The ability to enjoy M-Dolls and to look closely at their composition and coloring and appreciate their distinctiveness also seems to indicate a type of weakness. For even though it brings satisfaction, examining them so closely may not be a practical thing to do. As in medicine, one can forever analyze and contemplate and study possibilities, but limited time and imperfect information require acting. My potential weak points as a businessperson arise from my training as a doctor: I can be overly attentive to details and a perfectionist. I am a very responsible person and like to force co-workers to check off all the details. While being overly focused on details is necessary in medical practice, in business this may narrow the "panoramic view" of the problem.

Writing the "Greatest Accomplishments," "Leadership" or "Team-building" Essay

A "greatest accomplishments," "leadership," or "team-building" essay seeks to find out what you have done. One way to think about how all three of these essays are connected (particularly with respect to professional accomplishments) is to say that "greatest accomplishments" is the result, "leadership" is the process behind that result, and "team members" (team building) are the inputs in that process.

Sample Essay Questions

➢ "Discuss your three greatest accomplishments and why you view them as such."

➢ "Describe a situation when you acted as a leader and explain what you learned."

➢ "Explain a time when you worked effectively as a team member."

Common mistakes

Some of the common mistakes made when writing these essays include

- Mentioning only your work-related accomplishments as opposed to your non-work-related accomplishments;

- Not stating what you have learned from your experience;

- Not using a clear structure; not providing a preview of your accomplishment, leadership, or team-building experience before going into a full-blown description.

Winning approaches

Here are five tips to use when approaching the writing of these essays.

☞ *Tip #47:   Decide on the "mix" and order of your accomplishments.*

When asked for two accomplishments, consider choosing a personal accomplishment to complement a professional accomplishment. When asked for three accomplishments, consider choosing two non-professional accomplishments (for example, academic, extracurricular, community service) to complement your professional accomplishment. Obviously, if two of your three accomplishments are work related, then position them as your first and third accomplishments and sandwich a non-business accomplishment in between. Typically, your strongest accomplishment should be placed first.

☞ *Tip #48:   Ensure that your accomplishments have a "wow!" factor. Imagine yourself as a critical reader asking, "Is this accomplishment difficult? ... Why is this impressive?"*

Suppose you write in your essay that you did a benchmarking study while working as a consultant. Describing or summarizing what you did may not be enough. You know it was a difficult project. So play the devil's advocate for a moment. Ask yourself, "Is that difficult?" "Oh yes," you say to yourself, before citing a litany of reasons. Okay, now record what you are answering. Some of these details should be included in your essay. Make it action-oriented. This will help you prove the difficulty of your accomplishment. Do not buy into the assumption that just because something sounds difficult, it therefore proves it is difficult to achieve.

☞ *Tip #49:   Consider using "headlines" to summarize and highlight your accomplishment(s).*

Headlines, or captioned headings, exist to summarize or pre-phrase information and/or to capture the reader's attention. Examples of the use of headlines are seen in the upcoming essays of Vivian (page 89–90) and Shannon (page 91–93). Headlines, as used in MBA essays, are usually placed in quotes, but sometimes bolded or italicized.

☞ *Tip #50:   Do not define "leadership" too narrowly.*

Leadership has many dimensions. Depending on the nature of your particular work experience, leadership could be best shown by example, command, inspiration, competency, persuasion, empowerment, crisis, emergency, etc. Whereas one candidate chooses leadership by command and uses his or her involvement in the military as an example, another candidate chooses leadership in crises and cites his or her involvement in curtailing a public relations debacle. The point here is that there is no uniform definition of leadership and admissions officers will allow you much latitude in interpreting it and supporting it in the way you deem fit. That said, a classic definition of leadership might be, "Influencing the actions of others to achieve a shared goal."

☞ *Tip #51:   When writing team-building essays (or referencing team building within leadership or accomplishment essays), focus on those interactions among team members that require individuals to develop rapport, nurture trust, and maintain accountability.*

One way to think about team building is that it's a process involving four things: 1) setting a clear goal, 2) building trust and respect among team members, 3) ensuring commitment among team members toward the common goal, and 4) and maintaining accountability of all members while welcoming feedback.

Incidentally, an excellent book that chronicles the elements of team building in fable form, and which is well known in corporate training circles, is *The Five Dysfunctions of a Team: A Leadership Fable* by Patrick M. Lencioni.

Sample "Greatest Accomplishments," "Leadership," or "Team-building" Essays

Candidate: **Vivian from the U.S.**
Essay topic: **Discuss your three most substantial accomplishments and why you view them as such.**
Target school: **Harvard**

Extreme self-motivation, diligence, and a talent for leadership characterize the diversity and scope of my personal and professional accomplishments. My global work experience in Hungary, Hong Kong, and the U.S. and my educational background in communication and business has given me a broad perspective on the commercial world. These accomplishments have instilled in me a unique and formidable blend of skills and competencies.

Scholarship: Successfully completed General Electric's prestigious corporate Financial Management Program (FMP)

Upon graduation from General Electric (GE)'s two-and-a-half-year Financial Management Program (FMP), I joined the alumnae of GE's top finance managers and CFOs. I view this as my most substantial accomplishment because graduating from GE's FMP demonstrated my self-discipline, intellectual stamina, and strength in applied quantitative skills. FMP honed and sharpened my skills and gave me a firm foundation in finance and business.

   One of corporate America's most prestigious and most competitive financial training programs, FMP is an intensive and often grueling combination of a full-time, on-the-job finance experience and formal educational training. Concurrent to taking five graduate level finance courses such as Financial Reporting, Financial Accounting, and Auditing, trainees or 'FMPs' rotate through five six-month assignments in all functional finance departments, from General Accounting, Investment Finance, Sales and Marketing to Manufacturing Finance.

Global work experience: Attained key positions with General Electric in Eastern Europe, Western Europe, and Asia

For the past six years, I have held a series of intensive and challenging managerial positions in Eastern and Western Europe and Asia with General Electric. Achieving the responsible and visible level of these assignments demanded extremely hard work, excellent analytical and quantitative skills, and top management approval and support. I regard the attainment of these positions as my second most significant accomplishment to date. It took enormous diligence and dedication not only to be chosen for each position, but also to move quickly through the ranks at the relatively young age of 26.

   From my leading role as manager of the Western European Internal Audit Department for GE Lighting in Europe (GELE) to my present position as finance manager of the CNBC Channel for NBC Asia in Hong Kong, I delivered results and success. At NBC I created my position from scratch and provided financial counsel to management as the first financial manager of the channel. At GELE, I created all audit plans and led all business reviews throughout the Western European affiliates. I demonstrated not only my financial and business acumen through these varied roles, but also great adaptability, stamina, and a large threshold for hard work and rigor.

I took advantage of all avenues and opportunities to learn and grow professionally at GELE. Even during my first year of work, I requested and received additional assignments. One of my first assignments was to implement GELE's first investment tracking system for over US$44 million worth of capital investments. After its successful completion, I went on to help spearhead the company's first ever detailed analysis of product pricing and profitability by lighting product line. I received a management award for my recommendations which generated US$5 million in incremental margin in 20xx.

Above all, however, I value my work because I achieved success in vastly different and enormously complex environments. Environments that spanned different continents, cultures, and industries – from Eastern Europe to Asia and from manufacturing to broadcasting. I lived in foreign countries far from home for over six years and worked in new and often struggling companies.

Communication: Proven communications abilities as journalism major from Boston University and professional writing experience

I regard the acquiring of my strong communication skills as my third most substantial accomplishment. I graduated with a Bachelor of Science degree in Journalism and have proven my communication abilities not only by being the youngest intern at Boston Magazine, but also by having published an article in the magazine. As a first-generation American, I have also excelled in a language – English – that my parents never taught or spoke with me. They emigrated from Hungary in 1965 without being able to speak English. I have also achieved a complementary relationship between words and numbers, which is unique and very powerful. At times, one needs numbers to communicate ideas, and other times words. My strength lies in my ability to listen, synthesize ideas, and articulate concepts – whether quantitative, qualitative, verbal, or written – in a way that is concise and eloquent.

❖ ❖ ❖

Candidate: **Brett from the U.S.**
Essay topic: **Describe a situation when you acted as leader and explain how you were effective and what you learned.**
Target school: **Harvard**

As InterFraternity Council Chairman at Cornell, I led a 14-person, hand-picked fundraising committee and, over a period of six months, the committee managed to organize two events with a plus 200-person attendance. This endeavor also involved producing an hour-long video and an interactive class directory with photos. We raised $20,000 for the school, noting that neither was the Reunion an ongoing event nor was any support given from the school. During the process, we had an 85 percent attendance rate at all of our bi-weekly meetings and 96 percent of attendees were on time with delays of no more than 10 minutes. Given the "15 minutes late habit" for most social events, I consider this outcome exemplary.

My role as leader involved selecting the right people for each role, clearly identifying the responsibilities required and setting up a clear and accountable agreement, known as the Constitution. The structure precluded future miscommunications and confusion of roles. Furthermore, I never assumed I had solutions to any problems but instead relied on steering a group of intelligent people to the right direction by providing macro objectives then allowing the team to creatively deal with each situation. I often instigated laughter as a means of inspiration.

The structure I proposed also clearly identified those who were not committed and the system removed them naturally, which allowed the committee to remain enthusiastic through out the process. Of course good food was an added bonus since all of our meetings were held over dinner at selected or recommended restaurants.

Subsequent to the success of this fundraising event, I was invited to join the six-person fund raising development sub-committee for Cornell's Landmark Fund Raising Campaign, in order to raise $25 million in three years.

❥ ❥ ❥

Candidate: **Gautam from Hong Kong**

Essay topic: **Please describe your experience of working in and leading teams, either in your professional or personal life. Given this experience, what role do you think you will play in your study group, and how do you intend to contribute to it?**

Target school: **London Business School**

I find the analogy between shipping and leading and team building to be a powerful one. Leadership is like shipping because a ship must always have a destination before it sets sail. The objective must be crystal clear. And a ship provides a quintessential example of teamwork in action. Each individual must get along with other members because a ship in transit is home. There is no place to get off, no place for one to hide. Individuals on a ship form tight personal bonds, but professional rank must be observed and orders followed. Problems must be worked out and crises handled in quick order. Shiphands must be able to perform different tasks, and substitute for one another if sick or injured. With many nationalities on board, differences in culture and language must be accommodated for.

Apart from leading the Commercial department in Maritime Shipping, my other responsibility is working with the senior management team to win specialized and highly technical shipping projects. In Hong Kong the projects team consists of the Chief Operating Officer, Financial Controller and Technical Manager and together we form a good mix enabling us to be expressive, analytical, business driven, and skilled with working with potential customers. In my professional life, being a leader and a team member means setting clear objectives, letting individuals have the freedom to tackle details and complete their tasks and to customize as they deem appropriate, and concentrating on making the "journey" a pleasant one. Thus, as team leader for some projects, I must demonstrate balance between directing and empowering and delegating and following up.

In terms of my study group I'll be eager to break our work into manageable pieces. Then it's time to check to see that we're not overlooking key details. Sometimes we'll assign work based on what is best suited to a particular person's specialty; other times we'll assign work based on what a person is otherwise weaker in (for example, a group member who's a CPA can do the key marketing analysis or the group member who worked in advertising gets to work on cash flow analysis). I'll make a few phone calls just to check to see how everything is going and to provide encouragement (and hopefully others will do the same). Leadership commingles "offense" and "defense"; if one of my team members takes charge, my role will be to provide him or her with the support in order to accomplish our desired goal.

❥ ❥ ❥

Candidate: **Shannon from the U.S.**

Essay topic: **Describe your three most substantial accomplishments and explain why you view them as such.**

Target school: **Harvard**

Broke Guinness Book World Record for 109 hours of continuous debate to raise money for Oxfam

After a four-year high school debate career including a Georgia State Debate Championship title and a trip to the National Debate Tournament for public speaking, I was still not prepared for the challenge which awaited me in my freshman year of college. Our Debate Society at St. Andrews College decided to make an attempt to break the Guinness Book World Record for the longest four-person debate.

The existing world record was 104 hours, but used more than four people. However, we were determined to use the same four people for the entire debate. With world hunger as our topic, we set out to increase awareness on this issue, raise money for Oxfam (an international relief organization), and break the world record.

The team spent months gathering sponsorships, designing T-shirts, researching every aspect of world hunger and training our bodies to function with minimal sleep. We started our debate on the Thursday before Thanksgiving with the entire campus supporting our efforts. Individual dorms even took turns "camping out" with us overnight and by the third day, the student center looked like one big pyjamas party. During the five days, several close calls with physical exhaustion almost made us stop. But, on the fifth day, delirious from sleep deprivation and surrounded by reporters and cheering students, we broke the Guinness Book World Record. When we finally quit, we had surpassed the previous record by over five hours, using only four people, and raised well over US$1,000 for Oxfam. It took me three weeks to recover, but the satisfaction of our achievement will be with me always.

Uprooted myself from North Carolina to obtain my first international position in the watch/clock industry in Geneva as a fresh graduate of 22 years of age

The second accomplishment of which I am proud is the risk I took in moving overseas to gain international work experience in consumer products. While finishing my BA in International Business and International Politics in North Carolina, I spoke with several consumer product companies who indicated that only senior level employees could work in their international areas. With encouragement from my dean, I decided to move to Geneva to gain international work experience in the area of fast-moving consumer goods.

Geneva was the perfect choice as Geneva and Zurich collectively manufacture over 50 percent of the world's watches along with a vast majority of other related products. Thankfully, I had already spent one year studying in Scotland, so leaving the U.S. to live in a country I had never visited was not a difficult concept. Therefore, after graduation from college, I moved to Geneva, résumé in hand, to find a job in consumer products and to gain international management experience. Three weeks after arriving in Geneva, I was hired by a watch and clock manufacturer to work in their marketing department. Although I was the youngest employee when I started work at Silicon Watch Company, I was assistant manager of the watch division by the time I left to join Disney two years later.

Undertook emotionally charged work with Hospice of Scotland County

Although I have participated in numerous charity organizations, working with a group called Hospice of Scotland County in North Carolina was emotionally the most difficult endeavor I have ever undertaken. Hospice is an organization that takes care of terminally-ill individuals who have stopped receiving treatment for their illness. I was a volunteer caregiver in this group and had several patients that I would visit weekly.

I consider working in Hospice to be a significant accomplishment due to the emotional issues I had to overcome in order to spend time with these patients. Developing a relationship with them, while knowing they will soon die, can be a heart-wrenching experience. However, the knowledge of how much you can help a family or an individual far outweighs the emotional strain. Easing the pain of others, even if it is only on a small scale, is an accomplishment that only needs to be recognized by the individuals involved.

❧ ❧ ❧

Candidate: **Brian from the U.S.**
Essay topic: **Describe a personal achievement that has had a significant impact on your life.**
Target school: **Wharton**

Last year, I was involved in a very personal, challenging, and significant achievement that demonstrated the importance that family, love, and fellowship play in my life. It also highlighted personal qualities that have influenced my current career success, and will impact my future success as well. This involved locating my sister and her sons, and reuniting them with our family. Twenty-one years ago my sister converted and married into the Islamic faith. She and her husband were both African-Americans who chose to convert in the U.S. from their Christian upbringing to this religion. During their marriage they were blessed with five sons whom they planned to raise in their new faith. My sister's and my brother-in-Iaw's zealous beliefs created tension and distance between them and our parents as well as other family members. Gradually both my sister and nephews became more and more isolated from all of us. This distance was made more complete when nine years ago my sister moved to Cairo, Egypt with her five sons in order to raise them in an Islamic environment. Her husband had moved them to Egypt, but continued to live, work, and support them from the U.S. This left her husband as our most direct link to my sister but, by his choice, normal channels of communication with him had broken down.

Unexpectedly, my father received a distressing letter from my sister describing poverty-level living conditions and what appeared to be an abandonment of the family by her husband. The letter did not contain enough information to send any correspondence or help and we were unable to verify the contents of the letter with her husband. This made it necessary to personally visit Egypt in order to locate my sister and her sons. Based on my experiences and contacts developed while living overseas, it evolved that I would lead this effort.

In reflecting on the challenges and obstacles overcome in trying to locate and reconcile my sister with our family, I recognize several new discoveries about myself that were made on this journey. First, traveling to Egypt to find my sister uncovered my ability to quickly adapt, assimilate, and construct the tools or relationships needed to function effectively in a new environment. Egypt represented a region of the world for which I had little knowledge. Not only did I not speak the local language, but I also had never pursued any study of the region or its culture. The lack of advance warning for this trip limited my time to prepare for what I would experience. Egypt was my first experience in an Islamic country run under a dual bureaucratic and Koranic law. This would require me to work within the construct of Islam, which is unique in that it is at once an inseparable cultural, religious, and legal entity. Moreover, as a personal situation, I did not have the option of walking away from it. With limited time and financial resources, quick and efficient operation in this new environment was essential. My success in this matter resulted in finding my sister and nephews within three days of my arrival in Egypt.

This search might have taken weeks if it had not been for my ability to rapidly analyze the problem and find a path of communication in a foreign environment that would allow me to engage local people and obtain information. Using a local guide who spoke English, I was able to ask others in Arabic about the directions and address that I had of my sister from her letter to my father. The English translation of the Arabic address led us on a labyrinth-like search on the outskirts of the city. Eventually, my sister and nephews were found in a poor and isolated area. Despite the years apart with no contact, my sister lovingly greeted me and openly told me her story of isolation and abandonment by her husband who had left her without the financial wherewithal to support herself or to leave the country.

The trip to Egypt crystallized how much I had learned about tolerance and adaptability to other cultures. It also identified how communication is the key to bridging the gap between people and cultures. As I assisted my sister and nephews with their immediate needs, the application of the three-part principle of listening, observing, and adopting a non-judgmental attitude enabled me to deal with the new intricacies and mysteries of Islam and Egypt. Travel in other third world countries has shown me that success depends on a high tolerance for ambiguity. Method, priority, and urgency are measured differently in Western culture, with more time and patience required for anything needing to be accomplish. Being someone who likes things very well planned, this experience demonstrated that no matter what the task, there is a limit to the ability to prepare or plan for an event. One must be able to adjust quickly to situations in flux. This journey enhanced my ability to do this, as I recognized and seized opportunities and good fortune along the way.

Equally important in all of this was knowing when, and not being afraid, to ask for help. These qualities were manifested in my sourcing of a local guide who served as my primary means to successfully find my sister. Realizing my own limitations also meant that I did not go on this trip alone. Another sister, who is a doctor, accompanied me to help with any medical attention needed and to serve as a confidant to my sister in Egypt as we worked through the various issues we faced once she was found. In addition, I provided a daily e-mail journal of the events in Egypt to my closest friends in Hong Kong, Europe, and the U.S. This network of friends around the globe, through their direct guidance and assistance, or simply as confidants, served as a major support system while I struggled with the decisions and frustrations encountered during the trip. Each one, in some way, became a part of my journey and proved the many valuable friendships that I had developed over the years.

Lastly, this experience demonstrated to me my strength for building consensus. Before the trip, each family member held varying views on the goals of the trip. Much of the focus was on bringing them back to the U.S. These views did not consider my sister's original rationale for moving to Egypt and her possible desire to remain there. Nor did the family's views match my priorities of simply ensuring my sister's and my nephews' safety and health. Meeting the challenges of this situation required consolidating and reaching a compromise among these three separate views, priorities, and values. My sister's, the family's, and my own views all needed to be in sync in order to effectively pool the resources of the family in this effort. Shaping the focus and objectives of the trip led to one common purpose – locating and re-establishing communication with my sister. Any other desires such as bringing them back to the U.S. would not be a focus of this trip and it would allow everyone to be sensitive to their wishes to remain or leave Egypt. As a result not only were we able to locate her, but based on my sister's and nephews' own desire to return to the U.S., we were also able to successfully relocate her and my nephews back to the States and reunite her with our family.

My experiences with my sister in Egypt left me with a perception of the world as a smaller, reachable place with more in common across cultures than differences or separators. Communication is the first step. As shown in our family, establishing a dialogue that finds the common ground is the activity needed to cross borders and influence and guide people of all cultures. The result is the development of a universality in one's ability to communicate with others. This experience was about family and made me aware of the real importance of family structure to myself and the world in general. My family has not only shaped my values and priorities, but has also provided me much of my strength, drive, and determination to succeed. As part of a family, I as well as others in the world, contribute to this life and leave something for future generations as well. The success of my journey has helped our family, which was disparate, to pull together for a common good. There is now a more cohesive family and, through my nephews, a future beyond the present.

❦ ❦ ❦

Candidate: Tim from the U.S.
Essay topic: Describe a personal achievement that has had a significant impact on your life.
Target school: Wharton

I have always believed in this work ethic principle – as long as someone puts forward their best effort, good results will always arrive at the end. As one expression goes, "If you plant a melon seed you will get a melon, and if you plant a bean seed you will get beanstalk." I have been told that persistence and effort are rewarded while laziness and complacence are punished. The equation has always been easy to understand and to follow for me. By investing the proper time and effort I have been able to attain a fine high school education, a solid college preparation experience, as well as an opportunity upon graduation to work for a prestigious consulting firm. I believe that everyone has equal opportunity, equal access, and an equal understanding of how to be successful in this world.

"Stouffer Boy" – my nickname throughout my college years – reminds me of a life experience that caused me to re-evaluate a personal belief. It was a period of my life in which my own values and "hard work" beliefs were being challenged over a length of time. Most people saw little value in why I chose to work there – a 30-hour per week job at Stouffer Dining, one of the main student dining halls at Penn. Not only am I now proud of the fact that I was able to partially finance my college education, but also proud of the experience that has given me a new perspective on the challenges that others faced where equal opportunities might not exist.

Despite the rigors of working in the dish room, the dirty surroundings of the trash compactor, or the grueling task of cleaning up after students in the eating halls, I experienced and learned other things beyond the $8.50 an hour that Stouffer had to offer. I persisted in working at Stouffer for a few years and gained the well-rounded education that others did not value or see. My friends passing through the dining hall would jest at me and yell, "Stouffer Boy, what is the soup today?" They could not comprehend the reason why I was working there, "wasting" valuable time that could otherwise be spent hitting the books at Van Pelt. At Stouffer, students who operated the dining hall were looked upon different than the students who ate there. All of the student workers were not only bound together by the need of extra pocket money, but they also faced another level of adversity beyond the regular demands of school. While one fellow worker at New Jersey had divorced parents who could not support one penny in her education, another student from Texas had to send his wages back to support his family. I found that students under such pressures tend to develop a realistic, hardworking, and thankful perspective toward their education and their lives – something I had learned working side by side with them. For the student workers at Stouffer, the real challenge was not just getting admitted into Penn, but also balancing financial and academic requirements in order to stay and to succeed there.

Most people also did not see another opportunity I had at Stouffer – working closely, learning from, and building friendships with the local residents of West Philadelphia. Since Penn's environment is known to be quite hostile, many students in their four years at Philadelphia were afraid to interact closely with the people from the school's community. As I was promoted to be a Student Supervisor, I had to manage a team of seven to eight workers in one shift composed of both student workers and local workers. The local workers were varied in their backgrounds as well – some were lifelong union members in their 40s and 50s, while others were local high school students.

I felt initially that the local workers had an invisible wall separating themselves from the students. It was quite difficult at first to integrate the different groups and to understand clearly everyone's motivations and beliefs – many times I was even threatened by local workers as they did not like the assignments I gave them. However, I gradually learned how to gain their confidence through my work, and I was successful in breaking down some of their stereotypes of Ivy League students.

They eventually changed their initial confrontational attitudes with me to a more cooperative one. As I got to know several of the local workers over longer periods of time, I even found that some of them were more diligent and conscientious than us Penn students. Through my interactions with them I slowly learned that my strongly-held work ethic belief does not always apply. Most of them came from an under-privileged environment in some way or form – not only financially, but also other factors such as coming from a single-parent family, a background of drug abuse, or an environment of constant harmful peer pressures. No matter how many news or books I have heard or read about inner-city problems, I could never have understood the tribulations they have gone through. I realized how difficult and how "unequal" their circumstances were.

It was interesting to also understand the local people's perspectives of the school some were grateful of the school's contribution to the local economy, while many consider the students to be inconsiderate of the local people and the environment. Many of my younger fellow local workers were extremely smart but did not share the same opportunity to attend Penn, and often had stereotypes of the students. I felt that by leading through example, I changed some of their biases toward myself as I helped them to understand the school and the student body better. I invited some of them to several campus parties including our St. Patrick's Day party. They found the costumes to be extremely funny and they also found out that Penn students were fun, hardworking, and had interests similar to everyone else in West Philadelphia as well!

Working as a management consultant in Eastern U.S., clients and colleagues always seem to be surprised by the fact that I know how to fix a broken soda machine in a restaurant or how to operate a yogurt machine on-site at a client's cafeteria. They never guessed that I learned those skills at college. However, what I have carried forward in my life beyond graduation was not only a new set of finance, management, and dining hall operational knowledge, but a better understanding on the difficulties others faced and how greatly they differed from my own. I now believe that the traditional work ethic model, while still true, does not always guarantee success for everyone. Groups and individuals have their own unique set of circumstances and constraints to overcome, and people must be aware of those. There is simply no secret formula that applies to everyone. Today, the Students' Supervisor pin on my office desk serves as a symbol of "Stouffer Boy" days. It serves as a symbol of my persistence to defy popular beliefs and to see value in something where others did not.

Writing the "Overcoming Difficult Situations" Essay

Any "ethical dilemma" or "failure" type question is really a subcomponent of an "overcoming difficult situations" essay question.

Sample Essay Question

➢ "Describe a difficult decision or ethical dilemma that you have faced, how you resolved it, and what you learned from it."

Common mistakes

Some of the common mistakes made when writing this kind of essay include

- Not summarizing your writing in a clear way so that the reader knows for sure what is the "difficult situation";

- Not addressing the psychological aspects of the difficult situation;

■ Not showing how you are a better person because of the difficult situation—what did you learn?

Winning approaches

The following tips are useful guides when writing this essay type.

☞ *Tip #52:* *Signpost your difficult situation so the reader can more easily figure out what it is. Don't wait until the end of the essay to summarize the event or situation.*

Of all the essay types, the "overcoming the difficult situations" type is probably the easiest for the reader to get lost. The writer may take too long describing a difficult situation, leaving the reader to wonder, "where's this all going?" You may want to summarize the whole essay into one sentence before you start to write. For example, "My ethical dilemma involved weighing the risks of fitting unsafe contact lenses with the benefits of incremental sales and profits." The essay excerpt below shows how an essay can be framed with a minimal number of sentences:

> Ethically, I do not believe in trying to cheat government officials or in using my passport as a means of circumventing the law. I could have in all probability managed to take a couple of computers into Russia without declaring them. All I would have needed to do is to lie on my declaration form and play ignorant with Russian customs officials. I was reluctant to do so for a few reasons. First, if I were caught, I might be fined and face an embarrassing situation. Moreover, if I succeeded I might be inundated by other requests to do the same for our other Russian colleagues. The dilemma I faced rested with my desire to want to help my colleagues – colleagues who continued to give me valuable assistance in my joint-venture negotiation and translation work – and my duty to abide by the law.

☞ *Tip #53:* *Consider using quotes from people as a way to help the reader understand what you and/or other people actually felt.*

Difficult situations almost always have a psychological or moral component that brings emotion into play. Things actually said or thoughts held during these times, from you or others, can be key ingredients for understanding and relaying them.

☞ *Tip #54:* *In terms of describing your difficult situation and addressing what you have learned from it. A good weighting is to spend two-thirds describing and one-third writing what you've learned.*

Nowadays most business schools have begun asking, "What have you learned from your situation?" In the past this was an implied question, and one which was often overlooked by candidates. One closely related question is how much weight to give to describing the situation and how much weight to give to stating how much you learned from it. A good formula is "two-thirds describing it and one-third describing what you've learned." It is not necessary to break the two parts down into a 50-50 proposition.

Sample "Overcoming Difficult Situations" Essays

Candidate: Shannon from the U.S.
Essay topic: Describe a situation in which you failed and explain why you failed and what you learned from it.
Target school: Harvard

One of the greatest assets of any company is its people. Therefore, I view the loss of a "valued" team member as my biggest on-the-job failure to date. While at Silicon Watch Company, the Swiss watch manufacturer where I began my management career, our component purchaser resigned from her position. She had been with the company for six years and left only five months after I took over as her manager. She cited excessive workload and lack of support as the reasons for her departure.

As a first-time manager, I made several critical errors that actually led to her resignation. First, I imposed my own work ethic on her. I believed that everyone on my team should be willing to give 150 percent. I pushed her to finish urgent work before she left each day and held her accountable for giving timely feedback on production issues even when it meant working overtime. Her resignation showed me that not everyone's priorities are career-oriented and that sensitivity to my team's outside obligations is essential to being a good manager.

My second mistake was lack of communication. In an effort to learn more about our business, I met with some of our external suppliers individually. However, I did not properly communicate that in meetings with these vendors, I was not questioning my purchaser's abilities, but only trying to gain more insight into our product area. Since I did not make this clear to her, my purchaser misunderstood my intentions and felt that I was questioning her performance.

Fortunately, the next individual I hired for this position was actually much more dedicated. We were able to work together to decrease material costs and maintain a balanced work environment. Furthermore, I became much more aware of the work burdens on my team. Although I now do not hesitate to take action and provide relief when an employee is overloaded, I was only able to become a better manager through the process of losing my first purchaser due to my inexperience.

❥ ❥ ❥

Candidate: Marc from the Netherlands
Essay topic: Describe a difficult situation and what you learned from it.
Target school: Rotterdam

I faced a most difficult challenge in my work for a former senior accountant at Deloitte Touche Tohmatsu called Peter. Peter was known to be a bully to his subordinates. He earned his reputation for insulting subordinates' intellect, upbringing, capabilities, or personality. To make matters worse, since he was also a very demanding superior, he would seize upon any tiny mistake as an opportunity, in addition to the usual back-stabbing, to heap abuse upon colleagues.

Because of scheduling, I had to work for Peter on three assignments, stretching over a period of one-and-a-half years. Almost no day would pass without the two of us exchanging impressions of each other, and the whole department eventually got to know of our mutual disagreements. As I worked with him, I found out why he turned out to be such a "monster" – he was very scared of losing our managers' confidence in his productivity. He abused other colleagues, both as a way to vent his anxiety and as a means to extract the highest level of productivity with fear as the "motivator."

Since then, I began to deal with Peter in two ways. First, I tried my best to avoid any mistake, and would ask him to clarify each time I was not crystal clear about the results he demanded. Second, I came to regard Peter as only a very difficult tutor, and told myself that he was here to make sure I would not commit the same errors I had made in front of him. I ensured that I would remain upbeat when I worked for him. Each time he started his routine abuses, I would turn his attention away from the abuses themselves to the factors he wanted me to pay attention.

I was not able to stop Peter from bullying other colleagues, but I found that Peter gradually reduced the frequency with which he "abused" me. Moreover, because I must pay extra attention when I worked with him, I learnt a lot more from him than from many other senior accountants, both in terms of the detailed requirements of our work and of how not to become a leader. Peter eventually departed, but to my surprise, before he left, he actually mentioned to the managers about my attention to details and efficient execution of his order after clarifications as my good traits, something he had never done for anyone else.

♦ ♦ ♦

Candidate: **Vivian from the U.S.**
Essay topic: **Describe a situation in which you failed, with mention of why you failed and what you learned from it.**
Target school: **Harvard**

During my first managerial position at GE Lighting Europe, I faced the complex and diverse challenges of multi-cultural leadership. My efforts to foster an environment of cultural sensitivity and flexibility for my two Hungarian employees produced a dearth of direction and accountability. Ironically, it also brought a key cultural difference to the fore – Hungarians are often too proud to ask for directions or help. My plan of "empowerment" failed and left my staff without guidance. This lack of guidance caused our first project to veer irreparably off schedule.

My role as manager of the Western European Internal Audit Department was to create and lead comprehensive financial and business process audits for seven of our affiliate offices and three distribution centers. My team's first project in France did not go smoothly. The operational review of the business took twice as long as planned. Due to time constraints, our final report did not contain a complete balance sheet analysis.

When I hired my first Hungarian employee, Anita, I expected her to be a partner rather than a subordinate. Our deadlines were tight. We had two months to review both the financial accounts in the Paris affiliate and also audit the order-to-remittance process in the distribution center in Metz. This would necessitate us working not only on different reviews but also in different cities.

Although I anticipated that Anita might tackle her assignment from a different angle than I would have, I trusted her abilities and judgment. I wanted her to approach her work as she saw fit. Anita never called for advice or questions. Mistakenly, I never asked if she needed help. I interpreted her silence as affirmation that she knew what she was doing.

As an American, I took for granted that you ask for help if you have questions or are unclear about something. Only when an unplanned management request re-united us, did I realize we were over a month behind. Although I found that it is impossible to completely limit cultural misunderstanding, I did learn to better combine guidance and direction with cultural sensitivity.

♦ ♦ ♦

Candidate: **Peter from Australia**
Essay topic: **Discuss a non-academic personal failure, mentioning why you were disappointed in yourself and what you learned from that experience.**
Target school: **Columbia**

Martial arts has been an important part of my life. I learned Tae Kwon Do for five years, obtaining my black belt and instructor's degree while at university in Australia. I have continued martial arts training and currently have the privilege of learning from one of Hong Kong's most respected kung fu masters (Tam Hun Fan), who is from the same school where Bruce Lee began his martial arts career.

99

The personal failure that I would like to discuss involved a Tae Kwon Do tournament that I entered while I was still a student at the University of Melbourne. It was the State Championships and I qualified for the lightweight green belt division. Our club had ten or so entrants most of whom were exceptional fighters. In the months leading to the tournament, we all trained intensely and became very close friends. When the big day arrived we were all ready. The members of our school got off to a good start, and with the exception of two people, all progressed to the final of their respective divisions. I also made it to the final round of my division with a convincing victory over my semi-final opponent, gaining two knockdowns during the fight.

With all the final rounds completed and our club leading the trophy tally, one last match remained – mine. I was one of our instructor's favorite students. Before the fight he pulled me aside and said, "We want to finish this tournament with a big win from you. Do you think you can knock him out?" With my adrenaline pumping I thought I could do anything. He continued: "Look, I know I have taught all of you to go in hard as soon as the bell goes, but this time I want you to dance around the ring a bit and take a few hits. This will tire him out. After a minute passes, go in and knock him out."

The bell went off. The atmosphere was electric, reminiscent of a "Karate Kid" movie. I danced around the ring waiting for my opponent to tire so I could go for the big finish, but it did not progress as we had planned. My opponent kicked me in the face three times in quick succession. I was bleeding profusely from the nose and mouth. At this stage the referee stopped the fight and had a look at me; I wanted to continue, but he called off the fight. It was a tremendous anti-climax. It was lucky that the fight was called off at that moment because I found out the next day that my nose had been broken (I knew that something was wrong even before the X-ray. It had something to do with the green coloration of my nose).

What did I learn from this experience? Apart from learning that it is not healthy to be kicked in the face, this experience taught me that I should not be too greedy. If I had stuck to my normal technique I believe I would have beaten this opponent quite easily, but because I was over-ambitious I ended up not only not winning the division title, but suffering a painful loss. There is a Chinese saying that goes: Qing Chu Yu Lan Er Sheng Yu Lan (which literally means indigo blue extracted from the indigo plant is bluer than the plant that it comes from) which is sometimes translated as "the student surpasses the master." Before one can surpass the master he must master himself. And this means that a person should have the wisdom to follow a predetermined plan and not deviate from it. In my case, I should have followed my original plan for a quick sure-win victory.

❧ ❧ ❧

Candidate: **Steve from the U.K.**
Essay topic: **Please comment on a situation of personal or professional failure as well as what you learned from it.**
Target school: **IMD**

I have paid dearly for a lesson when I chose to quit in my first marriage, which ended in September 20xx.

I first got married in 20xx after six years of courtship. After a short and quiet while, trivial arguments often turned into big fights. Since both of us were young professionals and very righteous at that time, it was not long before we called it quits. It was a downhill journey from that point on and my first marriage had only lasted for a little more than one year. My life was shattered. I was deeply hurt and felt so ashamed to face people, especially those I knew before the marriage. Fortunately, I was able to recollect myself and focus on my career development.

I met my current wife, Elaine, in 2005. She was energetic, charming, and understanding and I knew she was the right one for me. However, I had difficulties shaking off my previous marriage experience and subconsciously I was driving her away. It was not until I became a Christian in late

20xx that I felt slightly more comfortable to accept my past and more ready to become someone's husband again. We eventually got married in March 20xx.

I am not suggesting here that we have been living happily thereafter. But, with God's teaching through the Bible, we are able to establish a very important ground rule "Quitting is not an option." This motto, together with vows we have pledged to each other, helps us through good times as well as bad times. We have the conviction that, with the help from our Lord, our relationship may be rocked but will never be broken.

❧ ❧ ❧

Candidate: John from the U.S.
Essay topic: Describe a situation in which you failed and what you learned from it.
Target school: Harvard

My literature professor under whom I studied at Phillips Andover Academy inspired me in a subject that I previously had not shown a great interest. Relating to his straightforward and captivating teaching style and his ability to draw themes between literature and life, I chose English Literature as my college major.

My university experience was brimming with activities and events. I was a member of the varsity wrestling team and also held two different jobs, one with a local restaurant, the other in the Anheuser-Busch marketing department. I also had an active role in the Marine ROTC Semper Fi Club. Throughout university, I struggled to find a passion for my liberal arts courses. I persevered and battled my way through the literature courses with the belief that the result would help me to achieve my career goal. I believed that the number-oriented, business courses could wait until I completed my Marine Corps commitment and went to business school. It was a mistake to continue a course of study which I did not have a great enthusiasm for. I should have majored in business and taken literature courses as electives.

Despite this stumbling block, I believe that learning to think with a critical literature mindset has been and will continue to be very advantageous in my professional career. Reading and writing about great literature has surely facilitated my written and verbal communication. In the military, it helped me quickly assess a situation, comprehend reports, and clearly and concisely communicate my operation plans and orders.

I have also enjoyed other benefits in the business world from the study of literature. I understand great writers and artists to be people who often test fringe ideas and concepts. As a reader of advanced literature, I learned to anticipate social issues arising from economic goals. For the greater part, based on my experiences to date, this is quite "optional" in the business world. Business leaders typically take the well planned, conservative routes as a means of achieving proven returns; they exhibit an ends-oriented, pragmatic thinking approach which typically does not entertain quixotic or figurative ways of thinking – the types of thinking that an artist would feel comfortable entertaining. For example, not so long ago executives of large multinational companies such as Coca-Cola, Nike, or McDonald's would have considered it a strange idea that certain groups within the international local culture perceived such multi-national companies as unwelcomed perpetrators of American Culture and eroders of local culture. Although such issues have not been critical at this juncture of my career, I am at least able to acknowledge these types of situations, including the social issues, peripheral or pivotal, that they give rise to.

❧ ❧ ❧

Candidate: Alfred from Austria
Essay topic: **Describe a situation in which you failed and what you learned from it.**
Target school: Harvard

In my senior year of university I participated in the Tyrol Cup, a snowboard halfpipe contest, held in the "Axamer Lizum" a ski resort close to Innsbruck, Austria. It was my dream to participate in that contest, which attracted many of the region's best snowboarders. As an avid snowboarder for many years, with extensive experience in skateboarding and wakeboarding, I gave myself a high chance to be among the top five. However, in the end I ranked 24 out of 50 contestants.

Ever since I was young, I developed a passion for board sports and snowboarding became a must for me in winter. The feeling of gliding in a forest through deep powder snow, with the snow reaching my waist, became an addiction. When I signed up for the event, I had one month to prepare. To better train for the contest, I chose to practice in a halfpipe (channel constructed in the snow) that was considered extra difficult with a steep radius. I spent three to four days a week on the "Seegrube" (ski resort above Innsbruck) practicing all the tricks I wanted to perform. My highlights were two extra difficult airs, one a "Frontside 540 Indy Grab" (a 5400 turn in the air grabbed with one hand and with a blind landing) and the other a "Backflip" (summersault in the air). To simulate the real conditions during the contest, I even practiced at night to adjust to the artificial light. I also went to the gym to strengthen my leg muscles and endurance.

On the night of the contest I was confident to get a top spot, given my rigorous and disciplined training. When I arrived at the site I was shocked to see that the halfpipe was very different from the "regular" ones. The radius was small and the half pipe was divided into two sections, which was combined by a flat section with a couple of small ramps. When it was my turn, I barely managed to do my tricks and I even fell once. It was a disaster and I was extremely disappointed. Although this setback seemed bigger at the time, it taught me a lesson. Practice and dedication are obviously important things but understanding the goal in context is critical. This is the same in sports or business. Today, for example, I would never just write a speech or prepare a report and get ready to present it unless I understood who my audience was.

Writing the "Analyze a Business Situation" Essay

"Business situation" questions cover great latitude, and therefore it is difficult to comment on all possible types in a specific way. This type of question appears to be gaining in popularity in recent years among business school admissions officers.

Sample Essay Question

➢ At Wharton, the Learning Team, which consists of approximately five first-year students, is often assigned group projects and class presentations. Imagine that, one year from now, your Learning Team has a marketing class assignment due at 9 a.m. on Monday morning. It is now 10 p.m. on Sunday night; time is short, tension builds and your team has reached an impasse. What role would you take in such a situation? How would you enable the team to meet your deadline? (Note: The specific nature of the assignment is not as important here as the team dynamics.) Feel free to draw on previous experiences, if applicable, in order to illustrate your approach. (University of Pennsylvania Wharton)

Common mistakes

Common mistakes made when writing an "analyze a business situation" essay include

- Not thinking about all aspects of a problem as required by an all-round thinking process;

- Not breaking the essay into distinct subcomponents as required by an analytical approach to problem solving;

- Not using a clear structure to break own your essay and signpost your discussion.

Winning approaches

Here are two useful tips to keep in mind when tackling this essay type.

☞ *Tip #55: Consider scenario analysis.*

Consider as many aspects of a business problem as possible. Occasionally, scenario planning is required if asked what might happen or what might be the problem and/or solution. One approach is to say that there are three potential problem areas and, therefore, three potential solutions to complement each problem. In the case where you are required to sketch a business plan, do not forget to mention each of these major components: summary, product, people, market and customer, competition, and financing.

In situations where you have an open-ended essay that does not specify a particular company, product, or person, you may want to center your discussion on a fictitious company, product, or person. The upcoming essay, written by Caroline, illustrates this technique through her use of a hypothetical employee named "David."

☞ *Tip #56: Signpost your discussion using enumeration.*

Enumeration refers to those tools—words or numbers—used to signpost your discussion. Examples include the words "first," "second," and "third" and the numbers 1, 2, 3 or i), ii), iii). Refer to *Chapter 10* for further explanation of this technique.

Sample "Analyze a Business Situation" Essays

Candidate: Caroline from Israel

Essay topic: **You are a successful manager and responsible for hiring people in your department. It now appears you may have made a mistake. An employee you selected six months ago is not performing at an acceptable level. You have confronted this person, reviewed performance expectations, and given constructive suggestions for improvement. However, the employee's performance has not improved and you have decided this cannot continue. How will you handle the situation?**

Target school: New York University

Let us take a hypothetical scenario in which I am sales director of ABC Co. who has made the mistake of hiring "David" for my department. Although David has not performed to an acceptable level by meeting sales goals in the past three months, I have decided to give him another chance.

Given that I am a compassionate person with good interpersonal skills, I see three options to consider in resolving this dilemma:

1. Keep him in my department but assign him to a different position; or
2. Transfer him to another department but keep him in our company; or
3. Terminate his employment.

First, my preferred action would be to give David another chance at another position within my department, provided he has the rudimentary skill-set. In my current job as a human resource consultant, one of the lessons I learned is that different people have different motivational levels. An intense line position with profit-and-loss responsibilities is more suitable for an ambitious achiever as opposed to a behind-the-scenes staff position. David may perform better in a support function with a base salary rather than in a sales position with a commission-based salary. He may not be as financially motivated as he is motivated by job stability.

Secondly, I would consider transferring David from my department to another department if his skill-sets are suitable to another department. Through my interactions with many department managers, I have found that because an employee cannot perform in one department does not mean he cannot excel in another department. In the case of David, perhaps his strong analytical skills are more attuned to finance models than to the marketing world.

As a last resort, if David is not responsive to my suggestions to stay within the company, then I will terminate his employment. I will suggest that he go to personnel for a career skills assessment test. It may be that he would be effective in a different industry and may not realize it. His failure in his job might be a blessing in disguise. I may have helped David save some time by encouraging him to find a job he can excel in.

◆ ◆ ◆

Candidate: **Rodriquez from Brazil**
Essay topic: **Imagine that, one year from now, your Learning Team (consisting of five first-year students) has a group marketing assignment due at 9 a.m. on Monday morning. It is now 10 p.m. on Sunday night; time is short, tension builds and your team has reached an impasse. What role would you take in such a situation? How would you enable the team to meet your deadline? Feel free to draw on previous experience, if applicable, in order to illustrate your approach.**
Target school: **Wharton**

Teamwork is my "specialty." Although I am not always a person who can draw insightful theories about teamwork, I am a team player who can always make significant contributions to the efficiency and effectiveness of the team. My understanding of team dynamics was strengthened by my experience in organizing activities in university, preparing team assignments during my Masters of Accounting degree program, and coordinating financing proposals at Credit Suisse First Boston (CSFB).

I see five steps involved in a team project. The steps are problem identification, data gathering, solution planning, implementation, and evaluation. As Wharton students are usually highly motivated individuals, by 10 p.m. on Sunday night, I assume that we would have at least gathered the necessary data and would be about to start our third stage, solution planning.

Given the time constraint, I see three potential scenarios that would overcome such an impasse. I would playa different role in each scenario to facilitate timely completion. The three scenarios are:

i)   We have the same solution.
ii)   We have different solutions.
iii) We have no solution at all.

In the first scenario, I would play the role of a coordinator. This is the most common situation that I face in the investment banking industry. At CSFB, we often already know the financing solution for a client company. However, the greatest challenge is often "tying up" our credentials, views, and methodologies together under immense time pressure. Based on my experience, once the solution is identified, there are four sub-steps in the implementation and evaluation process. First, I would suggest that my team outline the project. Once we agree upon the outline, we would first determine which part of the project is the most critical. The critical part would be done with priority and given most attention.

Second, each part would be drafted primarily by one person, and the most critical part would be drafted by two or more persons. We would also agree on the deadline for the first draft of each part, for example, by 4 a.m. Third, once we have the first draft (combined or not), each person would orally present his/her part and receive feedback from other team members. Each member would then further modify his/her own part to incorporate the additional suggestions. Finally, at around 6:30 a.m., we would circulate the second draft and finalize any changes if needed. From putting numerous proposals together under a tight deadline, I learned that time management and polishing the critical parts or key messages are most critical to the success of any project.

In the second scenario, I would play the role of a moderator. With two different solutions under time constraint, we could first continue to debate the solution indefinitely and end up putting minimal effort into actual implementation of the solutions, or even miss the deadline at 9 a.m. Clearly, the outcome is not acceptable. Second, we could impose a deadline for determining a solution, for example, by 2 a.m. From my experience in my Masters of Accounting program, we often had to determine the accounting treatment of many unusual activities. Although there is no one rule that specifically defined the situation, there are many conceptual statements or related pronouncements that would hint at the correct solution. My experience tells me that when there are different solutions, it is optimal to break down the solutions into different components. Understanding that each member has his/her own rationale, I would suggest that the team members present their ideas to other members. After examining and understanding the source of differences, we should either slowly narrow them down to one solution, or more likely, we should be able to integrate the best parts of different solutions and subsequently create a better approach to the problem.

However, if there is still no consensus by 2 a.m., we would then have to pick the two alternative routes. First, given the diverse background of my Learning Team, we can create a self-imposed hierarchy in the team and allow the person with the most relevant experience and background to determine the solution and drive the entire process. For example, assuming it is a marketing project about introducing new vehicles to Japan, our group member named "Keio," a Japanese who worked for Toyota as a sales manager, will become our team leader. Second, if there is no such person, we should simply take a vote and the majority would rule and drive the entire process.

In the third scenario, I would play the role of a leader. With no solution on hand, the deadline could be easily missed. In such a situation, there would be two options. First, I would impose the deadline for a solution at, for example, 2 a.m. Before the deadline, I would lead the team to attack the problem using an "analytical approach." I would take the lead to break down the project into as many little components as possible, and analyze the approach to each component separately. It is similar to my experience as the president of the Hong Kong USC Students' Club. As a newly elected president, one of my goals was to promote memberships. I also had no solution initially. However, once I broke down the problem into many components affecting memberships, for example, membership fees, nature of activities, club image and profile, and effectiveness of organizational structure, etc., I tackled each component separately. As a result, membership tripled to over 200 under my leadership. Therefore, I believe, the "analytical approach" should at least enable us to identify partial solutions to the project. Second, if we cannot identify a solution by 2 a.m., I would find one based on our partial results and our best estimates. As long as we can carefully explain our rationale, we should be able to get credit for our educated estimates. The bottom line is "something is always better than nothing."

In any scenario, effective communications, mutual understanding, commitment to hard work, and cohesiveness are key factors for successful teamwork. I am confident that I could contribute positively to those aspects of my Learning Team at the Wharton School.

❥ ❥ ❥

Candidate: **Alice from Hong Kong**

Essay topic: **A well-known, multinational company has a long-term contract to extract previous metals in an impoverished region in a developing country. Over the past decade, the operation has proven very profitable to the company. Recently, there have been peaceful, but highly disruptive, demonstrations by members of communities adjacent to the company's property. The ruling military dictatorship has been unresponsive in meeting the local communities' needs. The local communities are now demanding a share of the mining operation's profits in the form of approximately US$8 million to provide clean water and basic sanitation for the surrounding villages.**

You have recently been promoted and sent to this country as the expatriate general manager responsible for the operation. The mine is assessed US$20 million in annual taxes by the government. This year you will show a US$50 million after-tax profit if you elect not to address the request of the local community. Your team has worked very hard this year. A US$50 million profit is the minimum level to ensure that your team meets its bonus plan.

Please provide an analysis of your options, describing what you would do, discussing the rationale for your choice, and addressing your plan to communicate with any constituent affected by your decision.

Target school: **Dartmouth (Tuck)**

The case is a classic management dilemma of achieving profits while caring for the local communities. On one hand, our company must guarantee at least US$50 million after-tax profit to fulfill the bonus plan of my diligent team. On the other hand, we must promptly address the local needs to maintain the privileges of conducting business in the country.

To seek an effective resolution, we must first understand the three critical success factors of our mining operation:

1. The revenue drivers are rates of output and productivity. Therefore, our company's profitability relies heavily upon free access to abundant precious metals and cheap local labor.

2. We must skillfully balance the interests of all stakeholders: our operation, our employees, the local communities, and the ruling military dictatorship.

3. As we help settle the unrest by addressing the public's concerns, we will also build goodwill toward our brand.

After thorough analysis, as the operation's new expatriate general manager, I have identified and evaluated three options as follows:

Option 1: Maintain the US$50 million after-tax profit so as to fulfill the team's bonus plan.

This option is consistent with the objective function of commercial enterprises in a capitalistic world. As my team has worked hard, they are entitled to receive the financial rewards for their fruitful labor. However, this option prioritizes the short-term financial interests of our operation and our employees above the long-term well-being of the local communities. Therefore, Option 1 fails to address the needs of the local communities, and would cause the local military dictatorship to endure continuous public protests. As a result, this is a win-lose option.

Option 2: Recognize the concerns of the local communities and donate a portion of the profit to environmental projects.

This option prioritizes the long-term well-being of the local communities above the short-term financial interests of our operation and our employees. The donation would help improve the living conditions of the surrounding villages, and benefit the dictatorship by avoiding further disruptive public unrest while still maintaining the stipulated tax income. However, we would forsake the team's bonus plan and risk dampening their morale and our company's future performance. As a result, this is also a win-lose option.

Option 3: Jointly raise the US$8 million with the local communities, and establish a new profit-sharing plan for long-term community development. This represents a win-win situation and is the recommended course of action.

This option aims at attaining the long-term well-being of the local communities as well as the long-term financial health of our operation and our employees, through a new profit-sharing plan. The essence of the new plan is to bond the interests of, and share risks among all key stakeholders.

Under the new plan, our company would first establish a shared goal among employees and the local communities to enhance our productivity and develop innovative mining methods to increase output. The objective of enhanced collaboration is to achieve higher, sustainable profitability for our mining operation that would help fund local community projects in the long run. With the improved profitability, our company would donate, from after-tax profit in excess of US$50 million, up to US$8 million in the first year to provide clean water and sanitation facilities. Meanwhile, employee bonuses for this year would be paid out from the US$50 million after-tax profit. In the next five years, our company would donate five percent of the excess to community projects. We would distribute another five percent as additional bonuses to employees, while retaining the remainder for internal operations. At the same time, we would petition the government for tax credits on the ground that our plan has channeled the energy of a potentially large-scale social unrest, which would destabilize the business and political environment, to benefiting the development of the local communities.

This is a win-win option that balances the interests of all stakeholders. Our company would achieve a higher profitability while fulfilling its greater social responsibility toward the local communities. Our employees would benefit as the new plan promises additional bonuses, while their morale would also be boosted as a result of the public goodwill generated. The local communities would not only receive the donation required for providing clean water and sanitation facilities, but also take an active role in maintaining a healthy environment through participation in our plan. Finally, the local government would avoid unnecessary public protests.

Furthermore, Option 3 would also allow our company to build a solid foundation for long-term growth and profitability in the country along three dimensions:

1. Developing corporate citizenship. Externally, the plan is a bold expression of our commitment to the well-being of the local communities. Through sharing our profits, we would demonstrate our pledge to grow with the communities. Internally, the plan would help develop future generations of employees who can appreciate and shoulder corporate responsibility.

2. Establishing regional industry leadership early on. The plan would open new avenues for deepening our existing relationships with the local government and communities. It would also help us achieve competitive advantage over our competitors by establishing our regional industry leadership early on.

3. Achieving long-term economic viability. By drawing public interest to our success, the plan would enable us to leverage local manpower and expertise in exploring opportunities to streamline operations, increase productivity, and achieve long-term profitability.

At the execution level, I would propose a three-tiered communication approach targeting all stakeholders:

Communication to employees. This first-tier level of communication will solicit company-wide support and feedback. In forms of corporate memo and discussion forums, this communication will detail the rationales and policies of the new plan, and emphasize its important role in the long-term financial success of our company and our employees.

Communication to the government. This second-tier level of communication will petition government support of and contribution to the plan. It will be conducted through face-to-face meetings with key government officials, since government cooperation is critical to ensure our smooth transition into the new plan.

Communication to the local communities. This third-tier level of communication will formally announce details of the plan while soliciting public support. Conducted through press conference and advertising campaigns, this communication will also reinforce the primary objective of the plan: Help develop the local communities while furthering our growth.

Writing the "Wildcard" Essay

"Wildcard" type essay questions are used by schools to get an idea of who you are and, to some extent, take the place of the traditional "who are you?" essays. On another level, these essays are open-ended and are meant to assess your creativity.

Sample Essay Questions

➤ "Who would you choose to be for one day and why would you choose that person?"

➤ "Name three persons living or dead whom you would like to invite to dinner and what you would talk about."

➤ "If you were an animal what kind would you be and why?"

➤ "Mention one day you would like to relive and why?"

➤ "Propose a question that we, the admissions committee, should have asked and answer it."

➤ "The admissions committee has just reviewed your application. Write what has been written in your file."

➤ "Describe a teacher/mentor you admire and explain why you admire him or her."

Common mistakes

Two common mistakes made when tackling "wildcard" essays include

■ Not revealing enough of your personal characteristics through these essays;

■ Not briefly summarizing your experience and/or giving a brief answer to the question, before going into a full-blown description.

Winning approaches

Here are two time-honored tips for writing "wildcard" essays.

☞ *Tip #57:* *Reveal as much of your character and personal and professional strengths as possible—motivations, spiritual enlightenment, emotional balance, intellectual fervor, latent potential, insights, likes and dislikes. These essay questions invite (and expect) you to get "fancy" and take chances.*

☞ *Tip #58:* *Make sure you answer directly the question at hand. Often, it's best to do this in the opening sentence of the essay.*

Sample "Wildcard" Essays

In the sample essay that follows, William opens his essay with the summary, "The three persons whom I would invite to this special dinner would be Winston Churchill, Tang Tai long (the second emperor of the Tang dynasty of China), and my late father." In the sample essay written by Tiffany, her first sentence acts as an implied answer to the question at hand, "An apple is a most versatile fruit."

Candidate: **William from Canada**
Essay topic: **If you chose any three people who have ever lived to join you for dinner, whom would you invite and why?**
Target school: **London Business School**

The three persons whom I would invite to this special dinner, would be Winston Churchill, Tang Tai long (the second emperor of the Tang dynasty of China), and my late father.

Before being British Prime Minister, Winston Churchill warned about the ascent of Adolf Hitler in post-WWI years. Few people, even in his own country, believed in Churchill. He had even been ridiculed for his insight into the Fuhrer's ambitions. However, he never ceased to point out Hitler's true intentions and, when WWII finally broke out, he vindicated himself by leading the British Empire from the brink of defeat to victory. I would invite Winston Churchill to dinner, in order to be inspired by his decisiveness and strong leadership in the face of immense pressure.

When Emperor Tai long received the reign of the Tang dynasty from his father in A.D. 626, China was war-torn after more than three centuries of civil war and was vulnerable from invasion by the Turkish nomads in present-day Mongolia. He set out to recruit the best ministers he could find, built a team out of them, and with their conscientious counsels restored China's civil stability and military might. In A.D. 630, he started a campaign against the Turks which ended in the khanate's rout and westward migration. I would invite Tang Tai long to dinner because I want to learn how to recruit outstanding advisors, form a think-tank with them, and motivate them to give prudent counsel freely.

Unlike the first two, my late father was not a historically famous man. He served as the deputy chief engineer of a railway in China when the Communists marched down south in 1949. He escaped to Hong Kong as a refugee, only with the clothes on his body and a few dollars in his pocket. But, my mother told me, he never lost hope and confidence. When the construction industry took off in Hong Kong, my father managed to have himself hired by a big local construction firm, and eventually worked his way up to become chief engineer before leaving to launch his own subcontracting business. I would invite my late father to dinner, to remember old times and to be influenced by his dedication and optimism.

❧ ❧ ❧

Candidate: **Tiffany from England**
Essay topic: **If you had to choose to be a type of vegetable or fruit, which would you choose and why?**
Target school: **University of Cape Town**

An apple is a most versatile fruit. It can make cider or pie. As a raw liquid it is juice, as a cooked solid it is pie. Apples are a diverse lot. They can be described as red, green, yellow, tiny, large (reaching four pounds I believe), tart, or sweet. Famous names of apples include Delicious, Golden Delicious, Macintosh, Rome Beauty, Jonathan, Granny Smith, and there is even a Crab named Apple. Some companies have put apple in their names and grown as well. I am thinking of Apple Records before Apple Computers.

If I were an apple there would be many places I could visit and still feel at home. Apple is a truly pervasive fruit. It can be found on all continents and most countries including Canada and the U.S., China and Japan, France and Italy, Poland and Russia, Iran, Australia and New Zealand, and last but not least, South Africa. Apple is also a complementary fruit. According to the strict rules of juicing, only fruits can be mixed with fruits and vegetables mixed with vegetables. Apple is the exception. Apple and carrot are a winning combination.

Unlike a perishable peach or pear, an apple is durable and can stay for a while before getting too ripe to eat. An apple is an apple some might say. But there's no mistaking its identity. A tomato, on the other hand, is caught in a strange dilemma. It can be either a fruit or vegetable. Botanically it is a fruit because it contains seeds, but horticulturally it is a vegetable because it grows on a vine.

The apple is a recognized symbol of health and prosperity. It is said that "An apple a day, keeps the doctor away." And there are other sayings that adorn the apple. "An apple does not fall far from the tree" means we take on the characteristics of those around us or, perhaps, that we cannot escape our backgrounds and culture. Whatever! I'd rather be an apple on an orchard tree, basking in the warmth of a summer's day.

❧ ❧ ❧

Candidate: **Kyle from the U.S.**
Essay topic: **Which recent development, world event, or book has most influenced your thinking and why?**
Target school: **Oxford**

I studied the award-wining book *Siddhartha* by author Hermann Hesse during my philosophy course as an undergraduate. At first read, I thought this small novel was only about Buddhism.

But when I examined it more closely for the purpose of writing a book critique I could see many interesting things. Since I was majoring in business, I began thinking about how this book might be similar to business and wrote some thoughts in my journal. In order to answer this question, I have restudied the book and read through my journal and would like to recount how the book has most influenced me.

Siddhartha is foremost a story of objectivity. Where would the story have gone if Siddhartha had stayed in the palace and never questioned anything or had the courage to go out alone? His struggle is like that of a true entrepreneur who must pursue a dream and follow a tough "path" in the quest for accomplishment.

The story is about how Siddhartha (the prince) gets an idea, tests that idea, receives feedback, tests that idea out again, and finally reaches his goal. Each time he runs into problems, he must reevaluate what he is doing and how he will next proceed. For example, Siddhartha first believes that the way to live is to be a Brahman. He lives a life but is not satisfied. He reevaluates. Is the answer over there? So Siddhartha pursues a another pasture – he joins the Samanas and is still searching. With the pursuit of Gotama, he thinks he has found a place, but realizes he must reject this and travel yet again. Along anyone of these paths Siddhartha is actually successful. Through constant reevaluation he is able to make his experiences internal ("alone in the forest") and then go on to pursue a life in a village as a businessman for Kamaswami and confidant of Kamala. Each step of the way, he reevaluates his "success" and sets out again. Later he finds himself at the river learning from Vasudeva. Eventually he leaves to find his ultimate goal.

The story is also a study of perseverance. To some the story might seem like the ramblings of a philosopher. But it must be agreed that it is a story about a guy who gets dirty. It is about sweat. Siddhartha follows a grueling path toward the goal he seeks. His perseverance is interwoven with purpose. It's a purpose that is like a whip that has no mercy. Along the road to success are temptations and distractions. Some of these distractions almost led to his death. He lives on the edge. He is a maverick. This experience could be translated to the story of a top-notch business person, a Steve Jobs or a Bill Gates, fighting with feelings of self-doubt before the world knows them for who they are.

Perseverance requires courage and bravery. Even without vision or a purpose, the journey would have been wasted if efforts were not fully used. Siddhartha has talent and intelligence, but he also has courage. His courage – his spirit – it is a bird that can never die.

Lastly, *Siddhartha* is a story of appreciation. Appreciation is an offshoot of both objectivity and perseverance. How many times does Siddhartha think he has it figured things out only to be back at the drawing chart? We can't help but wonder how many times he will have to think again. The process of anticipating thinking again, engenders appreciation. The process of seeing two where there was previously only one is another sign of appreciation. Siddhartha does not become cynical by his experiences. He remains appreciative and balanced.

Siddhartha also holds strategic lessons in terms of understanding the roles of leader versus manager. Siddhartha played the role of manager when he worked alongside Kamaswami. As a manager Siddhartha confronted what it was like to be responsible for people and the daily operations of a business. This is a characteristic that most distinguishes a manager. A manager is responsible. The characteristic that most distinguishes a leader is a sense of vision or purpose. A leader is creative and doesn't always lead through words or instructions but often through emotions or feelings or inspirations. Siddhartha leads Govinda in this way. Not all the things he communicates to Govinda can be read, spoken, or heard. A leader exercises non-verbal communication. Siddhartha is all a worker, manager, leader, and individualist.

This book continues to have an effect on me because it reveals to me the many lessons to apply to business that come from places outside of business. If a person can use his or her mind fully, the ability to find lessons in one area of life and transfer them to other areas is of great benefit.

Candidate: Julianne from Canada
Essay topic: Which recent development, world event, or book has most influenced your thinking and why?
Target school: Oxford

Margaret Atwood's *The Edible Woman* is a fiction novel that has greatly influenced my thinking and has helped me reflect meaningfully on the various junctions of my life to date. This book is a celebration of the individual and is a metaphor for the aspiring individual's ongoing struggle to both fit in and stand out. Atwood takes us into the mind and experience of Marian, a young, educated, single girl living and working in the urban 1960s. Marian finds herself at a crossroads in her life when she accepts a proposal from her boyfriend Peter who rationalizes this proposition by concluding, "It'll be a lot better in the long run for my [law] practice". We see Marian's life through a variety of experiences that illustrate to us the struggle of a woman Marian's age in search of her "self" in Canada in the 1960s. The confusion surrounding her expected roles in society is captured through the lens of Marian's relationship to food. Eating in the novel becomes a symbol of power and destruction of self and character when, after accepting Peter's proposal, Marian becomes increasingly unable to eat.

I see this novel as relevant to Canadian society and culture today and useful in examining my own struggle to fit in and stand out in society. To demonstrate this, I need only to reflect on my decision to choose to study and pursue work as a nurse, to engage independent travel, and finally to focus my efforts on management and health promotion in the private health care sector. I relate to the theme of conflict that Marian faces throughout the novel and see similar conflictions woven throughout my years to date battling between the expected roles of society including struggling to find a career versus fulfilling my role within traditional society of having a family and settling down.

When I began my nursing training, it became increasingly apparent to me that I would be struggling to find a sense of individualism and a place to stand out in the large "machine" that is public health care in Canada today. Nonetheless, I grew to have a deep respect for the work that nurses currently do and the many progressions the profession has made from its role in the early days as "the physician's handmaiden". I found the intimate rapport I was able to gain with patients, as I shared in some of the toughest experiences of their lives, both extremely challenging and exceptionally rewarding. I was able to gain a new perspective both on death and on life as well as gain a sense of reality that comes from working first hand with terminally ill patients. I am grateful for this experience as I feel it has given me an enriched sense of empathy and compassion as well as allowed me to develop personal relation skills beyond what is taught in any classroom. The struggle I had throughout achieving my degree and becoming a part of the "machine" was that of finding a unique place for individuality and progression of achievement. I found that the limited room for career advancement in terms of recognized short- and long-term goal setting frustrated the drive I have to continually better myself and advance my career path. As Marian discovers when she signs up for the company pension plan, a sense of "this is it" was an increasingly common feeling as I examined the careers of my senior colleagues and options for Registered Nurses within the public health system. I was able to find a compromise of this position when I switched from the public system to the private system and transitioned to a position with Foothills Health Consultants. I recognized limitless opportunity in the large risk I took leaving a stable job with the region and taking a position with a private company that offered me no union backing or long-term promise of stability. I instantly felt the sense of relief Marian describes when she finally confronts Peter: "the force that was trying to destroy me". It is because of the risk I took leaving the "collective" to join a private company with no other nurses on staff and no set job description that I was able to create the job of my dreams and focus on larger, long-term goals I could not have even contemplated in the public system. In this way I identify with the struggle to find the individual among the collective Atwood so eloquently describes in the novel.

My second big struggle that I am reminded of when I reflect on this novel is a battle of a commitment versus independence or, perhaps, status quo versus change. This situation was also brought about by the feelings I had working as a Registered Nurse in the public health care system. After I finished my training in December of 20xx, and was able to work as a professional nurse before my degree was awarded in the spring of 20xx, I found myself struggling again with the feeling that "this was it". I had just graduated and it should have been one of the happiest times in my life; the time when I was able to join the real working world and create a living and career for myself like I saw my colleagues doing. Instead I felt a deep rooted need to explore and experience more life before I could even contemplate the thought of "settling down" as I felt was expected of me now that I was done school. I was able to find a perfect compromise for this situation when I decided to travel and work abroad.

My traveling experience began in the spring of 20xx, when I left on my own for Australia. I had such a renewed sense of adventure and excitement as I stepped onto the plane by myself and let my mind wander to all of the limitless possibilities that lay ahead. On that first trip I spent three months exploring Australia, Singapore, Malaysia and Thailand. The biggest thing I learned during this time was that there are so many more options and possibilities in life than what I had initially envisioned – finishing school, starting a career and eventually having a family in Canada. I was fortunate in this time to meet and stay with four families in Southeast Asia who took me in for the time I was there and treated me as one of their own. I learned a greater sense of hospitality and amazing generosity that I will remember for the rest of my life. When I returned home I knew I had to travel more it was just a question of when and how. I returned to work and became specialized in the area of neurology and it wasn't long before I was accepted to take a travel nurse position on a neurology ward in Edinburgh Scotland. This was to be my biggest adventure yet. In the following year I learned the ways of a completely new and different health care system from the one I was used to at home, I traveled through eight more countries again either independently or with friends I met along the way. I once again learned that I had the capability to survive on my own in a new environment miles away from home an experience that has shaped me for the rest of my life. I learned that the nursing skills I developed in Canada translated to the patients I treated in Scotland and I felt a deep connection to the patients I grew to know and who touched my life. I found it very interesting working with an international health care team from around the world and made many life-long connections and friends I now consider more family. I found that this experience satisfied in me the urge to break free of the routine I had at home while still allowing me to develop my skills as a specialized neurology nurse. I found the freedom of commitment to one job or one country and place of residence exhilarating and many times I packed up my bag and headed off to a new and unexplored part of the world amazed at how much l learned in each place. When I returned home I had a deeper understanding of health care and how the basic principles of humanity apply no matter where you are in the world.

The third major challenge I faced was my toughest yet. When I returned home from my travels I found myself back in the public health care system working on my old neurology unit with again few prospects for advancement or progression in my role as a Registered Nurse. My experiences in competitive sports instilled in me a deep-rooted belief in the basics of health promotion being exercise, good nutrition and risk awareness. With this idea in mind I began looking for a new job. I approached Liz Young who is the creator of Trym Gym, a health promotion and weight management program at the University of Calgary. Again this was a risk as it was a cold call and I had no formal teaching experience. I soon found myself with a new part-time position teaching for Liz and through this program was introduced to Foothills Health Consultants. It was with this company that I began to see the exciting opportunity for growth that I had been searching for. Through my development, and with the company initially defining a new role as the only Registered Nurse on staff, I became manager of the rapidly expanding nursing department. Having identified the career path I am passionate about, I now have a vision for myself that allows an individual identity. I am excited at the limitless potential I now face and can't wait to develop my skills and person further through an MBA program.

In conclusion, *The Edible Woman* has provided me with a point of reflection and basis to identify the challenges and successes I have had in my life thus far. Throughout the novel we are shown examples of the different paths women can take in life through the characters with which Marian interacts. I identify greatly with Marian in her struggle to both fit in and stand out and value the example Atwood provides when at the end of the novel she chooses independence. I have faced this choice on more than one occasion and it has proven to guide me to a place in my life where I feel I am on the right path toward finding a compromise that supports my drive to be successful in all areas of my life. I have begun to feel the reward of holding out for one path in life as my career choice. In the way that Marian at the end of the novel chooses to bake a cake in the form of herself and eat it as a means of emancipating herself, I too feel the unlimited opportunity stretched out before me. However, whereas Marian leaves only knowing what she does not want, I feel the course I have set for myself is congruent with my personal sense of self and purpose.

Chapter 5

Writing Optional Essays

Don't view your essay as an academic article or a business memo, but as a human interest story about yourself.

—Linda Abraham,
Admissions Consultant

Introduction

Ponder for a moment how a candidate would go about answering the following questions about his or her candidacy, particularly in light of the absence of essay questions that ask about them:

- How do I show my diversity of character?
- How do I truly differentiate myself from other candidates?
- Where do I address an anticipated weakness in my application?
- How do I show I am an interesting person?
- Where do I elaborate on my work experience?
- How do I further show my ability to handle detail as well as creative challenges?
- How do I illustrate my insight and intelligence?
- How do I embellish on my personal or professional strengths?

The above questions are very often answered only through the use of the optional or "blank" question.

Sample Essay Question

> "The Admissions Committee would like to know if you wish to address anything not mentioned in your essays or application. Please feel free to leave this area blank if you feel you have adequately presented your case."

Tips for Writing Optional Essays

A real secret to putting together a first-class application lies in taking advantage of the optional or "blank" question. The blank question is probably the most underutilized area of business school applications. It is estimated that only ten percent of business school applicants address this question. And when candidates choose to do so, it is generally only used to address an anticipated weakness in their applications, in particular, "Why I have a lower than average GMAT score or GPA?" But there are many more dimensions to the optional question. In fact, it is as much an opportunity to embellish your strengths as it is a place to address weaknesses.

A few well-developed optional essay entries can add a whole new dimension to your application. There are many things in your background—hobbies, interests, sports, awards, recognition, service projects, work projects, mentors, and virtually anything you feel is important—that could be the topic of an optional essay. Do not let something that you feel passionate about get reduced to just a single sentence and remain hidden away in your essay, employment record, or list of extracurricular and community activities. There may be no other place to draw attention to your piece and this may be just the kind of thing that could help your application catch fire en route to acceptance.

Even in terms of academic strengths, do not think that "everything" can be read from your academic transcripts or that the whole of your academic experience comes down to a single grade point average. You may want to help the reader understand what the full significance of your academic experience is. If you have a high GPA, take half a page in the blank question area and say exactly what it means to you and why it is important. You might mention some habits or ideas you picked up along the way that spelled success in the academic arena. At a minimum, you might say how you committed yourself to your studies and how commitment is the key to your future business success. Perhaps you do not have a high GPA, but were a double major, or perhaps you wrote a particularly interesting senior thesis or research paper.

Business schools want diverse, intelligent, and compassionate people to fill their classes. Your main essays alone are generally an insufficient medium to present yourself as a unique individual. In all likelihood, no business school application can really explore all the attributes of a complex and creative individual. The optional question provides you with an opportunity to explore some different areas. When you finish writing your standard application essays for a given school, ask yourself, "Do my essays, employment record, and extracurricular activities really describe me?" If your answer is yes, stop. If your answer is no, "they do not describe me in a complete way," then consider how to address these "missing areas" through additional entries. Most candidates will not put serious effort into the optional application questions and admissions committee members cannot help but be impressed by a candidate who knocks him- or herself out in preparing the application. It is recommended that all business school applicants consider creating at least two optional question entries. Possible topics follow in this chapter.

☞ *Tip #59:*   *Readability is of paramount importance. Try to keep each entry to the equivalent of a single page (approximately 500–600 words). You must make every effort to help the committee get through your optional questions. Think of the reviewer as skimming through your additional information.*

Make your entries well organized and of high quality, and the admissions committee will perceive you as a well-organized professional who produces high-quality work. The most common argument for not including anything in the optional area is, "Why should I do anything extra?...The admissions committee must consist of busy people; they do not have time to read this stuff." While it is true that admissions officers are very busy, they do have an allotted amount of time to spend on reviewing your application. Moreover, experienced admissions people develop a sixth sense for what is in an application. They know whether things are in order and whether there is substance to the application. Even if the admissions committee does not have time to read through all of your material, they can still go away with a favorable impression of what you choose to present.

Be extra brief and be hypersensitive about making it easy for the reviewer to get through your work. Unlike your essays and other required application components, "blank" questions are, after all, optional. Also, if possible, use one or more stylistic or readability tools for clarity—bolds, italics, indentations, enumerations, font sizes, shadings, as well as short sentences. See *Chapter 10, Packaging Your MBA Essays and Application.* Lastly, keep individual entries to three pages or less in length. Keeping each entry to one page, if possible, has the advantage of being psychologically manageable for the reader because everything is right in front of him or her.

The vast majority of business schools have an optional question. In fact, so does virtually every American undergraduate college. This is one of the hallmarks of egalitarian education. You are given every opportunity to express yourself and demonstrate your individuality. Although a few European schools go as far as to say "do not include anything extra," overall, for over 95 percent of the world's business schools, the blank question is exactly that—blank and wide open to use as you see fit.

☞ *Tip #60:*   *View the optional area as having four possible uses. Determine which of these four uses or combination thereof will best serve you.*

The four uses of the optional area include: (1) clarifying issues and addressing weaknesses, (2) showing diversity of background and character, (3) showing evidence of solid work experience, and (4) elaborating on reasons for wanting to go to a particular business school.

The Four Uses of the Optional Question

Use #1 – Clarifying issues and addressing weaknesses

Points that serve to support your current application may include a discussion of anticipated application weaknesses or points of clarification. Examples include: "I have a low GPA or GMAT score... You may wonder whether my three-year undergraduate degree is comparable to a four-year U.S. degree—let me explain... You may wonder whether my two years of work experience is sufficient; allow me to elaborate."

Use #2 – Showing diversity of background and character

Concentrate on those things which serve to show your versatility and uniqueness of character. This may include references to your favorite hobby, travel experience, cultural background, unusual experience, personal accomplishments, community service, volunteer work, artwork, creative writing sample, etc.

Use #3 – Showing evidence of solid work experience

Concentrate on those things that serve to support your solid work experience. These may include on-the-job projects, tasks, or assignments that show either breadth (variety) or depth (intensity) of experience. Your experience should highlight professional abilities, such as your decision-making skills, business acumen, integrity, character, or dedication.

Use #4 – Elaborating on reasons for wanting to go to a particular business school

It is prudent advice to sell a school on your reasons for wanting them in particular, rather than the MBA in general. If you feel, for any reason, that you have not been able to fully articulate this, then err on the side of writing more, not less. Refer to *Chapter 3* for coverage of the "Why XYZ School?" question.

What are Some Topics You Can Write About?

Use #1 – Clarifying issues and addressing weaknesses

- Lower-than-average undergraduate GPA
- Lower-than-average GMAT score
- Why a particular three-year college degree is comparable or equivalent to a four-year degree
- Why I cannot get a recommendation from my current employer
- Overcoming difficult situations, handicaps, illness, accidents, or tragedy

Use #2 – Showing diversity of background and character

- Interesting cultural background
- Special award, recognition, or unusual achievements
- Community service project or award
- Athletic achievements
- Difficult situations overcome
- What being from country X means to me
- My favorite hobby, sport, or outside interest
- The challenges of an interracial marriage or relationship
- A copy of an important speech

ca Articles written or books published
ca Excerpt from a published work
ca Plot summary of a book in progress
ca International travel or time spent as an exchange student
ca Special research completed
ca Proposed research project you want to undertake while at business school

Use #3 – Showing evidence of solid work experience

ca My most challenging work project
ca My most difficult customer
ca Sample analysis of a business situation
ca Where my chosen company or industry is headed
ca A brochure or promotional video containing information on my startup business venture or hobby

Use #4 – Elaborating on reasons for wanting to go to a particular business school

ca Location, geography
ca Post-graduate employment opportunities
ca Reputation or ranking
ca Academic specialties and courses
ca Teaching method
ca Length of program
ca Cost of program

Making Optional Essay Entries

☞ *Tip #61:   Consider using any "signature" essay as an optional essay.*

The easiest way to make an optional essay entry is to simply borrow a single essay that you wrote as a standard essay for another school. That is, if you have completed a particularly interesting essay—you might call this essay your "signature" essay—as part of an application for another school, then by all means, include it as an optional essay entry for your current school. For example, the essay written by Audrey (see *Chapter 3*, page 47–49) is an essay that can be used as her "signature" essay; the idea of using five Chinese elements—metal, wood, water, earth, fire—as representative of her life works well for her. Generally, an effective optional essay will be sent to all schools, other than those for which it is included as a main essay.

Suppose, on the other hand, that you want to create an optional essay—something creative, impressive, different—but you are not sure what it should be. First, start with your hobbies or interests. Say, for example, that you have had a long-standing interest in the game of chess, and as a result of your being stationed in Asia—Korea, Japan, China, or the like—you have taken to the game of Go, Asia's version of the game of chess. Second, you force a question: "Are these games just randomly different or is there some meaning behind the difference between chess and Go that reflect Eastern and Western cultural differences?" You also wonder if there might be some way these two games hint at understanding modern business strategy in each respective region of the world. Third, you come up with three major differences between these games based on the different kinds of playing pieces, the different types of moves possible, and the objectives of each game. Fourth, you fill things in and an outline emerges. You might present it exactly as it appears in *Exhibit 5.1* or re-craft it in written narrative form.

119

EXHIBIT 5.1   CREATING OPTIONAL ENTRIES – CHESS VS. GO

Game	Differences	Interpretation
Chess	♦ **Playing pieces** – called chess men. •diversity of individual playing pieces. •different pieces, i.e., King, Queen, Bishop, Knight, Rook, Pawn; individually carved pieces. ♦ **Movement** – varied and "uninhibited" directional movements based on the identity of a given chess piece. ♦ **Objective** – to remove players from the board and to bring into checkmate (capture, surrender) the opponent's King – symbol of the most important piece in the game.	♦ Belief in the individuality of inputs and the acknowledgment of human character and uniqueness. ♦ Ability to make varied moves of surprising capacity and significant consequence signifying the dynamics of individual input. ♦ Chess is a "connected, individualistic" game. Why? Chess pieces generally remain in close proximity to one another during the game (connected), but look different in appearance and share unequal values (individualistic). ♦ Chess signifies the idea of hierarchy and progression to the top, as there is only one King and one Queen – they stand higher than the other smaller pieces that exist to serve and protect them. Chess indicates the importance of individuality as well as the Western concept of annihilation and conquest.
Go	♦ **Playing pieces** – called stones. •uniformity of individual playing pieces. •identical small button-like objects. •set colors: black or white. ♦ **Movement** – simple forward movements are restricted to one space per move as analogous to pawns in the game of chess. ♦ **Objective** – to control the board by capturing the greatest amount of space on the playing surface and, secondarily, to remove pieces (stones) to achieve this objective.	♦ Belief in the expendability of resources and the intrinsic parity of all pieces. ♦ Simple directional moves show limitations of individual stones, but their ability to be placed in open "uncharted" regions that later become pivotal is the hallmark of long-term thinking. ♦ Go is a "disconnected collective" game. Why? Even though Go pieces need not be placed in close proximity of one another on the board (disconnected), they always look equal in appearance and share equal value (collective). ♦ Go signifies the Eastern concept of space and expendability of human or state property; space is the most valuable possession; pieces show parity of status and submission to the grand scheme; uniformity of pieces implies there is even more power in the holder of power – be it emperor, zaibatsu, company, etc.

Sample Optional Essay Entries

Use #1 – Clarifying issues and addressing weaknesses

Candidate: **Camilla from Denmark**
Essay title: **The Equivalency of My Three-Year Undergraduate Degree**

The purpose for this entry is to explain why the candidate's three-year degree from Denmark is comparable to and substitutable for a four-year U.S. degree. It is appropriate for candidates to address this type of clarifying issue through the optional question.

I am aware that XYZ school normally requires a four-year bachelor's degree in order to meet entrance qualification for your MBA studies. Therefore, I would like to take this opportunity to explain to the committee why my bachelor's degree is a three-year degree and also why I still believe I am at a sufficient academic level to qualify and succeed in your program.

The Copenhagen Business School, my undergraduate school, only offers three-year bachelor's degrees. A four-year bachelor's degree is not an option. In addition to my undergraduate studies, I studied one year in France and three months in a graduate school in the U.S., which further add to my academic skills and my belief that I will be qualified to complete your program successfully.

The level of education in Denmark is high and I am confident that my academic level is equivalent to those who hold a four-year bachelor's degree from other countries. This opinion is supported by the PIER report "Denmark, A Study of the Educational System of Denmark and Guide to the Academic Placement of Students in Educational Institutions in the United States" published by the American Association of Collegiate Registrars and Admissions Officers, NAFSA. This report, conducted by Valeria A. Woolston, Director of International Education Services, University of Maryland at College Park and Karlene N. Dickey, Associate Dean of Graduate Studies Emerita, Stanford University, recommends American schools accept the Danish bachelor's degree as an equivalent to the American four-year bachelor's degree.

◆ ◆ ◆

The following entry is to explain why the candidate could not obtain a recommendation from his current employer as is often requested by business schools. Since many business schools specifically request a recommendation from your current boss, candidates are generally required to write responses like the one that follows on the next page.

No Professional Recommendation From My Current Employer

Candidate: **Conrad from the U.S.**
Essay title: **No Professional Recommendation From My Current Employer**

I was unable to ask for a letter of reference from my current employer, because if I did, my chances of obtaining a future promotion or pay raise would greatly diminish. I talked to Ms Jennifer Merle of your admissions office by phone on October 11 about this matter. I conveyed to her the difficulty of securing three professional reference letters, as I have had only two jobs since graduating from university, and asked her if I could substitute with a non-professional letter of reference from a member of the American Chamber of Commerce here in Brussels. She conferred and said it was the best option in lieu of submitting a professional letter of reference.

What do you do if you have a "low" GMAT score and you think it will hurt your chances for admission? Why not address your lower-than-average GMAT score so that the admissions committee will not think you are underestimating the importance of the GMAT? You can also minimize the exam's effect on your overall application if you cite other cases where you have succeeded in your quantitative (numbers) and/or qualitative (verbal) endeavors. Also, refer to question #8 in *Chapter 2*, pages 30–31

♦♦♦

Candidate: **Bernadette from Switzerland**
Essay title: **My Lower-Than-Average GMAT Score**

My recent GMAT score of 550 falls below your average GMAT score of 650 as published in your admissions brochure for last year's entering class. My score also falls below my expectations because on my most recent practice tests taken under timed conditions, I achieved scores of 570 and 620.

I must admit to having some anxiety toward taking this kind of standardized test because these tests are unknown in the French education system. In addition, my extended overseas business trip just before the exam did not help either. However, rather than try to retake the test and miss your deadline for the second round, I have decided to apply with my 550 score. Upon examination, my math score of the exam was 490 while my verbal score was 630. Regrettably, my undergraduate major of sociology did not provide the chance for me to take many courses in mathematical subjects. Of the few courses I took while at university, I received grades of B in Operational Statistics and A in Quantitative Decision-Making. Moreover, I am well versed in using computers as a result of preparing computer and financial spreadsheets for my current boss. In order to be ready for fall business school classes, I am planning on enrolling in a spring session math skills refresher course offered through our community's continuing education service as well as a calculus course during the upcoming summer.

♦♦♦

Candidate: **Matt from the U.S.**
Essay title: **Why It Took Me Six Years to Complete My Undergraduate Degree**

"Academic peregrination" is a term I might use to describe my academic journey during my undergraduate education. Over a six-year period, from 20xx to 20xx, I attended three universities in three different States (US) and two universities in two different provinces in China. If I could have changed one decision that I have made, it would have been to begin my undergraduate career at Tufts University and to have pursued a more direct path toward graduation.

Upon my arrival at Tufts in the fall of 20xx, I had already attended two other universities, namely St. Lawrence University and The University of Iowa. St. Lawrence University, the first university I attended, was a small liberal arts college located in the village of Canton, in upstate New York. What initially attracted to me to St. Lawrence was its geographic location (the Adirondack Mountains were one-and-a-half hours away), its student body (primarily middle- to upper-middle class students), and its size (approximately 2,000 students).

After two years at St. Lawrence I soon found out that so many of the things that initially attracted to me to the school were the exact things that made me want to leave. I wanted to be close to a city that could provide an array of cultural activities, a globally diverse student body, and a larger school that had more academic programs and resources. But probably the most important reason why I wanted to leave St. Lawrence was its lack of academic competitiveness. For people familiar with St. Lawrence, it is sometimes referred to as "a four-year membership at an expensive country club," meaning, many students attend St. Lawrence not so much for its academic prowess, but to socialize and be surrounded by people with a similar socioeconomic background. As a result, in November of 20xx, I made the hard decision to leave St. Lawrence.

After I made my "big decision," I spent the next couple of months with my family in Des Moines, Iowa and spent two weeks in Colorado with some friends that attended Colorado University. This time was well spent. It gave me time with my family and friends and to think about my next steps. I decided that I would attend The University of Iowa as a visiting student and take a one class in Psychology and one in English on Geoffrey Chaucer's classics. It was during this time that I applied to Tufts University.

Tufts University opened up a whole new world to me. Greater Boston is home to more than 50 colleges and universities and more than 370,000 students. Being located in Boston, with so many students, museums, and cultural backdrops, I felt I was getting educated just by "breathing the air." Tufts provided me with an academic environment where the students were competitive, the student body was globally diverse, and the students could have easy access to the wonderful cosmopolitan and historical city of Boston. It was at Tufts where I was introduced to, and majored in, International Relations which then led to my intellectual passion to learn about China. Determined to put my newfound major to practical use, I traveled to China on three separate occasions to study Mandarin Chinese and to learn about the Chinese culture. Moreover, while in China, I completed two internships which gave me firsthand experience on how the Chinese conduct business. Then in the fall of 20xx, I interviewed with a Tufts Alumni at Chase in New York City, resulting in my first position as an Analyst in Investment Banking. In looking back, I find it amazing how much life experience I have garnered from my period of "Academic Peregrination." I attended both public and private universities, experienced large, small, and medium-size campuses, and met all walks of life from both the U.S. and abroad. I studied everything from Chaucer's classics to Mao Zedong's "Long March" and became proficient in Mandarin Chinese.

Use #2 – Showing diversity of background and character

Candidate: **Bidur from India**
Essay title: **On Five Continents**

I would like to provide the following snapshot to further highlight my distinctive cultural and geographical diversity.

I have lived in or worked in five continents (Asia, Africa, North and South America, and Europe) and have visited 65 of the world's countries to date. Having studied Nautical Sciences at the University of Newcastle, I am currently based in Hong Kong and work with the oldest and largest South American shipping company. Upon graduating with my MBA, I plan to focus on African Operations. Africa presents a place with growth opportunities, and also a place where I feel I could make the biggest strategic impact for my company and my career.

Although I hold Indian citizenship, I actually grew up in Nigeria. My father was transferred to Africa when I was three years old. I speak two languages of West Africa (Bini and Pidgin), as well as English, Spanish, Hindi, Urdu and Punjabi. Football was my game of choice in high school. But at an even younger age I can still remember a favorite hobby—crocodile hunting (it was legal then). Not only was Crocodile meat good to eat, it was also prestigious to bring one home to our mothers.

My father pursued his career as a Royal Navy Engineer. Incidentally, my grandfather was also involved with the navy, and was the first Indian Master to take a ship to British waters after India's independence. My mother, who now lives in India, was involved in social work in Nigeria. The "Oba" (Tribal-Chief) of Benin awarded her with the prestigious "Festosa" Mask for her contributions to community development in Edo state (Nigeria). My wife is also Indian, and is currently pursuing a MBA course at the Hong Kong University of Science and Technology.

Personally, I know of no comparable educational opportunity beyond INSEAD which could better embrace my diversity or allow me to learn from others.

❧ ❧ ❧

Candidate: **Camilla from Denmark**
Essay title: **What My Danish Nationality Means to Me**

My Danish nationality and upbringing are clearly reflected in my personality. Having being born and having grown up in a small country in Northern Europe of approximately five million inhabitants makes me different from many people in a number of ways. Therefore, I would like to tell the committee a little bit about my home country.

Denmark is one of the relatively few racially homogeneous countries in the Western world. We have a long history and a constitutional monarchy dating back to A.D. 900, and we do not have a long record of mixed cultures. Furthermore, Denmark is one of the few countries that really practices the welfare system. We have a high standard of social security and public services, including a high-quality educational sector. This means we do not have a big gap between poor and rich which is the case in many other countries. All this makes the Danes quite uniform and this is reflected in the average Dane's values and mindset. An example of a uniform belief is the Danes' belief in "The Jante Law," an unspoken law stating that you should not emphasize your own achievements over those of others.

Denmark is not only a small country in regard to population but also in area – 44,000 sq. km. Sixty-five percent of the country is farmland, which gives everybody the opportunity to go for a Sunday walk in the fields, and nowhere in Denmark is a person farther than 52 km from the sea, which means that every child and adult has the unmistakable distinction of having been for a swim in the ocean.

Denmark is governed by a democratically elected government and a parliament in a multiparty system. The Danes in general take interest in political issues and the rate of participation in elections is very high. This interest in politics concerns domestic as well as international matters. Recently, during the situation involving French nuclear testing, a group of Danes got on their bikes and rode all the way to France to speak their opinion.

Since I started traveling around the world my awareness of what it is to be Danish has become much clearer to me. I am probably more Danish now than when I was living in Denmark. And yet I appreciate so many other cultures and adopt some of these traits as my own. Although I do not applaud everything about Denmark or the Danish people, I am proud of my nationality.

❧ ❧ ❧

Candidate: **Ben from the U.S.**
Essay title: **Either With Friends or Alone**

Many applicants think that it is necessary to write on an obscure topic in order to have an interesting piece of writing. This is not so. The following memorable piece is written on an deceptively simple topic.

One of the activities I enjoy most outside of the work environment is travel, either with friends or alone. I have found that when traveling with friends, the opportunity to see them outside of their everyday environment reveals facets of their personality which I would not have seen otherwise. There is also a certain camaraderie shared while traveling that transcends the barriers put up in everyday life. And since the conveniences of home are not readily available, there is a sense of urgency that accompanies the need to work together as a team. This need for teamwork seems to be especially important while traveling overseas. When I was working in Venezuela, I spent my weekends traveling with a group of Canadian consultants. We found that we needed to pool our resources, both physical and linguistic, to get where we needed to go, but had a fantastic time in the process – climbing in the jungles north of Caracas, canoeing to Angel Falls and scuba diving off the western coast near Maracaibo. What I especially enjoyed about the group was their strong sense of adventure and their willingness to be experimental.

I also enjoy traveling on my own. For occasional periods, it can be lonely; however, the brief periods of loneliness are far outweighed by the benefits of getting to know a country and its people on a less superficial level. One time, I went up into the hills of northern Italy near the village of Asiago. I saw an interesting looking elderly man and sat down on the bench beside him. We had a two-hour discussion on what things were like before the war which few friends of mine would have the patience to bear. No doubt they would want to move on to see the "real sights," but discussions such as the one I had help me to understand the personality of a country with more depth than I can from just reading or visiting without interaction. For that reason, I sometimes travel on my own. Traveling on my own also has a few other benefits; on a one-month trip to Europe in 20xx, I received invitations to stay with new friends from over 30 countries.

❧ ❧ ❧

Candidate: **Soyoung from South Korea**
Essay title: **Tear Gas and Molotov Cocktails**

Tear gas and molotov cocktails take up a large part of my memory of my college years in Korea. My aunt and my cousin were both massacred during the protest staged by Korean students and civilians against the Chun Do Hwan regime in the Kwanju massacre. In spite of the howling 2,000 deaths during that massacre, no government officials were brought to account. No media could justly report the terrifying scene.

As I entered college, like many of the students at the time, I felt a strong moral obligation to fight against the government and bring democracy to Korea. My daily life during the first two years of college centered around the National Organization of Students and inter-school groups to discuss the alternative curricula or so-called leftist books. The anger and injustice we students felt toward our government would almost always end up in staging a demonstration, whether violent or not. After two years spent in blind outburst, I began to doubt the effectiveness of violence of any sort. Coincidentally, I became acquainted with a student at Yonsei who also shared my thoughts. He was involved in the student movement but started to seek other routes to sending the message to the students and the public. And because he was involved with the drama team at Yonsei School of Politics, we decided to work on a play toward delivering our thoughts. It took 30 members and a period of over a year from the initial meeting to write, produce, and stage a play. The subject of the play was how two men from the lowest-paid working class viewed the world and despite their feeling of injustice, how they became immune to it by finding a niche within that crooked society. It was a small stage with only a little over 200 students seeing the play over two nights.

Looking back, I do not regret spending my earlier youth for a just cause. The student movement together with the worker association is what after all brought democracy to Korea. But what I conceive as failure is that I was not mature enough to play the "tune" in harmony with society. The very people I thought I was fighting for were hurt along the way. I also realize the price I paid for losing a balance of reality. Instead of focusing on my main duty as a student, I failed to grasp the full benefit of an academic college education. After all is done I know that there are more effective and sensible ways to change the society. No one is completely free from his or her past. But it is how you look at it and grow from it that makes that difference. Now I understand that no one will view you with respect, let alone listen to you, if you neglect your primary duty. In the future, I intend to succeed in the field I choose. I understand that by doing this I will be able to return more to my society and my country.

❧ ❧ ❧

Candidate: Marie from the U.S.
Essay title: Rainbow Without a Beginning

My life is like a rainbow without a beginning. Just as dark clouds gather to produce the rain needed to create a rainbow, inexplicable events had occurred which led to my abandonment as a baby in front of an orphanage. I grew up in Hawaii and still vividly remember seeing single and double rainbows frequently during the tropical rainy season. Like so many people, I consider seeing a rainbow as a lucky sign, but I can never forget that rainbows can only occur as a result of dark clouds and rain. I now feel fortunate to be able to return to Latin America as a successful businesswoman. My life is full of colors and each color has a symbolic relationship to the different influences which shaped me at an early age.

Red is the color of Mayan clay and it represents my Guatemalan heritage. The official records only state that I was found as a four-six week old infant, at the door of the El Pablo Babies' Home, near the Honduras border in Guatemala, one September morning in 19xx. Although I cannot be absolutely sure, I have always assumed that I was born in Guatemala or Honduras. This was a year when tens of thousands of homeless and starving Guatemalan refugees were fleeing across the border into Honduras. Many babies were found abandoned in Guatemala during those turbulent times from the late sixties to the early seventies. Although I have long since come to feel at peace with the possibility that my birth parents may have been killed or forced to abandon me, I continue to wonder who they were and if they were among these refugees. I can only thank my birth parents for creating me and giving me a chance to live, if only in an orphanage, at a time when untold thousands of Guatemalans perished during the political instability and fighting in Guatemala caused by military extremists groups and the communist resurgencies.

Orange is like a sunrise. It symbolizes how I rose from being an orphan in underdeveloped Central America to becoming an infant adoptee in the USA. Unable to rely on my birth family, an important traditional source of comfort and protection, I had to become adaptable and self-reliant from the time I was just a few months old. For example, babies only a few months old had to quickly learn how to drink from a cup instead of a nursing bottle. This was because the chronic shortage of orphanage staff meant that it was more efficient for one staff member to sit six babies close together and feed them all at once by holding three cups of milk formula in each hand and tipping the nourishing liquid simultaneously into six hungry mouths. With dozens of babies requiring five daily feedings, there was simply no time for the staff members to take each baby in their arms and use a bottle to feed him or her.

When I was adopted by my Spanish-American parents in Hawaii at the age of 18 months, they told me that I was so overwhelmed by my new environment that I did not utter a sound for one whole week. Because I did not even cry, my mother and father were surprised when their family doctor said that there was nothing wrong with my vocal chords. Eventually, I did regain my vocal ability after another week in my new home, but my deepest psyche would be permanently scarred by the early loss of my birth parents, and sudden separation from my homeland.

Yellow is part of the sun itself. This color represents how I was influenced by growing up in rural Hawaii, because this color brings the brightness and warmth of the Aloha spirit to my mind. Although I did not know it at the time, going to public school in Hawaii was an invaluable cross-cultural experience. My elementary school classes were composed of ethnic Japanese, Filipino, Hawaiian, Portuguese, Samoan, Chinese, English-Irish, and Korean children. As part of my crash course in social conditioning, I learned to speak fluent Pidgin to communicate with so many different ethnic groups, despite my mother's constant encouragement for me to speak standard Spanish and English. With its unique history as a former Polynesian kingdom which closely allied itself with European royalty and its predominantly ethnic Asian population living as U.S. citizens, Hawaii became the site of some the world's first truly integrated, multi-racial societies. I was raised at an early age to feel comfortable and confident while communicating with people from diverse cultural, social, religious and economic backgrounds because of my real life experience of growing up among people of diverse backgrounds.

My life is like a rainbow without a beginning. Because I survived a traumatic early life, my parents wanted to give me a name that would remind me that I was one of the chosen ones, almost as if reborn while still alive. My Guatemalan name is the poetic word combination "Lora Mournel," literally meaning the brightness after darkness or the first glow of the morning sun, a new beginning. When my Aloha spirit meets my industrious side, the result is helping myself and others to find new beginnings. This includes using my knowledge of medicine to promote the well-being of others. Where do I get the strength to help others? The source of this strength is the joy that I get knowing that life is like a rainbow, full of color – a chance occurrence – which springs forth in a mighty arc and beckons us into the future.

❖ ❖ ❖

Candidate: **Claudio from Italy**
Essay title: **Experiencing the Culture Shock of a Sky Burial**

International living has played an important part in my personal and professional development. Living in a place like Geneva, encountering an abundance of cultural differences constitutes the norm. But one of the most significant cultural shocks I have ever encountered occurred when I saw a "sky burial" in Tibet.

Sky burial is a rather unique Tibetan cultural practice, which involves shredding the flesh of the deceased into pieces and feeding it to the birds of prey. When a commoner dies, the corpse is first bound in a piece of white cloth and left for a three- to five-day mourning period. The body is then transported to a sky burial site in the mountain where the Tibetan monks go through the process of flesh shredding and bone crushing. The eagles and vultures, which inhabit the area, devour the remains. I felt nauseous after watching the process, and lost my appetite until well into the next day. I wondered how such a barbaric habit could be practiced today. The question remained in my mind until the origin and necessity of this practice was explained to me.

I was made to realize that such a practice evolved over a period of time and was in fact a reaction to physical conditions and resource restrictions. In Tibet, where the climate is cold and dry, it is difficult for a corpse to decompose through land burial. It is also costly to cremate a body because of the scarcity of wood and the low concentrate of oxygen in the higher altitudes. The practice of sky burial makes perfect sense when viewed from the perspective of the local situation.

As a result of this incident, I developed a better understanding of different cultures, their motivations, and practices. Above all, I became determined to attempt to objectively understand other cultures from their own perspective rather than to judge them based upon my own culture. This habit has enabled me to develop a deeper understanding of others and assist me in improving my communication skills with people from different societies and cultures.

Use #3 – Showing evidence of solid work experience

Candidate: **Eva from Sweden**
Essay title: **My Intensive Investment Banking Experience**

The following essay is written by a candidate who portrays a strong record of employment despite having barely two years of full-time work experience. The essay serves the purpose of plugging an anticipated application weak point by making her one-year of banking experience seem as impressive as another candidate's two or three years of non-banking experience.

I realize that many of Oxford Said's applicants have several years of professional experience. Although I have only worked a short time, my professional experience has been immensely valuable. I am an analyst in a boutique investment bank, Pacific Rim Capital Asia Limited, based in Hong Kong. We now have three professionals as well as working partners in the U.S. and Hong Kong. Our work involves strategic advisory, mergers and acquisitions, and corporate finance, mostly private equity placements from Asian corporations to international institutional investors. Our firm is currently billing US$40-50,000 in retainers per month plus another US$15-25,000 in monthly expenses. We are presently working on over US$100 million worth of deals with potential success fees of over US$5 million, in addition to equity linked compensation.

Working for an entrepreneurial investment bank in Hong Kong is very intensive, not only because of the intensity of Hong Kong itself or the fast-paced nature of investment banking, but because I am working for a family business which my brother started a little over a year ago. Working for a family member means working around the clock, and is amazingly stimulating. Because of my brother's confidence in my ability and judgement, I have been able to take part in major negotiations and have gained exposure to top executives in major investment banks and merging companies. My responsibilities include all aspects of the business, from managing client relations and working with the team to pitch for new business, to creating financial models, market research, investment presentations, and selling documents for clients and investors. I am currently working with clients in Hong Kong, China, New York, and Germany as well as with investors and strategic partners from around the globe.

As a member of a small entrepreneurial firm, I have by necessity become involved with every aspect of our business including corporate registration, securities regulation, employee and partnership agreements, accounting systems, and other organizational matters in addition to my work with and for our clients. I have quickly come to appreciate the importance of both high-level professional activities such as pitching for new deals and the seemingly more mundane tasks of collecting accounts receivable and managing cash flows on a day-to-day basis. The combination of the small size of our professional team and the critical nature of the projects and dollar amounts with which we are dealing, has given me a level of responsibility in our organization beyond that of my peers in larger investment banks. I am playing a critical role in several of our transactions, including two "live" deals expected to bring us approximately US$3 million in fees over the next 90 days.

❧ ❧ ❧

Candidate: Caroline from Israel
Essay title: Diamonds in the Rough

The following essay adds a nice touch to the candidate's application package. The essay is personable and tells us a little more about her insights into the world of executive search.

As mentioned in my essays, my career goal includes obtaining an MBA and becoming a leader in the executive search field. Therefore, I would like to include a few insights that I have developed as a result of my current work in this field in Asia.

I have the good fortune of working for England's most successful headhunter, Ryan Portier. He has been written up in many news articles and has been quoted as saying, "Two things that make a good journalist and a great headhunter are the love of information and a love of people."

A love of information is important in order to locate a candidate once an assignment has been confirmed. How do you go about finding the "perfect" match? For sure, search takes initiative and creativity. I have to very quickly review information in books, magazines, newspapers, on-line searches, and word of mouth comments. I am a cross between an investigative reporter, management consultant, and sales person. I must know the industry, the people, the market dynamics, and be able to sell a potential candidate on the new "idea."

It is true that my boss is extremely charismatic, but I really feel it is his passion for people that enables him to focus on what is best for the search candidate. Top search executives know that there is a difference between the best candidate and the right fit. It is not whether we have the best candidate, but the right candidate. The right candidate may not be the best candidate, but the right candidate will fit the organization like a glove.

A search executive must be able to identify possibilities. You must view the long term. Certain corporate persons, unknown today, may become the stars of the future. The headhunting process is like finding diamonds in the rough. It may be true that you will occasionally work with a star candidate and place this person outright. But more often it will be true that you must place a candidate into a position that makes him or her a star. We must have a sixth sense about people and market opportunities. We must realize that diamonds do not look like diamonds in their raw state but rather are disguised as clumps of coal. Many of tomorrow's leaders of industry will remain disguised until we seek them out and match their talents with market opportunities.

❤ ❤ ❤

Candidate:	**Camilla from Denmark**
Essay title:	**Evita Peroni – The Next Benetton of Ladies Accessories?**

If you are working for a family-run company or are a self-employed individual, you may want to think of comparing your current company to that of a present day, leading corporate organization. The strategy here is to imply that you and your company will be a market leader in ten or more years. It is a little like saying, "Look over there, that's where we'll be tomorrow." This is likely to create a positive impression on the committee members and increase a candidate's chances of acceptance to highly competitive business programs. Admissions officers of major business schools desire to avoid rejecting applicants who may one day be giants in their respective fields. In the following essay, a young woman compares her family-run company, Evita Peroni, with Benetton because Benetton enjoyed initial success in Europe before a late entry in the U.S. market.

Basically all my practical experience is in our family fashion business Evita Peroni, and it is in this context that I am pursuing my long-term career goal – to become CEO. Therefore I would like to present the committee with more detailed information about our company. Although we are represented in 38 countries, we are not represented in the U.S. and therefore you may not be familiar with our brand. The strategy of Evita Peroni has been first to build up a good and stable business in Europe and Asia before reaching for the U.S. market. We have side-stepped the U.S. market deliberately, but now feel that we are ready and we are at the initial stages of making our market entry.

Under the brand Evita Peroni, our company has specialized in design, manufacture, and marketing of ladies accessories in particular hair accessories, scarves, sunglasses, and brushes in 38 countries around the world. The company has its origin in Copenhagen, Denmark where my father first founder the accessory business. Today, 33 years later, Evita Peroni's main office is in Hong Kong with the research and development office in Copenhagen, the design studio in Los Angeles, and the international marketing in London, England.

Evita Peroni is sold through franchise distributors in 38 countries around the world with Europe comprising 50 percent of our total turnover and Asia (including Japan) comprising 30 percent. The remaining business is spread over the Middle East, Australia, South America, South Africa, and recently the U.S.

Evita Peroni is mainly sold in medium to high-level department stores, such as Galleries Lafayette in France, Breuninger in Germany, Central Department Stores in Thailand, and Sony

Plaza in Japan just to mention a few. An average size department store like Zen Department Store in Bangkok has a yearly turnover of US$330,000 (retail) on a 40-foot-long wall display. Evita Peroni is also sold in perfumeries, specialty stores, duty-free stores, and in exclusive Evita Peroni shops. Two years ago, Evita Peroni was awarded the Most Dynamic Beauty Supplier in France in competition with brands like Estee Lauder and Lancome.

My vision is that Evita Peroni will be the next Benetton within ladies accessories. We are the only truly international brand within hair accessories, which is our present field of expertise and we are gaining good ground in the field of sunglasses, scarves, and brushes. I believe we are where Benetton was a few decades ago. We have firmly established ourselves in Europe prior to looking at the U.S. market. My vision is to make Evita Peroni one of the international leading brands within ladies accessories. I believe Evita Peroni has what it takes and I believe we will make it!

❥ ❥ ❥

Candidate: **Matt from the U.S.**
Essay title: **My Future Role as an Ethical CFO**

Many candidates do not fully capitalize on their major work accomplishments. The résumé (or employment record) can only tell so much. Furthermore, most candidates have had reasonably substantial work experience before applying to business school. If there is another angle you wish to show in which you have worked on a memorable project, then elaborate on it in a page or two. The applicant below highlights the role of ethics within the finance world.

With the ushering in of the 21st century, the role of the CFO at public companies has already undergone a significant transformation. The traditional roles of a CFO as the executive number-cruncher and the gatekeeper of financial reports have been relegated to secondary requirements. Today companies and investors are demanding that their financial executives possess superior communication ability, a broad range of skills, and ethical behavior. I believe that communication is the most important of these skills.

Now more than ever, there is little question that the media and the investment community are interested in how companies operate, perform, and account for their financials. In part this is due to high-profile accounting scandals, from the likes of Enron, Tyco, and WorldCom, but is also due to information flow and the ability of the average investor to comprehend financial data. Historically, CEOs have taken the center stage when addressing company results, but now this limelight is being shared with CFOs. How will this new "stardom" affect the role of the CFO? In short, the 21st century CFO will be required to be a great communicator.

The ability of CFOs to communicate efficiently and effectively will be integral to their personal successes as well as their companies' successes. There is a need to convey messages in simple terms to make points more striking and memorable. In particular, CFOs will need to express themselves succinctly and with an element of "salesmanship," especially in communication mediums such as television. In the end, the CFO who has superior communication skills will be the one who wins over the investment community with words, while backing these words up with actionable results.

Increasing complexity in the global corporate landscape will require that the 21st century CFO depart from the role as the corporate bean counter and become a well-rounded executive. For example, CFOs need to have more operating experience so that they can better understand the departments in their organizations. There is a need for proactivity, not just reactivity. Strategic thinking is necessary in order to evaluate capital raising, strategic partnerships, and M&A needs. The ability to be prescriptive will be crucial for CFOs because it will dictate the direction in which their company is steered. Similarly, as the role of the CFO and the CEO draw closer, the CFO will need to develop a strong trustworthy relationship with shareholders in order to share in a consistent and clear company vision.

Practicing good ethics will play an integral role for the 21st century CFO. CFOs will be called upon to set standards that govern the right conduct in how their companies make business decisions. These principles and values should be transparent at all levels of management to limit confusion or ambiguity in how companies account for their financial performance. In recent years, many companies were mired in corporate scandals. Although some of these companies did not technically break the law outright, they clearly did not practice good judgment. There is an ostensible difference between what is legally correct and what is ethically sound. As the government, Securities & Exchange Commission, and other regulatory agencies continue to close the gap between what is ethically sound and legally correct, the 21st century CFO will be on the frontline of determining first what is ethically right before making business decisions.

Use #4 – Elaborating on reasons for wanting to go to a particular business school.

In the sample essay excerpt below, note how the applicant finds a fresh voice. The best applicants find ways to push the limits in order to rise above the crowd. Try to write one level of detail beyond what the average informed candidate will write and be specific and be personable.

Sample essay excerpt:
The GSB campus would be an ideal place to spend two years. Its open walkways and shared courtyards speak to the collaborative atmosphere of the school. After four years living in high-rises of the urban jungle, the figure "8,000 acres" reads like a keyword for freedom! It must have been the vast acreage that inspired the Stanford motto: "The wind of freedom blows." I imagine tree-lined Palm Drive is actually the secret entrance to a Spanish-tiled cultural haven. One of my favorite artists, Richard Diebenkorn, occupies the galleries of the new Cantor Center. His sun-drenched abstract landscapes, painted in swaths of heat-colored vistas, are a reason to apply to Stanford GSB unto themselves. The new wing of the Cantor Center was designed by the same firm behind the Pequot Museum in Mashantucket, Connecticut, and the Rose Center at the American Museum of Natural History: my two favorite museums on the East Coast. I am excited to see the new Cantor wing's curved walls, cast in the high-finish concrete pioneered by my favorite architect, Louis Kahn. I plan to study by Maya Lin's new "Timetable" sculpture outside the Packard Engineering Building, the same way I relaxed to the murmur of her "Women's Table" water sculpture at Yale. Set among such cultural riches, Stanford GSB provides an ideal environment to study.

Sample essay excerpt:
I have met a number of INSEAD grads who have told me of their unbelievably positive experiences and have been the recipient of their lengthy emails and Facebook postings bragging about the diversity of the school – classrooms of more than 20 nationalities, study teams of half a dozen people who can speak 12 or more languages collectively, and students choosing between living in a flat in the center of town and a real castle 18 kilometers from the school!

❧ ❧ ❧

In the two essays that follow, each candidate creates a sense of excitement, preparation, and anticipation.

Candidate: **Alice from Hong Kong**
Essay title: **Reasons for Choosing the Tuck School**

I would like to take this opportunity to further elaborate on my reasons for choosing the Tuck School of Business.

My six years in the consulting industry, both in North America and South America, reflect a constant pursuit to mold myself into a distinctive management consultant, who has outstanding character and a broad yet balanced range of professional qualities and competence. Over the years, I have successfully transitioned from implementing tactical IT solutions to formulating strategic management game plans for top executives. As a former IT consultant at PricewaterhouseCoopers and IBM, I led transnational organizations to implement state-of-the-art IT solutions. Since joining McKinsey as a junior associate, I have re-shaped top CEO agendas, led Latin and South American companies to tackle their most burning business and technology issues, and shifted the fundamental way that businesses have been run.

Each successive career move has honed my professional qualities and competence: to master business and technology issues of broader implications to a corporation's competitiveness; to conduct fact-based and penetrating analysis with a strong sense of logic; to be imaginative and resourceful in developing original solutions to management problems; and to be a trusted team player. I have also learned to leverage important aspects of my character, including trustworthiness, honesty, and integrity, to deepening my relationships with client and team members.

Like that of any other distinctive consulting company, the future of McKinsey depends on the basic qualities, skills, and knowledge of its people. We need superior people with superior minds. In turn, the key to my future success at McKinsey depends on enhancing my management and leadership abilities. To achieve my goal, I require Tuck's interdisciplinary and pragmatic MBA education that effectively capitalizes on the intellectual capital and resources of a distinctive community to help me build sound management and leadership abilities. My recent visit to Tuck offered me a direct opportunity to experience your distinctiveness beyond the Tuck MBA brochures. The Tuck MBA program will help me achieve my goal in three fundamental ways:

Rigorous general management curriculum. To become an outstanding consultant, I must acquire strong management fundamentals that include the basic managing process, and the interdependence and interactions of various managing elements. Tuck excels in this area by systematically breaking down its management education into a set of functionally driven yet strategically coherent studies. I am particularly excited about the general management forum, where I would apply the concepts and skills I learned about economics and technology systems, toward developing a real-life project, such as IT-enabled productivity improvements in developing countries. Meanwhile, I would be exposed to an intense training on analytical thinking and innovative problem-solving, as I strive to develop recommendations that would be valuable to target organizations and executives.

Collaborative learning approach. From intimate class sizes to study groups, the Tuck approach to collaborative learning would allow me to capitalize on the diverse experiences and viewpoints of students at a personal level. It would also enhance my ability to understand others' perspectives. Everyone I met at Tuck, from the admissions officers to student hosts, demonstrated a high level of enthusiasm and passion toward building the community. Meanwhile, Professor Amy Hutton's accounting class, which challenged students to go beyond memorization of textbook principles to strategic analysis of accounting statements, reflected Tuck's commitment to superior teaching quality. What could be more satisfying than to be engaged in a learning environment, where every capacity or talent one may have is expanded, every lesson one may have is used, and every value one cares about is furthered? As your MBA student, Anne Heung, summed it up best, "Tuck has been an amazing experience so far. Tuckies are just the smartest, nicest, and most fun bunch of people I have been around."

Balanced leadership training. Tuck's commitment to providing balanced leadership training is exemplified in your weekly announcement of a variety of exciting extracurricular activities and social events. Given my background in women's issues, I am particularly keen on joining the Tuck Women in Business Club and Consulting Club to foster the next generation of female leaders in the consulting industry. These experiences would allow me to explore my enduring passions while cultivating in me strong fundamentals for a lifetime of caring leadership for the community. Furthermore, the daily visits by high-level executives, the breath and depth of topics covered, and the opportunity for up-close and personal discussions would allow me to stay abreast of the latest management thinking.

A premier education institution like Tuck requires committed students to advance its legacy of academic excellence and rich tradition of collegiality. Given my multi-cultural upbringing and diverse professional background, I will help inject greater cultural diversity to the Tuck community and stronger international focus to classroom studies. Specifically, I was raised and educated in three different countries through which I have honed my multi-language skills and appreciation for cultural differences. As an international consultant, I have traveled to and worked in numerous countries to serve a diversified portfolio of clients on strategic and management issues. Coupling my global experience with my capability to relate to people on a personal level, by speaking their languages and understanding their unique cultural challenges, I will add valuable inputs and context to classroom learning and student interactions at Tuck. Furthermore, I will leverage the extensive business network that I have cultivated over the years with the business communities and governments in Asia to further the global reach of Tuck's alumni circle and strengthen Tuck's representation in the global business community. Finally, my passion in volunteer work will help expand the horizon of the student life at Tuck.

❥ ❥ ❥

Candidate: Amar from the U.S.
Essay title: Reasons for Choosing the Chicago GSB

During the course of the past year, when I first became interested in attending a graduate program in business administration, I had the privilege of attending a number of presentations by top U.S. business schools. All of the presenters were informative and portrayed their respective schools in a positive manner. However, their information, in conjunction with my own research, led me to the conclusion that there were only a few business schools that could help me achieve the goals that I had set for myself.

As a business professional and an aspiring student, my goals are straightforward: (1) To further develop the technical, financial, and intellectual skills that will enhance the techniques I have already gained from working in the credit markets of New York and Hong Kong; (2) To study under innovative scholars in order to solidify the academic knowledge that I gained at Vassar and the London School of Economics; (3) To prepare for work in the international arena and bolster my chances of becoming a development finance professional at an international organization such as the World Bank or the Inter-Americas Development Bank.

For the last three years, I have learned the business of credit analysis and the debt capital markets in an "on the job" basis or in hurried training seminars. To my firm's and my colleagues' credit, I have learned a great deal about high yield bonds, the leveraged loan markets, mergers and acquisitions, credit analysis and, most recently, emerging markets. However, I am certain that there are gaps in my professional knowledge that need to be filled if I am ever to be a productive participant in the financial markets. I do not think these gaps can be filled by on-the-job training or the knowledge-sharing of my everyday work environment. I strongly believe that a rigorous academic setting that provides access to both the theoretical and practical issues is important to the development of a young professional.

I see the University of Chicago as the ultimate intellectual platform. First, the university is revered as a "graduate school." Only one out of every three students on campus is an undergraduate; two out of every three students on campus are either graduate students or PhD students. Second, the influence of Nobel Laureates on the university as a whole is astounding. Elaborating on the fact that the University of Chicago has won more Nobel prizes than any other university in the world, a school administrator put it in a memorable light: "If the University of Chicago were a country, it would be ranked number three in the world in terms of the number of Nobel Prizes received. In first place would be the United States of which the University is a part of; in second place would be England; and in third place would be the University of Chicago." Third, the reputation of Chicago grads among employers is noteworthy. There is a saying: "if you don't know an answer, go ask a Chicago grad."

The second major reason for choosing Chicago as my first choice is my desire to study with scholars of the GSB. During my senior year at Vassar College, I had the opportunity to study advanced labor economics. During the course of that year I was able to study the work of Gary Becker, George Borjas, and Jake Mintzer and their important contributions in understanding the consequences of labor policy. Taking part in a class that Gary Becker teaches at the GSB would allow me to take part in what I anticipate would be a unique academic experience. Students rarely have the opportunity to study under any scholar who helped lay the foundation of modern labor economics theory. I work in an environment filled with the sophisticated concepts of trading, risk management, and deal execution. However, despite the sophistication of today's financial markets, labor market issues still manage to be of critical importance in driving or hindering economic growth and policy. IG Metal still has a powerful voice in German industrial organization, newly laid state workers in China protest the growing "rustbelt" in the northwest provinces and pension obligations have crippled U.S. steel companies despite newly installed tariffs. Structural rigidities or, conversely, a lack of social protection have been detrimental to the European, Asian and, to a lesser degree, the U.S. markets.

At institutions like the IFC within the World Bank, one has the opportunity to use the knowledge gained in both financial markets and labor economics to assist still-developing economies overcome illiquid financial markets and structural weaknesses. I have been fortunate in seeking my professional experiences and in finding mentors during my career. I was able to be an intern economist during my LSE Masters program at JP Morgan in London during the Euro's first year in existence. I was able to serve in UBS Warburg in New York as a credit advisory analyst during one of the most trying credit cycles in a generation, and I have had the opportunity to help rebuild Asian financial institutions in the wake of volatility and crises. The GSB offers the opportunity to deepen these experiences, particularly in the international arena. Tackling new studies, developing new perspectives, participating in lectures and group work, talking with fellow classmates, and making new friends, who will be partners in the future, are all essential ingredients in making this happen.

Chapter 6

Résumé and Employment Record

Your résumé is ready when your mother looks
at it and doesn't recognize who it is.
—Anonymous

Introduction

How will your work experience be evaluated?

The admissions committee will rate your work experience in two general ways—depth and breadth of experience. The depth or intensity reflects the amount of time you have worked and your accomplishments; depth of work experience is sometimes evaluated from looking at your job titles, responsibilities, accomplishments, promotions, and/or salary increases. Breadth or variety of work experience, on the other hand, reflects the number of different tasks or job functions that you have performed or have been exposed to in the workplace. Breadth of work experience may also refer to your ability to acquire people skills (also team building) as opposed to technical skills. There usually exists some degree of trade-off between acquiring depth and breadth of work experience, and it is unclear whether it is more important to have depth or breadth of work experience. For instance, it is also unclear whether it is better to work for one company for, say, four years, or two different companies for two years each. However, it is not well regarded if you work for four different companies each for a single year.

What is the difference between a résumé and an employment record?

Business schools generally require that you submit an employment record as part of your completed application. Sometimes your résumé (also known as CV or curriculum vitae) is required in addition to your employment record. The Adcom (admissions committee) may give your résumé to your prospective interviewers. The employment record, as required by business schools, differs in three basic ways from a standard résumé. The first is format, the second is length, and the third is content. In terms of format, think of an employment record as a "reformatted" résumé. A résumé is broken into "lateral" thirds: (1) education, (2) work experience, and (3) extracurriculars. An employment record is usually broken into "vertical" thirds: (1) company or organization placed in the first column, along with job titles, (2) places and dates in the second column, and (3) job responsibilities and/or accomplishments placed in the third column.

In terms of length, a résumé is typically one page in length whereas an employment record is usually three to five pages in length. This added length results primarily from the format of the employment record, which necessitates placing the bulk of job description and work accomplishments into the right-hand column.

In terms of content, a résumé also includes a summary of an individual's educational history and extracurricular involvement, but these items are not included in the employment record. Business schools require separate forms to be completed with regard to educational institutions attended and extracurricular activities undertaken.

Both a résumé and an employment record contain five standard pieces of information regarding each job experience. These include: (1) name of company or organization, (2) title or position, (3) geographical location of company or organization, (4) dates of employment, and (5) job responsibilities and/or accomplishments. However, employment records usually include two additional pieces of data, namely starting and ending salaries for each position <u>and</u> reasons for leaving each job. Candidates sometimes wonder why schools ask for beginning and ending salary. In the words of one admissions director: "When times are good, salaries move but titles don't. When times are bad, titles move but salaries don't." In an era where titles do not mean as much as they once did, salaries give an added indication of responsibility level.

EXHIBIT 6.1   SAMPLE RÉSUMÉ – TODD A. GILLMAN

TODD A. GILLMAN
Apt 22B, Exchange Towers, 64 Grant Street, Hartford, CT, USA 06501
Bus/Tel: (203) 782-4200 Res/Tel&Fax: (203) 785-1717

EDUCATION

BOSTON UNIVERSITY, Boston, Massachusetts
Bachelor of Science in Business Administration, May 20xx
Concentration in Accounting, GPA 3.65, Cum Laude

*PROFESSIONAL
EXPERIENCE*

20xx–present   **BANK OF AMERICA** Hartford, Connecticut
Associate and Financial Analyst
- Analyzed branch performance and devised new strategies to improve regional market share. Formulated two-year marketing plan for two branches.
- Developed new commission system and assisted in implementation.
- Tax-saving strategies and advice on investment portfolio compositions for principal clients.

20xx–20xx   *Financial Analyst*
- Evaluated clients' corporate credit ratings based on credit history, performance, and financial ratios. Developed structure of interest rate, loan maturity, and payment schedule to ensure maximum net income.
- Managed foreign exchange transactions involving US dollar and Japanese yen. Served as consultant to corporate clients on foreign exchange transactions by predicting short-term exchange rate fluctuations and suggesting appropriate time to engage in transaction.
- Issued, confirmed and negotiated letters of credit and authorized issuance of official import and export licenses on behalf of US government.

20xx–20xx   KRESTER and JONES New Haven, Connecticut
Tax & Audit Staff
- Prepared consolidated financial statements for medium-size companies.
- Prepared tax returns for individuals, corporations, and partnerships.
- Resolved tax matters with IRS and CA Franchise Tax Board for clients.
- Tested and analyzed new accounting and audit softwares.

Achievements: Passed all four parts of the November 20xx CPA Exam in one sitting.
National Association of Accountants Scholastic Achievement Award.
Membership to Beta Alpha Psi and Beta Gamma Sigma Honorary Society.

Skills: MS Office, QuickBooks, and ACCPAC tax and audit softwares. Fluent in Spanish.

Interests: Translator and Guide at International Exposition in São Paulo, Brazil.
Enjoy skiing, tennis, mountain biking, and weight training.

EXHIBIT 6.2   SAMPLE RÉSUMÉ – SONIA KHAN

SONIA KHAN

Current Address:
House 22, Belgravia Square
London, England SW114DG
Tel: (4471) 917-8754

Permanent Address:
5B Sunita, Ridge Road
Karachi 6, Pakistan
Tel: 91-22-366-1635

EDUCATION

INDIAN INSTITUTE OF TECHNOLOGY, New Delhi, India

Degree/Concentration: B.Sc. in Electrical Engineering, May 20xx
Academic Distinction: High Honors Graduate; McEnery Scholarship Recipient
Extracurricular Activities: Captain, Women's Field Hockey; Recreational Cricket

*PROFESSIONAL
EXPERIENCE*

BAIN CONSULTING
Consultant, Business Process Design

London, England
Jan 20xx to Present

• Conducted comparative studies on existing marketing strategies and tools utilized by leading Fortune 1000 Office Automation companies. Project results were subsequently sold to 12 companies.
• Re-engineered a local client's sales billing system to empower sales representatives, increase customer service and reduce cost. Resulted in 23% increase in sales and 34% reduction in costs.
• Helped lead seven-member team in designing and developing a system to automate a shipping process through an online software package with centralized data repository.
• Presented seminar Logistics in Action to 400 persons at London Exhibition and Trade Center.

INTEL CORPORATION
Technical Marketing Support Liaison

Bombay, India
Aug 20xx to Dec 20xx

• Worked on team of ten engineers, technicians and college interns in providing technical and marketing support for Pentium chip processors to South Asian client base.
• Promoted from Grade 3 to Grade 5 for outstanding project management of pre-Pentium processors.
• Received Intel Recognition Award for Results Orientation – for meeting tight deadline in developing test procedures and validating client motherboards, which were displayed in ROMDEX, biggest Computer Show in India.
• Received Intel Recognition Award for Customer Service – for creating documents for online tools, which resulted in increased client downloads by 30%.

OTHER

• Worked part-time while pursuing full-time study; earned 40% of university expenses.
• Junior Achievement – (20xx) Taught Algebra weekly to eighth-grade class during University. Encouraged students to learn geometry by seeing practical application of these skills.
• Public Relations Representative – (20xx) Arranged lectures for Intel Senior Management, coordinated philanthropic activities; set-up recreational trips for 200-plus members.
• Fluent in English, Hindi, Punjabi, and Urdu. Enrolled in intermediate-level French course.

Seven Tips for a More Impressive Résumé or Employment Record

The following seven tips can help you make your work experience look more impressive:

☞ *Tip #62:* *Use corporate profiles, especially if your company or organization is not well known.*

Corporate profiles (or company descriptions) are essential if a company is less than a household name. Adding descriptions helps the reviewer clarify immediately what industry a company is in. Say, for example, your résumé or record of employment contains the company name, Goliath Industries, Inc. The reviewer will have to guess at the nature of the industry that this company operates in. Providing a corporate description will clear up the confusion.

> Goliath Industries, Inc. is a Vancouver Stock Exchange public-listed company that trades under the symbol GOL. The company specializes in oil and gas and mining ventures. Its subsidiary, Goliath Mining South America, is currently involved in gold-mining operations in Bolivia.

To be consistent, consider adding corporate descriptions for all companies, even if the companies are well known.

> KPMG is a U.S.-based international "big four" accounting firm specializing in audit, tax, consulting, search, and investigative work.

☞ *Tip #63:* *Choose a professional format for your résumé.*

Exhibits 6.1–6.2 present two standard résumé formats. *Exhibit 6.1* follows a format with dates placed on the left-hand side. This gives a more open, airy feeling. It's also appropriate for candidates with less rather than more work experience because the left-hand column takes up a significant amount of space. *Exhibit 6.2* follows a format that places dates on the right-hand side of the page. This format is appropriate for individuals with more rather than less work experience because it enables information to be placed flush against the left column.

☞ *Tip #64:* *Use bullet points to start each line of your résumé, when highlighting a description of your work experience (i.e., responsibilities and/or accomplishments). Compared with previous jobs held, use an equal or greater number of bullet points when listing your most recent job experience.*

Putting more bullet points under your latest piece of work experience will give the reviewer the impression that you are gaining more and more experience and responsibility. This is an especially good technique if you have worked for your current company for less than one year. A rough rule of thumb is to try to have five bullet points for your most recent work experience and at least three bullet points for any other work entry.

☞ *Tip #65:* *Use verbs and consistent verb tenses to begin each bullet point.*

Each line of a résumé or employment record will typically begin with a bullet point followed by a verb expressed in the past tense. Verbs in the past tense usually end in "ed." Examples include the verbs "achieved," "maintained," or "counseled." The one exception occurs with your current job in which you have the choice of beginning each line using a verb in the "ing" form (that is, an "ing" verb, present tense of the progressive verb form) or a verb in the past tense (that is, an "ed" verb, past tense of the simple verb form).

☞ *Tip #66:   Quantify your work-related accomplishments with number-based modifiers.*

When listing your responsibilities and accomplishments on your employment record (or résumé), begin each entry with a verb and, when possible, list a quantitative measure of your accomplishment. Some of the examples are as follows:

- Worked on project Y, which increased company revenues by 10 percent while decreasing expenses by 5 percent.

- Installed a new computer system and trained two employees.

- Involved in a deal-making process that resulted in a 10-million-share initial public offering (IPO).

- Organized a company picnic for 700 employees.

Concentrate on your work accomplishments, not simply a description of your experience, and do not overlook what may be accomplishments. For example, perhaps you used less time, limited expenses, increased safety, bolstered corporate reputation, or raised employee morale.

In evaluating work accomplishments, it is meaningful to contrast achievements with responsibilities. Responsibilities are the tasks or duties a person is required to perform as part of his or her position. Responsibilities are typically detailed in a job description. Achievements, on the other hand, are results accomplished on the job. For example, "managed the company's sales force in San Antonio" is a responsibility; a "20-percent annual growth in sales for five consecutive years" is an achievement.

From a content standpoint, one of the key differences between the sample résumés seen in *Exhibits 6.1–6.2* relates to the "quantification" of work experience. Because the résumé of Sonia Khan contains a sufficient number of numerical quantifiers, she comes across as more proactive. Note the following number-based qualifiers: "sold to 12 companies...23% increase in sales...34% reduction in costs...seven-member team...increased client downloads by 30%."

Contrast this with Todd Gillman's résumé which contains virtually no quantifiers. For example, he mentions having "analyzed branch performance"..."formulated two-year marketing plan"..."developed a new commission system..." The reviewer is likely to ask, "What was the result?...what was the impact?...how effective?...how much?...how many?" This is perhaps the most common "mistake" candidates make with respect to résumés—they do not add enough numerical qualifiers. When a résumé contains too few qualifiers, the candidate's experience looks weak and unsubstantial. Their inclusion, on the other hand, makes the candidate's résumé or employment record look meaty; the candidate comes across as a doer.

☞ *Tip #67:* *Add "employment summaries" to explain what you found significant about each of your job experiences.*

Company or organization	Location and dates	Responsibilities/accomplishments
KPMG *Junior Consultant* KPMG is a U.S.-based international "big four" accounting firm specializing in audit, tax, consulting, search, and investigative work.	Chicago, IL June 'xx – May 'xx	• Worked… • Installed… • Spearheaded… • Involved… **Summary:** "I learned to…"

Company names and job titles rarely tell the whole story. They mean a lot more when accompanied by the reason the candidate thinks his or her work experience is important or significant. The headings "Summary" or "What I Learned" or "Why this is Significant" are used in upcoming examples (see *Exhibits 6.4 & 6.6*) to signal use of such summaries. Ideally, if your summary is well phrased, the reviewer may adopt your comments as his or her own interpretations. If nothing else, they will serve as well-organized and purposeful summaries. It is an excellent idea to mention why your job activities were important or significant and what work themes arose from your employment opportunities. Employment themes are discussed in the next section.

☞ *Tip #68:* *Review "employment themes" as the basis of writing meaningful employment summaries.*

Thinking about how to summarize your work experience is an important part of the business school process. You need to think about what your employment record means and strategize about how it impacts your whole application. Your work experience indirectly, sometimes directly impacts, the quality of your letters of recommendation, application essays, and interview sessions. Work summaries help to show the meaningfulness of your work experience. Work summaries can also help show that your career has developed in a systematic and coherent way. Give the reviewer the impression that everything about your experiences is linked together—that it has a rhyme and reason. Your previous work experiences must be viewed in terms of your ultimate career goal. A major problem many candidates have is the inability to explain why their job experiences are meaningful. Show off the richness of your professional experience, not only by citing your accomplishments, but by mentioning your work themes.

There are three potential groupings of work themes: (1) working across different job functions or across different departments, (2) working across different industries or sectors, and (3) working across different geographic or international settings.

Working across different job functions or across different departments:

In terms of job functions or skill sets, there are several key ones, including accounting and financing, marketing and selling, manufacturing, and engineering or researching. In days gone by, people used to refer to work in one of three ways—you could "make, sell, or count." In other words, you were effectively a manufacturing person (factory worker or engineer), a salesperson (or marketer), or an accountant (including financial analyst). In terms of departments, the major departments within companies still includes administrative (management, legal, personnel), marketing (and sales), finance (and accounting), production (engineering, technical), and research and development.

Example: "As a bond trader, I gained exposure to the different product areas of bond sales, trading, and research."

Example: "We anticipate conflicts to take place between the finance and marketing departments, but not between the marketing and sales departments. As a brand manager, I see the brand as the company's most important long-term asset. Salespersons, on the other hand, are motivated by short-term objectives, (for example, price discounts), which may or may not be beneficial to overall brand management."

Another way to view work themes according to job functions or departments is in terms of scope or job responsibility. For example, draw attention to some combination of experience you have as a specialist or generalist, manager or technical person, line-person or support person, self-employed individual or corporate employee.

Example: "I have worked as an investment specialist for a retail bank and as a self-employed individual. Working as my own boss in my own small business helped me see all areas of a business. I was responsible for writing checks, drafting proposals, and soliciting clients. It was an opportunity to see a complete business cycle, which includes paying for expenses and supplies, selling a product or service, collecting the money, and even licking postage stamps."

Example: "I learned, firsthand, the difference between being a financial controller and a financial stock market analyst. While the former sees things from an operational point of view, the latter sees things from a financial market point of view. I learned of the different things that a corporate manager feels are important in running a successful business from the 'inside' versus the kinds of things that a stock market analyst views as important in evaluating a public-listed company from the 'outside.'"

Example: "I found that 'leadership by command' was useful and necessary for leading our sales team, but 'leadership by example' worked best for motivating our company's research scientists."

Working across different industries or across different sectors:

If you have held a variety of different jobs prior to applying to business school, this is your opportunity to emphasize the diverse nature of your work experience. If you have worked steadily for one company prior to attending business school, look at diversity in terms of work in different industries or departments, or projects or clients you have served. For example, consultants often work across many different industries. Have you worked in different industries (for example, marketing versus finance, manufacturing versus wholesaling or retailing), or in different sectors (for example, private versus public or government)?

Example: "My legal background helps me to set up businesses within a legal context whereas my banking experience helps me evaluate whether a business deal makes economic sense."

Example: "As a member of the asset management team, I was able to better understand how individuals or companies operating in different industries measure the key drivers of performance. Retailers measure profitability by sales per square foot whereas leveraged buy-out firms measure profitability by internal rates of return."

Working across different geographical or international settings:

If you have worked overseas, this is your chance to emphasize the value of your international experience. On the other hand, it is still possible to have gained considerable exposure to international business without having left your home country, particularly if you have worked for a multinational company. In short, draw attention to the fact that you have a combination of international versus domestic experience, or national versus regional experience (for example, east versus west, north versus south).

Example: "I have worked in three geographically diverse continents of the world, namely Europe, North America, and Asia."

Example: "I have worked in both developed and developing countries, and gained exposure to doing business in both free-market and socialist-based economies."

☞ *Tip #69:   Anticipate strengths and weaknesses in your employment record.*

In terms of the number of companies or organizations you have worked for (from the time you left college up until the time you apply to business school), you will fall into one of three categories:

1)   You have worked for one single company or organization.
2)   You have worked for exactly two companies or organizations.
3)   You have worked for three or more companies or organizations.

The typical MBA applicant works approximately three to five years before applying to business school. In the event that you have worked for three or four different companies within a three- or four-year period, you will likely be faced with the problem of "weaving" your experiences together into a cohesive whole. You must address the otherwise implicit question of why you have worked for, say, four companies each for a single year rather than one company for an entire four years. Unless you address it, this will create a problem because you will look unfocused. The solution is to weave your three or four experiences together and make them look connected. Try to compose an "employment summary sheet," de facto cover sheet (see *Exhibits 6.3 & 6.5*), in which you summarize your employment experiences as if you were preparing a cover sheet. If you cannot add this within the fields ("data boxes") supplied by the online application, consider adding it in the optional essay area.

An employment summary sheet can show employment themes resulting from diversity in terms of work over differing geographical, industrial, or functional areas. In the particular case of candidates who have worked as consultants, a cover page can work marvelously for highlighting diverse work endeavors gained from having worked on different projects or for different clients.

Sample Presentations – Employment Summary Sheets and Employment Records

The following section includes the employment records of two MBA candidates: Kevin and Vivian. These two employment records are very much juxtaposed. Whereas Kevin has worked for three different companies in five years, Vivian has worked for one single company for seven years. Kevin benefits from an "employment analysis summary sheet" in order to consolidate his experiences and sell the admissions committee on the merits of his work diversity. He is effectively saying, "Hey, three different jobs in three

143

different industries is the best thing that has ever happened to me." His eclectic work background proves beneficial to his career as a fund manager. Vivian also benefits from an "employment summary sheet" because her seven pages of impressive work experience might otherwise simply blend together in the eyes of the reviewer. Note also how the use of employment summaries or anecdotes helps both candidates in making their experiences more personable and meaningful.

EXHIBIT 6.3   SAMPLE EMPLOYMENT SUMMARY SHEET – KEVIN

Employment Record Summary
Application to XYZ MBA School

My career objective is to lead in the fund management industry. Business people working in the fund industries need to be well acquainted with broad-ranging issues and disciplines. My work experience has helped me gain broad exposure in a short time frame. Only as a result of these diverse experiences do I now feel that I am best prepared for an MBA education and a career in Fund Management.

Full-time employment

From/To	Company	Nature	Categories of experience
Apr xx – Dec xx	Nedcor Asia Limited	Banking	Financial analysis
Mar xx – Mar xx	Shougang Concord Steel	Steel business	China trading
Mar xx – Feb xx	Decor Field Corporation	Import/export	Trading/entrepreneurship

Summer/part-time/internship employment

From/To	Company	Nature	Categories of experience
Jun xx – Aug xx	Decor Field Corporation	Import/export	Trading/entrepreneurship
Sep xx – May xx	Univ. of San Francisco	Teaching	Education
Jun xx – Aug xx	Decor Field Corporation	Import/export	Trading/entrepreneurship

---

Exhibit 6.4   Sample Employment Record – Kevin

NEDCOR ASIA LIMITED
Credit Officer/Financial Analyst   Macau, PRC   Apr 'xx – Dec 'xx (Present)

Corporate Overview:
This company is a restricted license bank (restricted license limits the bank in certain aspects, such as the ratio of capital to loan, nature and amount of deposit, etc.) wholly owned by Nedbank, South Africa. It has a client portfolio of about 220 accounts and annual turnover of over US$240M each year from 20xx to 20xx. There is about 70 staff in the Macau office.

Responsibilites:
- Evaluated corporate credit ratings of existing and prospective accounts based on clients' credit history and financial ratios. Minimized problem loans and reduced delinquent accounts to about one per month.
- Developed new financial packages to encourage clients' utilization of credit lines. The aggregate utilization rate was improved from 65% to 83% after implementation.
- Designed new operation procedures to re-engineer the existing operating system. This helped to simplify and standardize work flows.
- Developed a system to delegate daily operational duties to respective departments. Supervised the handover of tasks. Restated credit department's function in risk assessments and strategic duties.
- Assisted in managerial duties to prepare credit agenda and credit reports for credit manager's presentation in the weekly credit meetings and annual board meetings.

Summary:
"I took up the role of a financial analyst to analyze, assess, and restructure over an average of 20 new or review proposals each month, together with approving and administrating over 120 applications of excess each month. We interact with 11 marketing staff who continue to expand their portfolios by either increasing the number of clients or making larger volume of loans to clients. In such a fast-paced environment, my credit-analyzing skills were growing at the same horizon."

SHOUGANG CONCORD STEEL INTERNATIONAL TRADING COMPANY LIMITED
Marketing Executive & Assistant Manager   Macau, PRC   Mar 'xx – Mar 'xx

Corporate Overview:
Shougang Concord Group is a public-listed red-chip steel enterprise in Hong Kong. Its parent company, Shougang, was the No. 1 state-owned steel production plant in Beijing, China. The company has US$600M in annual turnover with 60,000 staff in Beijing and a staff of 100 in the Macau office.

Responsibilities:
- Designed shipment, conversion and repayment schedules in form of barter trade for 30,000 tons of iron from the iron mine in South America to China.
- Placed purchase orders on basis of marketing trend and performed sales analysis to avoid overstock. Resulted in 15% decrease in expenses in stocking of steel products.
- Participated in infrastructure tender in China and serviced a portfolio of active clients. The income contributed to the group by the tender projects was about US$300K. My previous portfolio of clients constituted 15% of the group's turnover.

Summary:

"Our trading department contributed over 40% (or US$379M) to the group's turnover in 20xx and 20xx, and represented over 14% profit contribution (or US$4.5M) to the group. As the second staff member to join the department, I played a critical role in many of those transactions. This job has given me solid China Trade experience and specialized marketing and operational management skills, applicable to a career in a globalized economy."

Reasons for leaving:

To establish my career path in the finance field – banking. After gaining some China trade experience at my two former jobs, I aim to lay the foundation for my career objectives.

DECOR FIELD CORPORATION

Assistant to General Manager   Macau, PRC   Mar 'xx – Feb 'xx

Company Overview:

Decor Field Corporation is a family-owned trading company specializing in trading sundry products, such as artificial plants, ceiling fans, photo frames and Christmas decorations. It is a small company with 10 staff. The annual turnover was about US$7M.

Responsibilities:

• Responsible for account entries, preparing tax returns, and reconciling bank statements.
• Established a computerized accounting system, ACCPAC and trained two employees to operate the system. Resulted in 15% reduction of expenses.
• Promoted a new item, photo frame. Duties included organized exhibitions and negotiated contracts with clients, suppliers. Contributed 8% to sales turnover in four months.

Summary:

"Assisting the general manager in a family-owned business translated to working unlimited overtime. Yet, this was the best way to learn about entrepreneurship in a real-world setting. The training from opening a bank account to negotiating business gave me solid experience in managing a small business."

Reasons for leaving:

To seek China trade experience in preparing myself for my future business role.

DECOR FIELD CORPORATION

Management Trainee   Macau   Jun 'xx – Aug 'xx; Jun 'xx – Aug 'xx (summers)
Hours: min. 40 hours/wk

• Handled full set of shipping documents.
• Responsible for daily account entry.
• Replied to all in-coming business correspondence from clients, manufacturers, shipping companies, and other trading agents.

UNIVERSITY OF SAN FRANCISCO

Teaching Assistant, Mathematics Dept   San Francisco, CA   Sep 'xx – May 'xx
Hours: min. 20 hours/wk

• Tutored students in Calculus classes.
• Corrected students' homework and examinations in Calculus classes.

EXHIBIT 6.5   SAMPLE EMPLOYMENT SUMMARY SHEET – VIVIAN

The following cover sheet serves to summarize my professional work experience. All of my work experience has taken place under the umbrella of General Electric. I have worked in both European and Asian markets; this includes experience in financial management, internal auditing, and investment analysis. I feel that the depth and variety of these experiences will play an integral role in preparing me for my ultimate career goal: Becoming a global marketing executive at GE.

Company & Position	Dates	Location
NATIONAL BROADCASTING COMPANY ASIA (NBC Asia) Manager, News Finance and Special Projects	Feb 'xx – present (as at Jan 10)	Hong Kong, China
GE LIGHTING EUROPE Manager, Western European Internal Audit Department	Nov 'xx – Feb 'xx	Based in Hungary, (extensive Western European travel 2–3 wks/mth)
GE LIGHTING EUROPE Investment Analyst, Incandescent & Halogen Product Lines	Sept 'xx – Nov 'xx	Budapest, Hungary (monthly travel to the U.K.)
GE LIGHTING EUROPE Cost Analyst, Budapest Light Source Factory (6-month Financial Management Program [FMP])	Apr 'xx – Sep 'xx	Budapest, Hungary
GE LIGHTING EUROPE Financial Analyst, Financial Planning & Analysis (FMP Rotation)	Jul 'xx – Apr 'xx	Budapest, Hungary
GE LIGHTING EUROPE Financial Analyst, Technology Finance (FMP Rotation)	Feb 'xx – Jul 'xx	Budapest, Hungary
GE LIGHTING EUROPE Financial Analyst, Sales & Mrktg Finance (FMP Rotation)	Jun 'xx – Feb 'xx	Budapest, Hungary

EXHIBIT 6.6   **SAMPLE EMPLOYMENT RECORD – VIVIAN**

Firm name:	**NATIONAL BROADCAST COMPANY (NBC ASIA)**
Job title:	**Financial Analyst, Technology Finance (6-month FMP Rotation)**
Job location:	**Chai Wan, Hong Kong**
Dates:	**Feb 'xx – Present [Jan 'xx]**

Firm size:	Approx. 298 employees; US$4M	
Nature of business:	Broadcasting company	
Annual base salary:	Beg. US$84,000	End. US$90,600
Add Cost of Living & Location Premium Adj:	Beg. US$42,000	End. US$45,000

List and description of responsibilities:
• CNBC Asia Business News Channel's first financial manager.
• Working closely with CNBC Asia management to develop annual business and operating plans for channel and establish monthly and quarterly budgets.
• Tracking and reporting expenditures and providing variance analysis versus budget on a weekly, monthly, and quarterly basis to CNBC Asia management and quarterly results and analysis to NBC NY headquarters.
• Performing monthly internal closings of all CNBC Asia accounts and account reconciliations and reconciling inter-company expense and liability accounts for purchased programming with NBC NY headquarters and NBC Super Channel in the UK.
• Responsible for approving of all CNBC Asia expenditures and performing various financial analysis for the channel.
• Responsible for NBC Asia's total head count reporting to NBC NY headquarters.
• Working closely with NBC Asia technical staff to create budget and track over US$35M of annual expenditures for satellites and link charges for company. Providing variance analysis versus budget on a monthly basis to local management and quarterly results and analysis to NBC NY headquarters. Performing monthly internal closings of all satellite and link accounts and account reconciliations.
• Providing financial support to legal department and helping negotiate contracts with suppliers such as stringers, newswire agencies, and production houses.

Most significant challenge of this position:
• I am responsible for controlling spending and redirecting resources to opportunities in line with CNBC Asia's goals. At the same time, I have to maintain a good working relationship with CNBC Asia's management as the channel's first financial manager.

Reason for leaving:
• N/A

Firm name:	**GENERAL ELECTRIC LIGHTING EUROPE**
Job title:	**Manager, Western European Internal Audit Department**
Job location:	**Based in Budapest, Hungary; extensive Western European travel 2 to 3 weeks per month**
Dates:	**Nov 'xx – Feb 'xx**

Firm size:	9,000 employees; $700M in revenue	
Nature of business:	Manufacturing; Lighting Industry	
Annual base salary:	Beg. US$55,650	End. US$56,700
Add Cost of Living & Location Premium Adj:	Beg. US$48,000	End. US$50,925

List and description of responsibilities:
- Created new organization. Led and managed two employees.
- Planned, organized, and headed all financial and business process audits at GELE sales offices in France, Spain, England, and Hungary.
- Audited office's financial statements for accuracy and adherence to generally accepted accounting principles (GAAP).
- Interviewed employees, process mapped office's activities, and conducted transactions tests to verify routines and controls.
- Conducted compliance audits with management and key staff to ensure knowledge of and adherence to GE Spirit & Letter Integrity Policies.
- Audited information system security and deleted unnecessary and/or conflicting system access of staff.
- Presented findings and made recommendations on issues uncovered to local and upper management.
- Worked in multicultural teams to resolve issues and implement recommendations.
- Provided financial analysis as member of a cross-functional team setup to reduce excess inventory in the Incandescent product line.

Most significant challenge of this position:
- Although the job description and responsibilities were vague, I was able to create a new organization, quickly identify major business issues, and successfully incorporate business goals into the audit program.

Reason for leaving:
- Promoted to Manager, News Finance and Special Projects at NBC Asia in Hong Kong

Firm name:	**GENERAL ELECTRIC LIGHTING EUROPE**
Job title:	**Investment Analyst, Incandescent and Halogen Lighting Product Lines (6-month FMP Rotation)**
Job location:	**Budapest, Hungary; monthly travel to the U.K.**
Dates:	**Sep 'xx – Nov 'xx**

| Annual base salary: | Beg. US$49,050 | End. US$55,650 |
| Add Cost of Living & Location Premium Adj: | Beg. US$28,000 | End. US$31,500 |

List and description of responsibilities:
- Responsible for analysing, approving, and tracking of over 90 projects totaling US$6M in capital investment in Hungary and the U.K for the Incandescent and Halogen lighting product lines.
- Conducted financial analysis of proposed capital investments using DCRR, NPV, IRR, and financial modeling techniques. Worked in cross-functional and multicultural teams to gather financial and operational information to perform analysis, and made recommendations to management based on results.
- Financial representative for GELE's first major rationalization project, coordinating pan-European information gathering, analysis, and tracking of US$5M of fixed assets transferred from the U.K. to Hungary as a result of plant shutdowns.

Most significant challenge of this position:
- I was able to successfully gather and analyze financial and operational information in an environment where data was scarce and project team members were located in different plants throughout the U.K. to Hungary and had conflicting objectives.

Reason for leaving:
- Promoted to Manager of Western European Internal Audit Department.

Firm name:	**GENERAL ELECTRIC LIGHTING EUROPE**
Job title:	**Cost Analyst, Budapest Light Source Factory (6-month FMP Rotation)**
Job location:	**Budapest, Hungary**
Dates:	**Apr 'xx – Sep 'xx**

Annual base salary:	Beg. US$49,050	End. US$49,050
Add Cost of Living & Location Premium Adj:	Beg. US$28,000	End. US$28,000

List and description of responsibilities:
- Prepared investment analysis for new Incandescent manufacturing line in Budapest Light Source Factory using DCRR, NPV, IRR, and financial modeling techniques. Worked within cross-functional teams to gather financial and operational information to perform analysis.
- Audited routines and controls for movement and sale of scrap lamps and components from factory. Made recommendations to change process involving use of environmentally hazardous materials in order to ensure greater safety.
- Financial representative for GELE Asset Committee – a cross-functional team set up to dispose of buildings and houses owned by Tungsram in Hungary. Responsible for the financial analysis of the rental and disposal of this property. Helped committee members negotiate with real estate agents and company representatives for the sale and rental of buildings/houses.

Most significant challenge of this position:
- I was accepted by the Light Source Factory plant management and employees and gained their trust to accurately complete investment analysis.

Reason for leaving:
- Promoted to off-program position as Investment Analyst for GELE's Incandescent and Halogen product lines.

Firm name:	**GENERAL ELECTRIC LIGHTING EUROPE**
Job title:	**Financial Analyst, Financing Planning & Analysis (6-month FMP Rotation)**
Job location:	**Budapest, Hungary**
Dates:	**Jul 'xx – Apr 'xx**

Annual base salary:	Beg. US$47,100	End. US$49,050
Add Cost of Living & Location Premium Adj:	Beg. US$28,000	End. US$28,000

List and description of responsibilities:
- Responsible for the information retrieval, tracking, and reporting of US$65M worth of Purchase Accounting (PA) expenditures. Personal investigation yielded US$1.6M of undiscovered PA.
- Conducted an in-depth investigation into entire system of passenger transportation at Tungsram. Recommendations were used as basis for management decisions.

Most significant challenge of this position:
- I had to communicate regulations and proper accounting methods of Purchase Accounting, a complex GAAP procedure, to a group of non-English-speaking factory accountants who were unfamiliar with US accounting standards and practices.

Reason for leaving:
- Six-Month FMP rotation (General Electric's Financial Management Program).

Firm name:	**GENERAL ELECTRIC LIGHTING EUROPE**
Job title:	**Financial Analyst, Technology Finance (6-month FMP Rotation)**
Job location:	**Budapest, Hungary**
Dates:	**Feb 'xx – Jul 'xx**

Annual base salary:	Beg. US$45,750	End. US$47,100
Add Cost of Living & Location Premium Adj:	Beg. US$17,200	End. US$28,000

List and description of responsibilities:
- Successfully implemented GE Lighting Tungsram's first fixed-asset investment tracking system (RKP) for the purpose of tracking US$44M worth of capital investment and program expenditure.
- Trained and instructed all users of system.

Most significant challenge of this position:
- I was responsible for implementing a complicated information system without the support of the designing team (spearheaded by an FMP and information systems consultant who left the project) while under strict deadlines.

Reason for leaving:
- To continue the 6-Month FMP Program rotation (General Electric's Financial Management Program).

Firm name: **GENERAL ELECTRIC LIGHTING EUROPE**
Job title: **Financial Analyst, Sales & Marketing Finance (6-month FMP Rotation)**
Job location: **Budapest, Hungary**
Dates: **Jun 'xx – Feb 'xx**

Annual base salary: Beg. US$45,750   End. US$45,750
Add Cost of Living & Location Premium Adj: Beg. US$17,200   End. US$17,200

List and description of responsibilities:
• Responsible for the first-ever detailed analysis of pricing and profitability by Lighting product line and for recommendations for price increases.
• Created a transportation spreadsheet program to calculate per product transportation cost by product line and destination.

Most significant challenge of this position:
• I generated incremental margin through pricing increases despite internal resistance from local sales and marketing personnel and lack of reliable sales and contribution margin information.

Reason for leaving:
• Six-Month FMP Program rotation (General Electric's Financial Management Program).

Chapter 7

Letters of Recommendation

I always know when candidates write recommendations themselves. They never brag about themselves in the way a recommender would.

—Admissions officer of a
leading business school

Introduction

How many recommendations do you need?

You are generally required to obtain two or three recommendations in order to apply to business school. Nowadays, business schools generally want both your recommendations to be work related, with ideally one written by your current boss. When a third recommendation is required, it may be professional, academic, or community service in nature.

A typical candidate will be required to submit two or three recommendations as follows:

1. Professional
2. Professional
3. Academic, professional, or community service

The rule of thumb is that unless your third recommendation is going to present another aspect of your work experience, not merely repeat information contained in your first or second recommendations, then you should go for diversity on your third recommendation. Think of a person you have interacted with outside of work or school, particularly a person working in community service, or politics.

How are your letters of recommendation evaluated?

There are two dimensions along which letters of recommendation are evaluated. The first is the objectivity dimension: "Who says it?" The second is the content dimension: "What is said?" Both dimensions combine to lend a sense of credibility. The person "who says it" should be someone capable of observing your work (or academics or volunteer work). The strength of "what is said" is ultimately linked to the examples (or lack thereof) used by the recommender in support of what he or she says. Content will vary depending on the type of recommendation, namely professional, academic, or community service.

Regardless of whether a recommendation is professional, academic, or community service in nature, the reviewer will look for evidence of a candidate's personal traits and qualities. Thus, a professional recommendation should ideally touch on those personal traits and qualities that have been important to your career development. Likewise, an academic recommendation should ideally touch on those personal key traits related to your intellectual development.

Two methods to complete recommendation letters

The first method involves having each recommender answer all questions on each individual recommendation form, which is submitted online. The second method involves having each recommender type a generic, all-purpose letter, which is either emailed or mailed to the school.

Individual Question Method. Business schools prefer that recommenders follow the Individual Question Method. Here the recommender must answer each individual question asked in the recommendation and submit online the completed form required by each school. See *Exhibit 7.1.*

Generic Letter Method. Using this method, recommenders type separate letters, usually two-thirds of a page to one-and-a-half pages long, and staple a copy of each typed letter to the specific recommendation form of the school (see *Exhibit 7.2*). Each recommender is required to check off the boxes directly on the recommendation form in order to rate the applicant on cross section of personal and professional traits and abilities. The recommendation will be either emailed or mailed directly to the school.

EXHIBIT 7.1   LETTERS OF RECOMMENDATION – INDIVIDUAL QUESTION METHOD

(front side)   (back side)

Confidential Recommendation
The ANDERSON SCHOOL AT UCLA MBA PROGRAM

Name of Applicant _____

TO THE RECOMMENDER:
The person whose name appears above is applying for admission to The Anderson School MBA Program. The Admissions Committee values the direct contract you have had with the applicant and asks for your personal and candid assessment of his or her potential for senior management. The most helpful recommendations are those that present a balanced view and give detailed descriptions of an applicant's abilities.

Please answer the following questions and send them by e-mail. Alternatively you may type a letter and return it with this form in a sealed envelope with your signature across the seal. We will send you an acknowledgment card informing you that your recommendation has been received by our office.

Name of recommender _____ Telephone _____

Position / title _____ Firm / school _____

Address _____

1. How long have you known the applicant and in what context? Please comment on the frequency of your interaction.

2. What are the applicant's principal strengths and special talents?

3. In what areas can the applicant improve? Has he or she worked on these areas?

4. Compared to others with similar responsibilities in your organization, how would you rate the applicant? Why?

Confidential Recommendation
The ANDERSON SCHOOL AT UCLA MBA PROGRAM

5. Please rate the applicant on the qualities listed below, identifying here the group to which you are comparing the applicant: _____ _____. If you are unable to comment, please place N/A in the appropriate box.

	<50%	>50%	>25%	>10%	>5%	>2%
Ability to work with others						
Analytical/quantitative skills						
Intellectual ability						
Oral communicating skills						
Written skills						
Motivation/initiative						
Leadership potential						
Maturity						
Sense of humor						
Respect from peers						
Respect from management						
Potential for career advancement						

Recommender's signature _____ Date: _____

In practice, recommenders often prefer the Generic Letter Method because they can type a single letter to be used by a candidate for all the schools that he or she is applying to. Consider, for a moment, the task that faces a recommender (especially an investment banker or senior-level consultant) who is assisting seven people apply to business school in a single year, in which each candidate is applying to seven schools. Can you imagine being burdened with filling in some 50 individual recommendation forms! Admissions officers understand why recommenders might prefer this procedure and will not reject a candidate simply because he or she did not have recommenders fill in answers directly on each recommendation form.

EXHIBIT 7.2   LETTERS OF RECOMMENDATION – GENERIC LETTER METHOD

staple

(typed letter)   (backside of recommendation form)

Jan 17, 20xx

Admissions Director:

It is my pleasure to serve as a reference for Richard Tyler in his application for admission to your Graduate Business School. I have known Richard for fourteen years, first as an associate of his father (we worked together in a large U.S. conglomerate from 20xx to 20xx). Later Richard worked for me at Xerox Corporation as an accountant and financial analyst.

Richard demonstrated a high level of intelligence, strong technical skills, and a very effective and positive way of interacting with people. He gained quickly the respect and support of his peers and seniors. He made a substantial contribution at Xerox Corporation during his period of service. I would particularly like to cite his originality and desire to innovate new systems and procedures.

Another remarkable quality worthy of mention is Richard's wide range of interests – from the specific and exacting profession of accounting and quantitative analysis to the broad interests that took him to Beijing for study and international experience. This is a unique range.

Based on my 32-year career in the financial management of high tech companies, my own XYZ School MBA degree, and knowledge of many applicants and young graduates over the years, I would rank Richard in the top 10% of his peers now applying for admission.

Sincerely,
Frank B. Moore, Jr.

Frank B. Moore, Jr.
VP Finance & CFO
Xerox Systems of America

Confidential Recommendation
The ANDERSON SCHOOL AT UCLA MBA PROGRAM

5. Please rate the applicant on the qualities listed below, identifying here the group to which you are comparing the applicant: _____ _____. If you are unable to comment, please place N/A in the appropriate box.

	<50%	>50%	>25%	>10%	>5%	>2%
Ability to work with others					X	
Analytical/quantitative skills				X		
Intellectual ability					X	
Oral communicating skills				X		
Written skills			X			
Motivation/initiative						X
Leadership potential				X		
Maturity			X			
Sense of humor						X
Respect from peers				X		
Respect from management				X		
Potential for career advancement					X	

Recommender's signature *Frank B. Moore, Jr.*   Jan 17, 20xx

Getting a Detailed Recommendation

A common problem with recommendations is similar to that of application essays—namely superficiality and a lack of concrete examples to support what is being said. The recommendation written for you is, in part, only as good as the information that a recommender has to use in writing about you. Your objective is to get each recommender to mention specific things about you, in order to make what that recommender says both credible and forceful.

With a tad of cynicism thrown in, many recommendation letters sound like: "Johnny is a nice boy" or "Suzie is a good girl." In other words, the reader is left with no measure of how to judge the applicant's qualities and credentials. Superficiality stems from two sources:

- The recommender really does not know the candidate. This is very often the case of recommendations received from CEOs and high political officials. They are referred to informally as "letters of support," rather than letters of recommendation.

- The recommender knows the candidate but cannot express it through his or her writing. This is often true of recommenders who are either unfamiliar with the MBA admissions process (or other graduate level undertaking) or who are less than proficient in the art of writing (more often true of recommenders whose first language is not English). Such letters lack concrete details and examples, and may be full of unsupported adjectives and platitudes.

The following letter is rumored to have been obtained by a candidate who apparently met the U.S. vice president at an official government function.

Dear Admissions Committee:

I recommend this candidate for admission to your school. I met the applicant at an official function and he impressed me with his honest-looking face and firm handshake.

Sincerely,
Mr. Vice President of the United States

This letter has become part of the folklore of graduate school admissions. Regardless of whether the letter is completely authentic, it has nonetheless become a metaphor for any vacuous letter with unsupported details. Such a letter would contribute more in terms of comic relief for overworked admissions personnel than to the advancement of the applicant's application.

Seven Tips for Getting Good Letters of Recommendation

The following are tips on how to get good letters of recommendation.

☞ *Tip #70:   Decide as early as possible who your recommenders will be and prepare to "recruit" them.*

Give your recommenders sufficient time to receive forms and/or type letters. If you haven't been in touch with a potential recommender for some time, it might be a good idea to drop them a line to say hi first. Then in a couple of weeks contact him or her and ask for a recommendation. This way you massage the awkward situation that arises if you directly ask for a recommendation and give the recommender the impression that that is the sole reason for your contacting him or her. Some candidates prefer to send a postcard from a travel destination a few months before asking for a letter of recommendation!

☞ *Tip #71:   Send your résumé or employment record, along with a personal letter, to each recommender.*

In order to ensure that the recommender puts details into your letter, try to supply each recommender with the following:

- First, a copy of your professionally formatted résumé or employment record.

- Second, a personal letter (suggested length, approximately two type-written pages). A personal letter is needed in order to highlight for the recommender what your career goals are, why you want an MBA, and to elaborate what you believe are your key personal traits, your achievements, perhaps your own assessments of your strengths and weaknesses, etc.

☞ *Tip #72:* *Update your résumé and/or employment record and complete summaries on what you feel you have learned or what you feel is significant about your experiences. Think of your experience as divided between hard skills (quantitative skills) and soft skills (qualitative skills).*

An employment record should ideally contain a summary of what you found significant about your work experience. See Tip #67 in *Chapter 6*. The objective here is to get the recommender to reinforce those things that you believe are highlights of your work experience.

☞ *Tip #73:* *Communicate to your recommenders where you feel your career is heading.*

Based on a well-written personal letter, your recommenders will have specifics—both professional and personal—to use in writing your recommendation letters or in filling out your recommendation forms. It is vital that you have your goal statements and vision statements written before you ask recommenders to write recommendation letters for you. Do not let recommenders guess at your career goals; help them to figure out what you are doing. Most candidates send recommendation forms to their recommenders with only a copy of their résumé. However, without a candidate first deciding on his or her post-MBA and long-term career goal, and subsequently communicating this to his or her recommender, the recommender is likely to be left feeling confused by not having a better idea of what the candidate expects to do with his or her MBA and where his or her career path is heading. Having a clear career goal will serve to impress the recommender and give him or her the added confidence in writing you a better-than-expected recommendation letter.

You ideally never want the admissions committee to think of you as a clueless applicant. Below is the last paragraph of an actual recommendation letter. Consider how detrimentally it would affect the candidate's chances for admission to a top-tier business school.

> Eric is a "good person." He is very intelligent, yet with an ego under control. He has principles and morals by which he lives by. I am not sure if he is fiercely ambitious and has a clear vision of what he wants to do with his life, but in a stimulating MBA program, I am sure that this will soon change.

☞ *Tip #74:* *If your recommender insists that you draft your own letter (or draft answers to the individual recommendation questions), then ask a friend to draft the letter based on the input you received from your recommender. Your recommender will still have to vouch for what is written in the letter.*

Admissions officers frown upon the practice that occurs whenever applicants draft their own letters of recommendation and have recommenders sign these letters. Recommenders who agree to write recommendations should fulfill their responsibilities and write the letters themselves. In reality, your recommender may, for reasons of overwork, unfamiliarity, or laziness, ask you to write your own letter to be presented to the recommender for modification and signing. If you have no other way to get a letter of recommendation done for you, here is a sensible tip for helping you tackle the process. For purposes of style and voice, if your recommender is female, then have a female colleague draft the letter; if your recommender is male then have a male colleague draft the letter for you. This will help you to disguise your writing style. Also, the writing styles or tones of males and females are often generically different.

☞ *Tip #75:* *Think detail. The goal is to get the recommender to write in a specific and concrete manner, typically highlighting one or two major work accomplishments, one or two distinguishing personal traits, or one or two strengths or weaknesses.*

If your recommender allows you to see a copy of your recommendation letter, and you do not see sufficient detail, you may want to ask your recommender to add more in the way of specifics. As diplomatically as you can, suggest to your recommender that you understand that top ranked business schools are looking, above all else, for written details to support what you have done. Here is an opportunity to coach your recommender. You might say, "I was reading in the online application that admissions officers are looking for detail and really want specific examples so they can understand how a particular candidate excels as well as gets things done in the workplace."

☞ *Tip #76:* *Welcome any opportunity to involve yourself in this process. If recommenders allow you to view your recommendations before they are submitted, check to see that each letter contains sufficient supporting detail, and that all letters work as a unit to address your background in a meaningful and varied way.*

The above tip is fairly self-explanatory. Although you want some form of consistency across different letters, you also do not want to repeat the same information. Case in point: If one letter talks about your attention to detail, the other can talk about your ability to get things done. If one letter talks about you ability to lead by example and other can talk about your ability to manage resources competently. If one letter talks about your involvement in project A, the other can detail your accomplishment with respect to project B.

☞ *Tip #77: Send thank-you notes or e-mails to your recommenders.*

Your recommenders have done some good work for you, which required time and effort. You may decide to apply to more schools at a later point in the application process, and you may need to approach your recommenders again. Moreover, you will likely submit the names of your recommenders as job references when looking for work both in and outside of business school. Develop and keep rapport.

The Mechanics of a "Good" Letter of Recommendation

The following five things are generally present in a quality letter of recommendation:

1. The recommender mentions in what context he or she knows the applicant.

2. The recommender mentions what the applicant accomplished on the job (or in school).

3. The recommender mentions how the candidate ranks in comparison with others.

4. The recommender mentions what he or she believes are the applicant's best personal and professional traits.

5. The recommender mentions one area of perceived weakness or one area of needed professional, academic, or personal improvement.

Sample Letters of Recommendation

The following are examples of two fairly standard letters of recommendation as seen in the business school application process. A critique of both letters follows.

EXHIBIT 7.3   SAMPLE RECOMMENDATION LETTER – FRANK B. MOORE

Admissions Director:

It is my pleasure to serve as a reference for Richard Tyler in his application for admission to your Graduate Business School. I have known Richard for fourteen years, first as an associate of his father (we worked together in a large U.S. conglomerate from 20xx to 20xx). Later Richard worked for me at Xerox Corporation as an accountant and financial analyst.

Richard demonstrated a high level of intelligence, strong technical skills, and a very effective and positive way of interacting with people. He gained quickly the respect and support of his peers and seniors. He made a substantial contribution at Xerox Corporation during his period of service. I would particularly like to cite his originality and desire to innovate new systems and procedures.

Another remarkable quality worthy of mention is Richard's wide range of interests – from the specific and exacting profession of accounting and quantitative analysis to the broad interests that took him to Japan for study and international experience. This is a unique range.

Based on my 32-year career in the financial management of high-tech companies, my own XYZ school MBA degree, and knowledge of many applicants and young graduates over the years, I would rank Richard in the top 10 percent of his peers now applying for admission.

Sincerely,

Frank B. Moore, Jr.

Chief Financial Officer
Xerox Systems of America

EXHIBIT 7.4   SAMPLE RECOMMENDATION LETTER – ELIZABETH LEE

Dear Admissions Committee:

I still remember the first time I met Judith Chan. She was a bit shy when she applied to work in our firm as a sales support person in March of 20xx. As a sales representative at the newly opened branch of Avon Cosmetic Products in Hong Kong, she would be responsible for monitoring the phones and walk-in customers, answering their questions and helping them with whatever we could offer them. As this was a new center for Avon International and women's accessories was a brand new product area, it had to be adapted for Hong Kong and PRC consumers. Judith not only exceeded her sales quotas, but also became our regional expert on how to adapt, modify, and package all our local products.

Besides having a very special organizational ability, Judith also has a wonderful way with her co-workers and customers. Co-workers listen to her advice and customers continue to buy from her. Judith is always willing to put in that extra effort to get things right. We have all watched Judith develop her marketing and sales skills. If she were not planning on going to graduate school, we would have offered her the position of director of our Beijing Avon office where she would not only administrate but also train sales staff to open up the China market.

As an XYZ school college grad myself who started the Avon Hong Kong office and hired Judith, I am most proud of "finding" her for our company. She is extremely talented, diligent, and innovative, and all without business school training. Although we hate to "lose" her, we know that she would gain so much from further studies at business school, as I know that I did. As a teacher and administrator myself, I have to admit that I have never met another person who has greater potential to be a truly great marketer. She already is our most valued one and will be greatly missed. Thus, I unreservedly and enthusiastically recommend her for your program. The school would proud of such a graduate.

Elizabeth Lee

Director
Avon Cosmetics (Hong Kong) Ltd.

Exhibit 7.5   Sample Recommendation Letter – Norman Kravics

Massachusetts Institute of Technology Sloan School of Management
Master's Admissions Office, Room E52-101 50 Memorial Drive
Cambridge, MA 02142-1347

To Whom It May Concern:

At the request of Julie Munzer, I am writing this recommendation in strong support of her application for admission into your graduate program.

Julie has been reporting directly to me for the past two years as a financial analyst at Goldman Sachs in Australia. In my current role as the Regional Head of Utilities Research, Julie and I interact frequently on a daily basis. Significantly, Julie's performance and contributions to the team have been nothing short of outstanding. Appropriately, she was promoted to associate analyst in August of this year, a position typically occupied by post-MBA graduates.

The ability to handle multiple projects and service widely varying end-customers (investment banking, corporate clients, institutional investors, sales and trading, or others) is a requirement for success in equity research. Along this metric, Julie is a superstar. In my estimation, her capacity for carrying heavy workloads for sustained periods of time is among the top one percent of all financial analysts I have worked with globally. Julie has been instrumental in helping to expand our research coverage universe roughly three-fold in the past 18 months. She developed and maintains ownership of the firm's Utilities Weekly research product. She has been a key coordinator of our annual Utilities Symposiums, the largest conference of its type in the region and one of the firm's most visible annual client events. On the investment banking support side, Julie has contributed research directly or indirectly in several major transactions, including Initial Public Offerings (IPOs), secondary stock offerings, block trade executions, convertible debt transactions, and mergers and acquisitions. I am convinced that Julie's resourcefulness and ongoing contributions were an important factor in our utilities team being named to Institutional Investor magazine's All-Asia Research Team.

It has been personally gratifying to me watching Julie's analytical abilities mature since the time I have worked with her. I am entirely comfortable with having Julie meet with and interview company management teams when I am unavailable. She asks probing questions and has developed "an ear" for what is important and increasingly how to interpret various (and sometimes conflicting) data points. In our latest new coverage report (Symbiotic Industries), Julie constructed the basic financial models and projections, as well as a major portion of the written material and investment thesis. She handles herself flawlessly in working across geographic regions, as companies that we actively research include multi-billion dollar corporations in Taiwan, China, Singapore, and Korea. Perhaps the strongest endorsement of our confidence in Julie's analytical ability is the fact that she is slated to soon begin introducing her own research franchise and senior coverage of stocks. Again, senior or lead coverage of stocks is typically not mandated to new analysts until a year or more after graduate business school has been completed.

Earlier this year, I was asked to spend a few days in Japan with other Goldman Sachs analysts visiting major institutional clients as part of a global marketing initiative. Due to scheduling conflicts, I was unable to participate. Feeling that she was up for the assignment, I asked Julie to take my place. Although it was clear to me that she was somewhat intimidated at first by this request – and with good reason, as to my knowledge, there had been no financial analyst at her level at the time that had assumed such a prominent role in a research marketing trip – she accepted the challenge without hesitation. For my part, any cautiousness I had came from the fact that Julie had historically spent most of her time performing grassroots research and interacting with company management, not doing face-to-face institutional investor meetings. Julie spent a good deal of time preparing for the trip, probing me with insightful questions and studying the art of "stock positioning" versus "company positioning." She prepared herself to market her stock ideas with a strong "ground-up" approach, focusing on competitive positions and valuations of companies within the region, driving our ultimate investment ideas. Needless to say, the trip was a great success, with some of the other senior analysts coming back to me with feedback about how impressed they were regarding her performance on the road show and accompanying luncheon presentations (one of which featured more than 100 attendees).

Julie works effectively and cooperatively in the team environment, one of the cornerstones of our organization. With regards to managers and supervisors, she may sometimes come off as a bit shy to those she does not know well. I believe that some of this may be attributed to her sense of modesty. With regard to peers, Julie is very successful in nurturing cooperation and getting things done. For example, she maintains good relationships with counterparts in various departments (sales, strategy, economics, etc.) and was praised by others in international offices for her cooperation and timely sharing of news flow. With respect to subordinates, Julie has begun the task of mentoring two new financial analysts that joined the team in June of this year. With the best of intentions, I have asked her to "clone herself" in the training of our new teammates. She has taken the task to heart, providing daily guidance in everything from financial model building to networking around the firm. One of the new analysts has even moved his own chair into her office.

I rate Julie's leadership potential as high. Although she has spent most of her career with me in support of group initiatives, Julie has clearly demonstrated key traits that I believe are critical in leadership: focus, teamwork, responsibility, and integrity. As mentioned above, she has recently taken on a mentoring role, and I believe has been successful in integrating these new analysts into the team in a very short period of time.

Within the organization, Julie has been giving of her time on several fronts, including college campus recruiting (sometimes requiring her to fly to other countries, such as Taiwan where her language abilities are a major benefit for the firm's recruiting efforts). In addition, Goldman sponsors an ongoing program called "Community Teamworks" where employees volunteer their time outside of work to help the local community in projects ranging from public cleanup initiatives to tutoring to construction programs. Julie is an active member of Community Teamworks and I trust will provide more details of the various projects she has been staffed on in her application.

In summary, I am in strong support of Julie's application for admission into MIT's Sloan School of Management. I believe she has given careful consideration of her plans to enroll in an MBA program, as we have talked about this subject on several occasions. To be quite frank, while I am less than thrilled about the prospect of losing her contributions to the team while she pursues a graduate degree, I believe her motivations are sincere. Additionally, I believe Julie will share a unique global perspective with other students in the classroom setting. I welcome the opportunity to speak directly to the admissions committee should you feel you require additional information on Ms. Munzer.

Respectfully submitted,

Norman Kravics

_____

Executive Director, Goldman Sachs

The following serves as critiques of the three previous letters of recommendation. These recommendations are examples of the "generic-letter" method.

Recommendation #1 (Exhibit 7.3)

This recommendation letter follows a traditional format for a business school letter of recommendation. It cites at a minimum, the context in which the recommender knows the candidate and a quantifiable comparison of how the candidate compares in his or her peer group. This letter constitutes a solid endorsement; the only criticism is that it misses on a few opportunities to cite details in support of things said. For example, the reviewer is likely to respond to the recommender's statement, "I would particularly like to cite his originality and desire to innovate new systems and procedures" by asking what these new systems and procedures were. Moreover, the best professional recommendations may also make mention of a candidate's career aspirations, as well as areas of needed development. Sometimes the recommender cites anecdotes or quotes that other persons have made about the applicant in order to support some of the comments made by the recommender.

Recommendation #2 (Exhibit 7.4)

This recommendation is another example of a good one, written in a lighter, more colloquial tone. It comes across as warm and personable. A criticism of this letter, similar to the preceding one, lies in the lack of concrete details to support the things stated by the recommender. For example, the reviewer may want to know how much Judith did exceed her sales quota—1 percent or 200 percent—and perhaps how much sales of the Hong Kong office have grown and how much of this growth may be the result of Judith's efforts. The recommender should give one example of how Judith adapted, modified, or packaged new products for the local market because the reviewer is no doubt interested. Perhaps the recommender could cite a quote from one of Judith's favorite customers. Lastly, the reviewer may want to know at least one area where Judith is weak in order to balance out the recommendation.

Recommendation #3 (Exhibit 7.5)

This recommendation provides an example of a longer appraisal, which is some 1,200 words in length. A "longer" appraisal might be defined as any recommendation that has a word count of more than 1,000 words in length. Lengthy recommendations are more commonly found in the world of management consulting and investment banking because recommenders working in management consulting and investment banking (including private equity and venture capital) are usually more familiar with the writing of recommendation letters, more likely to be graduates of top-tier business schools themselves, and more likely to be writing recommendations for candidates applying to the most competitive business schools.

There is some truth to the idea that "more is better." In this respect, a recommender who writes more is signaling to the reader (Adcom) that the candidate is indeed "good" because the recommender is expending more time and effort to write the recommendation.

In Julie Munzer's recommendation, all five mechanics regarding a recommendation letter are present. The recommender mentions the context in which he knows her, her rank relative to others, her accomplishments, her best personal and professional traits, and one area of perceived weakness or area of needed improvement.

In summary, if we step back and look at recommendations from a distance, we see that regardless of length, recommendations generally say two basic things: "The candidate has good technical skills and good people skills," or stated another way, "the candidate is competent and has demonstrated leadership potential."

Chapter 8

Extracurricular Presentations

You don't need to have done something really exotic or esoteric to stand out in the pool, and that's what I want applicants to understand. There are a lot of people we admit who haven't done anything out of the ordinary, but the passion they bring to the job and to other activities is something that's going to carry over to the community here and really inspire others.

—Marie Mookini, former Director of
Admissions, Stanford Business School

Introduction

When applying to business school, you will be asked in the application to chronicle your extracurricular involvement. Extracurricular involvement may be thought of as a composite of any of the following three things: (1) your extracurricular involvement while in college, (2) your community service, either during college or on the job, and (3) your awards or recognition. In the case of your awards and recognition that are of a personal nature, you may go way back, and even include things that occurred in your childhood, if significant, for example, "grade school national guitar finalist."

The generic format followed in business school applications is shown below. Actual online applications require that such information be placed in fields.

Exhibit 8.1   Generic Format for Presenting Extracurricular Activities

---

Extracurricular and Community Activities

List in reverse chronological order your major extracurricular and community activities in college and since graduation:

Dates	Activity	Office Held	Distinctions, Honors, and Awards
_____	_____	_____	_____
_____	_____	_____	_____
_____	_____	_____	_____

Leading business schools view favorably candidates who show all-roundness of character as depicted by achievement in extracurricular or community involvement. Why do schools care if you partake in such activities? There are at least four reasons for this. First, business is primarily a group-oriented activity. Business schools prefer leaders to loners. Group participation in a non-business environment mirrors teamwork within a business organization. Second, by showing a certain level of leadership or achievement in one single area of your life, it is believed that you could, by analogy, achieve a similarly high level of leadership or achievement in another area (positive transference). Your ability to excel in an extracurricular activity or endeavor is, therefore, interpreted as an indication of your ability to succeed in other areas of your life, including business. Third, you might say that schools are interested in interesting people. Think of the reader as a person who wonders whether he or she would like to spend four hours with you while stuck at the airport. Fourth, you might say that schools are interested in well-rounded individuals. This dovetails with the idea of balance. If a person has a number of outside interests (for example, sports and hobbies), these hobbies and interests act as a buffer should that person have a bad day on the job, or worse yet, suffer personal trauma.

You are encouraged to judiciously develop this area of your application. It is highly recommended, in the absence of having a solid record of extracurricular activities, that you go out and join an organization or volunteer your time to a worthy organization. It might seem opportunistic to run out and join an organization just because you are prompted to do so by the need to strengthen your business school application. On a practical note, some evidence of involvement is better than no evidence of involvement.

And who knows, you may become a volunteer junky and thank the business school application process for getting you started!

There exists a kind of trade-off between recent involvement and past involvement. A candidate who was heavily involved in college activities requires less in the way of current involvement; someone without much collegiate involvement would benefit from evidence of recent involvement. If the latter situation applies to you, consider joining a public speaking club. Two professional organizations specializing in personal development through public speaking, which are easy to join and have worldwide locations, include Dale Carnegie and Toastmasters International.

Two Tips for Presenting Extracurriculars

☞ *Tip #78: Mention why you feel an extracurricular entry is significant.*

A key to presenting your extracurricular activities is your ability to wow the reviewer with your insights and personal commentary. You should think in terms of why a special achievement is important or significant regardless of whether a school specifically asks for a reason in the application. The "story" behind an award, extracurricular collegiate activity, or community service project is often as important as the actual accomplishment itself. Do not simply state your accomplishment on a single line, place a date beside it, and expect the reader to know exactly what it means. For example, if you were a member of the Oklahoma State Swim Team, explain what it means to you, why you feel being a team member is significant, what you have learned, or perhaps why it is important to your future success in business school and perhaps your business career.

Adding summaries allows a person's record of extracurricular activities and community service to become one of a kind. In the sample presentation, per *Exhibit 8.2*, Masumi captures her personal comments under the heading of "thoughts." The next candidate, Tim (*Exhibit 8.3*), presents a general summary of each activity and then follows up with personal blurbs enclosed by quotation marks. In terms of drafting your presentation, you can choose to use either a portrait (vertical) format or a landscape (horizontal) format as depicted in the exhibits that follow. However, for the purpose of applying online, you must follow the format required by each school's application.

☞ *Tip #79: Present hobbies and interests in lieu of extracurricular activities.*

Occasionally schools will even ask you to list your hobbies and interests. The difference between a hobby and interest and an "extracurricular" is that an extracurricular takes place in a structured environment and requires a fixed commitment of time, usually on a weekly or monthly basis. *Exhibit 9.3* provides a sample presentation for one candidate's "hobbies and interests." As is the case with your extracurricular presentation, do not just list your hobbies and interests—personalize them, embellish them, and/or articulate what makes them special for you.

When hobbies and interests are not asked for, and you are struggling to find entries to "fill up" your extracurricular presentation, why not list and elaborate on a few of your hobbies and interests in lieu of extracurriculars? The entry in *Exhibit 8.2* titled Graphology was chosen to give you an idea of how to elaborate on a hobby and interest, by presenting it alongside extracurriculars in order to make your presentation look more substantial.

If you really do not have any extracurricular activities to speak of, but you chose or found it necessary to work during your free time while attending college or university, then present this additional work record to help the reviewer understand why you are not listing extracurriculars in your application. Refer to *Exhibit 8.5.*

Sample Presentations

EXHIBIT 8.2   SAMPLE PRESENTATION – EXTRACURRICULARS – MASUMI   (Page 1 of 2)

Language Student
Korean Language Student, AIFS Educational Exchange Program
Place: Yonsei University, Seoul, Korea
Date: August 20xx to June 20xx

Activity: Studied (full-time) as an exchange student and lived in Korea at Yonsei University's foreign dormitory along with 150 international students.

"My language studies have allowed me to converse in Korean which helps me do business more efficiently and to understand Korean culture. Learning to speak Korean, however, is only the tip of the iceberg. Direct communication is important, but the ability to understand what Korean people think is more critical. In becoming fluent in Korean, I started to gain a sixth sense about what Korean people were thinking before they could even speak. In business negotiations this is a real asset."

Rafting Guide
White Water Rafting Guide, Ultimate Descents
Place: Katmandu, Nepal
Dates: July 20xx to August 20xx

Activity: Acted as a local guide (35 hours per week) for tourist groups of up to 50 persons making a three-day journey down the Karnali River in Nepal; responsible for the safety of one raft of eight persons; helped organize campsites, tents, and supplies.

"Successful guide work requires not only careful preparation of supplies and improvisation (you never can plan for everything) but also good people skills to combat those few "crazies" who flout safety rules. Rafting is one of the best ways to get to know people. The challenges of the rapids helps get everyone to work as a team and overcome obstacles. (Try getting back into an overturned raft by yourself). It comes down to forcing people to have a common goal – and a great time."

EXHIBIT 8.2   SAMPLE PRESENTATION – EXTRACURRICULARS – MASUMI   (Page 2 of 2)

Volunteer
Volunteer for disabled children
Place: Melbourne, Australia
Date: January 20xx to March 20xx

Activity: Worked ten hours per week while at university; helped two disabled children: one 11-year-old orphaned boy, and one mentally challenged 9-year-old girl. Received a certificate from Collins Institute in appreciation of time and services given.

"My time spent volunteering allowed me to make some concrete contributions to deserving children and to reevaluate my own beliefs about my personal limitations. One aspect of my volunteer work struck me in an unexpected way. I remember talking to Steven, the 11-year-old orphan, about the untold opportunities he had ahead of him, when I realized that there was not a single thing that I had said to him that could not apply equally to me. Personal impediments, like handicaps, are relative."

Graphology
Handwriting analysis
Place: Melbourne, Australia
Date: Plans to start a 16-month certification course.

Activity: Learning to analyze handwriting for the purpose of revealing a person's personality and character traits.

"Graphology requires that a person be detailed minded and requires deciphering a number of details in handwritten script – writing slant, impression, size, etc. – as well as weighing the details relative to one another in order to judge, in context, what a writing sample is really telling you about the person's handwriting you're analyzing. My interest in graphology is purely avocational, but I would like to advance my learning by taking a full IGAS (International Graphoanalysis Society) course by correspondence and obtain certification."

EXHIBIT 8.3   SAMPLE PRESENTATION – EXTRACURRICULARS – TIM   (Page 1 of 2)

Activity	Location/Dates/Hours	Description & Summary
Tennis 3X Participant, National Junior Tennis Championships	While residing in Sarasota, Florida 20xx to 20xx Time: Daily practices and frequent tournament travel throughout the U.S.	Description: •Participated three straight years in U.S. National Junior Tennis Championships •Ranked number 4 in Florida and number 21 in the Eastern US Summary: Tennis taught me two important things: •Be persistent and never give up •The importance of training and conditioning "I found that the secret to winning close matches is actually the ability to reduce an important match down to its smallest components. A set is a series of games, a game is a series of points, and points are reduced to individual strokes. The closer a match becomes, the more important it is to concentrate on the smallest details and forget about winning the match."
Debate Varsity Team Member	Arizona State University Sept 20xx to May 20xx Time: 7 to 10 hours per week excluding library research and occasional weekend travel	Description: •Competed in intercollegiate NDT debate and participated in individual speaking events; won two regional debate tournaments – Pomona and West Coast Challenge. Summary: Debate taught me four things: •To organize and defend coherent arguments •To speak well under pressure •To develop excellent research skills •To formulate strategies for beating tournament competitors "My time spent in debate taught me to develop affirmative and negative briefs to support and defend the resolution at hand. I learned to be ever mindful of the importance of anticipating both sides of an argument. For every argument there is an equal and opposite argument. It is here that I gained my first real insights into an old tenet of philosophy: "Only through contrast do we have awareness.""

EXHIBIT 8.3   SAMPLE PRESENTATION – EXTRACURRICULARS – TIM   (Page 2 of 2)

Activity	Location/Dates/Hours	Description & Summary
Sigma Chi Social Fraternity Alumni Liaison	Arizona State University Sept 20xx to May 20xx Time: 15 hours per week	Description: Acted as alumni liaison and was present at all meetings to schedule events both within the fraternity and for off-campus venues. Summary: My days spent working with members of my college fraternity have helped me work within a large corporate structure. Large companies frequently have unwritten rules ("do's and don'ts") based on a tier system of bosses and workers, and the fraternity gave me a head start in understanding how to maintain favorable protocol with older and newer members alike. "My early involvement with my fraternity, however, brought me frustration. I remember wanting to take charge to organize and 'fix things.' But in the end, it was the fraternity that taught me to relax, be spontaneous, and accept chaotic circumstances. As a businessperson, I see the benefit of approaching every situation as if it can be solved – it can be fixed. But outside of business, I also see the value in learning to live naturally without always finding definitive solutions."
CPA Credential Arizona State Board of Accountancy	Phoenix, Arizona August 20xx Time: Weekly study including eight hours per week attending Daubermann Chaykin CPA Review	Description: Passed all 4 parts of the CPA exam – Audit, Law, Financial and Managerial Accounting; only 15% of candidates pass all 4 parts on their first try. Summary: Passing the CPA exam is testimony of my ability to work with large amounts of information. I followed a rigorous, systematic study schedule. I came away seeing the advantages of strong theory as the driving force behind understanding practical, on-the-job problems. "The key to passing the CPA exam was using both books and videos. In addition to mnemonics, I really like learning with the help of anecdotes whenever possible. For example, the following anecdote was useful in differentiating between gift and inheritance tax: 'Your uncle is on his death bed. He says you can have his house. Do you say yes and accept it as a gift now (gift tax) or say no and wait to inherit it and be subject to inheritance tax?'"

The presentation below is a good example of how a candidate can create "energy on paper." Angel's genuine excitement about her activities is contagious.

Exhibit 8.4   Sample Presentation – Hobbies and Interests – Angel

INTERESTS – Each activity I choose to engage in gives me a different kind of satisfaction. The common thread is comradeship. I enjoy spending time with friends and consider myself an outgoing individual. Through these activities, I make new friends and form stronger bonds with old ones.

Scuba Diving – "Serene" is the word I would use to describe the underwater experience. It is so quiet yet so full of life. It is a world so close to us yet so mysterious. Diving allows me to travel beyond land, a world three times expanded. (Certified Advanced Open Water Diver by PADI in 20xx.)

Culinary – Having lived in New York, I really enjoy fine food. I took a professional course at Peter Gump Culinary School in 20xx because I wanted to be able to tell the ingredients, herbs and spices that made those beautifully garnished dishes so good to taste. Knowing the culinary arts makes me appreciate not only the taste of my food more but also the effort behind it.

Photography – I started photography in 20xx, and received a Silver Key from Boston Globe Scholastic Award in the same year. For me, photography is a means of showing the world in a personal perspective, from the subject I pick to the way I choose to frame it. When I find people who like my work, it is like finding a friend who shares the same "view."

Dancing – I love dancing, whether it is Ballet, Jazz, Ballroom, or Folk Dance. I love it because it combines art, music, rhythm, and above all it tells stories. When I dance, I forget my nationality, my age, my sex, and totally immerse myself into the music, using my body to express all the non-spoken feelings. (Received a Commendation Award at the Schools' Dance Festival in 20xx.)

French Language – I studied French since I was 13 years old for six years, of which I received five academic awards. I had a great teacher who taught me that language is not an empty train; it comes loaded with culture. And culture is what interests me most. Through a French film and theatre class, I learned a lot of things that I identified myself with, and the most important of all is the passion for life.

Outdoor Activities – Rock climbing and trekking are two of my favorite outdoor activities. My senses are enhanced. Breathing the fresh air, feeling the sunshine upon my skin, stepping on earth and not concrete, hugging a tree or a rock, and being at awe with the power and beauty that nature inspires. (Received a Bronze Level in Expedition from the Duke of Edinburgh Award Scheme in 20xx.)

TRAVEL – I have visited, lived in, or worked in the following places:
• North America (United States, Canada, and Mexico)
• Europe (England, France, Italy, Switzerland, Denmark, Sweden, and Norway)
• Asia and other (China, Japan, Singapore, Taiwan, South Korea, Thailand, Indonesia, Malaysia, Maldives, and Australia)

Exhibit 8.5   Sample Presentation – Work in Lieu of Extracurriculars – Vivian

While at Boston University, I pursued a variety of work experiences in lieu of more in-depth involvement in extracurricular campus activities.

Dates	Employer/activity	Location	Duties	Hours/Week
Sep xx – Dec xx	Allied Irish Bank (Part of BU's London Internship Program)	London, U.K.	Credit Analyst	24 hrs/wk
Jun xx – Aug xx	Mrs Miller's Muffins	Martha's Vineyard, MA, U.S.	Waitress/cashier	30 hrs/wk
Jan xx – May xx	Smith Barney, Harris & Upham	Boston, MA, U.S.	Intern	8 hrs/wk
Sep xx – Jan xx	Pierre Deux, French lifestyle store	Boston, MA, U.S.	Salesperson	10–15 hrs/wk
Jul xx – Aug xx	Interview Magazine	New York, NY, U.S.	Editorial intern	40 hrs/wk
Feb xx – Jun xx	Houghton Mifflin Publishers	Boston, MA, U.S.	Intern	10 hrs/wk
Jun xx – Jul xx	Madame Figaro, magazine	Paris, France	Editorial intern	30 hrs/wk
Jan xx – Jan xx	Boston Magazine	Boston, MA, U.S.	Editorial intern	12 hrs/wk
Sep xx – Dec xx	Coffee Connection	Boston, MA, U.S.	Waitress/cashier	8–10 hrs/wk

Chapter 9

Interviews

Poised, confident, knowing.
—Motto of the perfectly
prepared interview candidate

Introduction

Interviews can be a potential variable in the MBA application process. Interviews are, depending on the school, either required for admissions, encouraged but not required, or simply not part of the normal admissions process. That said, virtually all top business schools in the U.S., Canada, Europe, and Asia require interviews in order for candidates to be accepted. See *Exhibit 9.4.*

Why do schools interview? The answer to this question begs two follow-up questions: "Would you hire a person on the basis of his or her résumé alone?...Would you agree to marry another person on the sole basis of biographical information?" Business school interviews are thought to be important tools to help avoid false positives and false negatives. A false positive translates to, "We accepted you (positive), but when you arrived at the school and we met you, you're not the person we thought you were." A false negative translates to, "We rejected you (negative), but you turned out to be the businessman or businesswoman of the century." Both of these mistakes are embarrassing for a business school.

In cases where the interview is required, most schools follow the policy of offering interviews to a pre-selected number of applicants based on an initial review of their application packages. Schools will then make a final review of an applicant's application package along with interview results and make final selections. To illustrate the process with some very simple numbers, a competitive business school will reject 50 percent of the applicants based on an initial review of their applications and offer interviews to the remaining 50 percent of the applicants. The school will then accept approximately half those applicants who interview, with a resulting acceptance rate hovering around 25 percent. For schools that have acceptance rates below 25 percent, these schools will either offer interviews to fewer students or accept a corresponding smaller percentage of those students who have completed interviews. By following the practice of making "initial cuts" and interviewing a limited number of students, business schools can succeed in interviewing every admitted applicant. The substantial number of applications received at top-tier business schools is a major reason behind the current popularity of this policy. Nowadays, it is a practical impossibility for schools to allow every prospective applicant a chance to interview.

Do not forget to schedule your interview well in advance (in the case that the interview is optional and you wish to interview) by contacting the admissions office of your selected schools, especially if you are working overseas. Waiting until the last minute will only help delay your application. Also, as a general strategy, try to interview first at schools that are not your first or second choice—"best schools second, lesser schools first"—as you will invariably get better at interviewing through practice. Remember to send thank-you notes or emails.

Should I interview?

Given the option, the decision to interview pivots on whether you feel you can favorably advance your overall chance for admission. If you do not feel you can present yourself as a stronger applicant compared with the application package you have sent or are sending to a school, then it may be best not to interview. In this case, sit at home and let your application do the work for you. If you feel, however, that your "paper" application is weaker than you—the person behind that application—and you can articulate this, then by all means get out and get an interview and make an additional "application" to the school you are applying to.

Where do interviews take place?

Interviews, when required or encouraged by a school, may take place on campus, off-campus, or even over the phone. Off-campus interviews are carried out by alumni of each respective business school who live and work in that city. This is also true of interviews in international locales, where the interviewer is not only an alumni of the school in question, but also a member of the local business community. Occasionally, over-the-phone interviews are given when it is not possible to schedule actual in-person interviews.

How are interviews structured?

Interviews may follow either a structured or an unstructured format. The advantage of following a structured format is that it is easier for business schools to compare interview results across a number of candidates. *Exhibit 9.1* is modeled on an actual interview evaluation form used by a top school. It requires their interviewers to fill out an interview form by rating the interviewee from 1 (low) to 5 (high) over five categories including personal presentation, maturity, motivation, self-confidence, and communication skills. Regardless of the interview format, however, the ultimate question from the perspective of an alumni interviewer is, "Would I like this person to have the same degree from the same school as I do?"

Four interviewing points that are always worth adhering to include:

- Do be on time for your interview.
- Do dress conservatively.
- Do not tell jokes (but it's okay to laugh at them).
- Do not get opinionated (remember the interviewer is always right).

Twelve Things to Do for Your Business School Interviews

What twelve things do you need to do to prepare for your business school interviews? Different schools look for different things, and individual interviewers may use different interviewing techniques. In general though, you, as an interviewee, need to have a good handle on what your career goals are, why you want an MBA, and why the particular business school you are interviewing for is a good match for you.

1. Review the school's website.
2. If you know who your interviewer will be, learn as much about them as you can.
3. Be able to "defend" every line of your résumé in the event an interviewer asks about it.
4. Be able to articulate to your career goals and career vision.
5. Be prepared to define and/or contrast the terms "leadership" and "management."
6. Be able to articulate the advantages and disadvantages of the case-study method versus the lecture method.
7. Practice with mock interview questions.
8. Relax and be yourself.
9. Answer questions in a succinct manner. Don't waffle.
10. Remember: For interview purposes, every school is your ideal school.
11. Have questions for the interviewer.
12. Send a thank-you note or email.

Exhibit 9.1   Sample Interview Evaluation Form

Confidential Interview Report   XYZ School of Business Administration

Date: _____

Name of Applicant: _____

Name of Interviewer: _____ Class of: _____

Interviewer: Please supply short answers to each of the following questions based on your interview. Grade the candidate on a 1 to 5 scale with one being the lowest and five being the highest.

1. Personal presentation and punctuality   Rank __ 5 __

Interviewee (candidate) was on time, neatly dressed, and professional in appearance.

2. Career motivation/energy/maturity   Rank __ 4 __

A lot of energy. I have the impression she gets things done quickly and with flair. Quite mature. I think she needs to think more deeply about her career development. She stumbled somewhat on the "where do you see yourself in 10 years' time?" question. Good raw ingredients. B-School should prove helpful in refining career objectives.

3. Communication skills   Rank __ 5 __
(If applicant is not a native English speaker, please comment
on spoken English ability)

Confident speaker. Clear and concise. Astute in fielding different types of questions asked. Sharp with some wit.

4. Fit with our business school   Rank __ 3 __

The candidate cited International Finance as her proposed area of academic concentration at XYZ Business School. However, she seemed a little unfamiliar with the details of our international program offering. This is probably the result of not researching adequately.

5. Other points noted including possible red flags

None cited. No red flags.

6. Overall recommendation   Rank __ 4 __

A solid candidate. I think her strong sales and marketing experience will contribute nicely to the program. Very outgoing and thoughtful. My criteria is: First, does she have the background and second, is she an interesting person. Answer: A strong "yes."

☞ *Tip #80:   Review the school's website and/or any multimedia promotional materials.*

Learn as much as you can about the school's business program you are applying to—its academic and program specialties, professors, course offerings, geographical location, internship opportunities, special programs, etc. Some of these special programs include leadership classes, new product laboratories, and overseas or independent study opportunities. In short, why is this particular business school right for you? Your interviewer will perceive you as an informed candidate. Certain information can be gleaned by contacting alumni of the university who can give you their own personal insights about their school and the business school process, which can't be obtained from the school's website. But a great deal of information can be obtained simply by reading any material put out by the school, including promotional videos. Schools spend time, money, and effort to produce materials and information that aim to be comprehensive and meaningful.

☞ *Tip #81:   If you know who any of your interviewers will be, learn as much as you can about them.*

At a minimum, find out your interviewer's nationality, what industry they work in, their job title, and where they obtained their undergraduate university degree.

☞ *Tip #82:   Practice with mock interview questions.*

One way to think about the interview is that the interview exists to find out things about yourself that are not necessarily mentioned in your application. Mock interview questions can be used to prepare you for your interviews. They are used extensively by the job placement centers and career service centers of major universities to prepare candidates for their job interviews. Most people find mock interview questions tough, which is why practice is needed in order to be able to field such questions during a regular interview situation. Remember the adage, "If you want to interview without thinking, you must think when not interviewing."

The following are examples of possible interview questions. You should practice answering these as part of a mock interview.

- ଔ Tell me something about yourself.
- ଔ Why did you choose to attend XYZ college or university?
- ଔ Why did you choose X major as the focus of your undergraduate study?
- ଔ Where do you see yourself in your career in five years from now?
- ଔ Why in particular do you like XYZ business school?
- ଔ What do you see as your three biggest accomplishments?
- ଔ What are your strengths and weaknesses?
- ଔ What do you like or dislike about your current job?
- ଔ Why did you leave a particular job?
- ଔ What do you do in your free time? What are your hobbies?
- ଔ What do think is the world's most pressing problem and why? Any solution?
- ଔ Who are your heroes, historical or contemporary?
- ଔ If you could change something about yourself, what would it be?
- ଔ On a scale of one to ten, one being technical skills and ten being people skills, how would you rate yourself?
- ଔ How would you define the word "leadership"?
- ଔ Can you give an example of leadership both on and off the job?
- ଔ Give an example of how you use people skills?

- What movies have you seen lately?
- What is your favorite book, and why?
- What magazines and/or newspaper do you read regularly?
- What other schools are you applying to?
- Do you have any questions for me (as asked by the interviewer)?
- What else would you like the admissions committee to know about you that has not been covered in your application?

If practicing by yourself, here is a good list of questions for conducting a mock interview:

- Tell me where you're working?
- Where did you go to school? What did you take? Where did you grow up?
- Where do you see yourself in 10 years time?
- As you know, leadership is a desired ingredient in the b-school application mix. Give an example of leadership both on and off the job.
- What do you see as your greatest personal strength?
- What is one thing you would like to change about yourself?
- What do you do in your free time?
- Why in particular do you like our business school?
- How has your diversity helped you? Hindered you?
- Do you have any questions for me?

☛ *Tip #83:* *Be able to "defend" every line of your résumé (or employment record) in the event that an interviewer asks about details of a previous job or project.*

Being familiar with your résumé or employment record is not the same thing as being able to defend each and every line in this document. The ability to explain each bullet point of your résumé will enable you to respond to the most specific questions about your responsibilities or accomplishments. There are two reasons why interviewers cannot always defend each "line" of their résumés: Either they are not used to giving a detailed, analytical account of their accomplishments, or they have simply forgotten about earlier jobs due to the passing of time. Should the interviewer focus on one of these previous jobs, the interviewer may struggle to recall past details. The good news is that the ability to defend each line of your résumé is a skill needed to prepare for job interviews, whether for summer internship positions or full-time positions.

Lastly, be able to explain what your work experience means to you apart from your responsibilities and accomplishments as listed on your résumé. This was covered by Tip #68 on page 141.

☛ *Tip #84:* *Articulate your career goals and your career vision.*

Do not assume that the interviewer has seen your application. In fact, due to the confidential nature of your application, schools will not release an entire application package to any interviewer, unless of course the interviewer works in the admissions office. And even if the interviewer has seen your résumé, there is no way you can be certain that he or she can remember details of your background. Bring a copy of your résumé just in case.

Try to mention early in the interview what your career objectives are, both over the long term and the short term. Ideally these can be linked to your vision statements. This is an excellent opportunity to dazzle the interviewer. Few candidates will supply vision—that idea of where their chosen industry is headed and how they will contribute or capitalize on this knowledge.

☞ *Tip #85:   Be prepared to define and/or contrast the terms "leadership" and "management."*

Although there is no single "right" answer as to what differentiates leadership from management, occasionally interviewers will ask about how you are defining these terms. One way to explain the difference is to say, "Leadership is management plus vision, where management is defined as planning, implementation, and control (feedback)." This would suffice as a textbook definition. An age-old distinction is to say that leadership is about "people" and management is about "things." Of course, the deficiency with this definition is that both management and leadership have to do with people. A slightly more sophisticated distinction is to say that leadership is about effectiveness while management is about efficiency. Effectiveness is about picking the right courses of action; efficiency is about completing tasks in the quickest, most cost-effective manner.

☞ *Tip #86:   Be able to articulate the advantages and disadvantages of the case-study method versus the lecture method.*

Most business schools use a hybrid of lecture method and the case-study method. Certain business schools, such as Harvard Business School and The University of Virginia (Darden), rely almost exclusively on the case-study method. The goal of case study work is to help you see broad themes across a number of unique business situations. Students are given a case that contains background information about a business or venture, which requires a management decision in order for the company or venture to proceed forward. The discussion pivots on the question, "What would you do?" From an academic standpoint, success in case-study work results from two complementary aptitudes: inductive and deductive thinking. Whereas the study of new and unfamiliar cases requires seeing the details before shaping them into a more complete picture—inductive thinking, the recalling of important and related previous cases, requires seeing the whole picture before engaging in details—deductive thinking. Students who have studied science, engineering, or law generally have an advantage in terms of their inductive thinking capability whereas students who have majored in political science, philosophy, or business generally have an advantage in terms of their deductive thinking capability.

The lecture method (driven by professor lectures, students questions, homework assignments, and tests) is arguably the best method for teaching skill-based subjects, particularly technical courses such as accounting, statistics, and micro-economics. The case-study method works best when you have the basics down and able to "dance" with those basic skills. Otherwise, it's a difficult proposition to try to master the basics and simultaneously apply them in a case-study setting.

☞ *Tip #87:   Relax and be yourself.*

Remember the motto of the perfectly prepared interview candidate: "Poised, confident, knowing."

☞ *Tip #88:   Answer questions in a succinct manner. Don't waffle.*

We have all experienced rambling conversationalists. We are torn between mustering the boldness to cut them off and maintaining the courteousness to let them keep speaking. We listen but secretly wonder where this is all going. We want to say "What's the point?" or "Do you mind fast-forwarding to the future?"

Just because a listener listens without blatantly interrupting you, it does not mean he or she is not annoyed. Keep your responses shorter rather than longer. Rest assured the listener will probe for more. Observe leading talk show hosts and expert interviewers including Oprah Winfrey, PBS's Charlie Rose, and the BBC's Zeinab Badawi. These interviewers have the ability to redirect and cut conversations with relative ease. And the reason each interviewer has to do this with a majority of guests is because they ramble. Most people like to say more rather than less, with nervousness being a contributing factor. Interviewers who can make a point and have the confidence and control to wait for the follow-up response will definitely chalk up points in the eyes and ears of the interviewer.

> *Tip #89: Remember: For interview purposes, every school is your ideal school.*

Each and every interviewer should believe you are sincerely interested in the school you are interviewing for. Always find reasons why a particular business school represents the ideal fit for you and don't hesitate to let your enthusiasm shine through.

> *Tip #90: Have questions for the interviewer.*

Candidate:	I am here for an interview.
Associate director:	Yes, I am the associate director of admissions and I am in charge of your interview. What would you like to tell me?
Candidate:	Yes...well...
Associate director:	Can I ask if you have any specific questions for me?
Candidate:	Well...

Toward the end of the interview, the interviewer will customarily ask, "Do you have any questions for me?" Your answer may say a lot about how prepared you are. If you reply "no," this may impact you unfavorably. Interviewing for a job and interviewing for a place at business school is analogous. As one headhunter remarked, "If a candidate has no questions for the job interviewer, then this is perhaps the worst sign of all." For your business school interviews, prepare at least one question ahead of time in the event that one does not arise in the natural course of the interview.

The following is a list of some questions you may choose to ask of the interviewer:

- Why did you choose to attend XYZ business school? How did you narrow down your choices?
- If you had to do your MBA all over again, would you choose the same MBA program?
- What aspect of doing an MBA do you feel is most helpful in your current work? In your current life endeavors?
- How does the placement office help students find summer internships and/or full-time employment opportunities?
- What were your favorite MBA courses? Least favorite courses? Favorite professors?
- What one thing did you not like about doing an MBA? What one weak point would you cite about XYZ business school? (assuming the interviewer also has an MBA degree)
- How is the social life at XYZ business school?
- How does the program teach ethics?
- What kinds of giving programs does the school sponsor?
- How strong is the alumni organization in XYZ city?
- How can I get the most out of business school?
- What advice could you give me for my future interviews?

Sometimes interview questions are used by an interviewer to confirm or deny stereotypes stemming from job functions or occupations. Without becoming preoccupied with this idea of job stereotypes, review the list, per *Exhibit 9.2*, in light of your own background, recognizing that the interviewer may choose some questions in order to test your perceived strengths and weaknesses. Your goal is to emphasize your strengths while minimizing your perceived weaknesses.

EXHIBIT 9.2   PERCEPTIONS OF THE PROFESSIONS

	Perceived Strengths	Perceived Weaknesses
1. Accountant	• Good technical, quantitative skills • Good at reality checks • Diligent	• Not dynamic; not a leader • Lacks big-picture view despite exposure to different industries
2. Administrator/ Personnel	• Organized; detail minded • Trained to take care of people; team player	• Doesn't know how to build a business • Stuck on rules and procedures
3. Artist	• Flexible mindset; creative • Unique viewpoint	• Not quantitatively skilled • Doesn't know how to manage people
4. Computer/Internet/Techno Geek	• Quantitatively skilled • Understands technology and uses hands-on approach	• Lacks people skills • Lacks big-picture view
5. Consultant	• Can think outside the box; good business sense • Articulate; smart	• Doesn't care about detail • Too theoretical; too much style at the expense of substance
6. Engineer	• Methodical; hardworking • Quantitatively and technologically skilled	• Myopic; can't see the forest for the trees • Lacks communication skills
7. Entrepreneur	• Dynamic; high energy level • Hands on; a real doer	• Chaotic; disorganized; easily bored; impatient • Averse to theory
8. Investment Banker	• Savvy; resourceful; knows the bottom line; good at networking • Facility with numbers	• Callous; uncaring; arrogant • Focuses on the "ends" at the expense of the "means"
9. Lawyer	• Smart; clever communicator • Well trained; good organizational skills	• Works alone; set in his or her ways • Not quantitatively skilled
10. Marketer/ Salesperson	• Strong personality; self-confident • Understands the consumer	• Lacks number sense • Doesn't see value in theory or book learning
11. Military	• Obeys rules; disciplined • Team player	• Commercial misfit • Too focused on executing orders; not enough vision
12. Scientist	• Intelligent; unique viewpoint • Quantitatively skilled	• Lacks business sense; inhibited • Can't "bullshit"; unwilling to develop soft skills

☞ *Tip #91: Send a thank-you note or e-mail.*

This is a courtesy, but it can also be a strategy. Say, for example, you did not feel your interview went well. The interviewer may have caught you off guard with a series of more detailed questions than you anticipated. The wording of your thank-you note could still help to influence the interviewer before he or she writes, types, or emails a response to the admissions office for inclusion in your application file.

The following short note, captioned in *Exhibit 9.3*, was written by an applicant as a follow-up to his interview. Although he thought his business school interview was so-so, he was later accepted to his first-choice business school. This letter may well have resulted in the interviewer writing a more favorable response.

EXHIBIT 9.3   SAMPLE THANK-YOU NOTE

Dear Mr Alumnus:

Thank you for taking valuable time from your busy schedule to interview me. I feel that our interview not only provided me with insightful information about XYZ business school, but also provided me with a learning experience. Your many detailed questions made me think in real depth about the particulars of my own business and the changes taking place in the marketplace. If my business school education can help me develop a similar mindset, I know it will make a striking difference in my future business endeavors.

Sincerely,
Candidate Hopeful

Interview Policies at the Leading Business Schools

EXHIBIT 9.4   INTERVIEW POLICIES AT THE WORLD'S LEADING BUSINESS SCHOOLS   (Page 1 of 3)

The schools listed below offer full-time, one- to two-year, MBA programs. EMBA programs (Executive MBA programs) are not full-time programs and are, therefore, not included. The business schools listed in this exhibit are those that are likely to appear in various business school rankings and newsworthy articles. Such a listing is subject to change and is not meant to be authoritative.

	Interview is required	Interview is not required
U.S. Business Schools:		
Berkeley (Haas)	✓	
Carnegie Mellon (Tepper)	✓	
Chicago (Booth)	✓	
Columbia University	✓	
Cornell (Johnson)	✓	
Dartmouth (Amos Tuck)	✓	
Duke (Fuqua)	✓	
Harvard Business School	✓	
MIT (Sloan)	✓	
Michigan-Ann Arbor (Ross)	✓	
New York University (Stern)	✓	
North Carolina-Chapel Hill (Kenan-Flagler)	✓	
Northwestern (Kellogg)	✓	
Pennsylvania (Wharton)	✓	
Stanford University	✓	
Texas-Austin (McCombs)	✓	
UCLA (Anderson)	✓	
Virginia (Darden)	✓	
Yale University	✓	

EXHIBIT 9.4   INTERVIEW POLICIES AT THE WORLD'S LEADING BUSINESS SCHOOLS   (Page 2 of 3)

	Interview is required	Interview is not required
Canadian Business Schools:		
McGill (Desautels)	✓	
Queen's University	✓	
Toronto (Rotman)	✓	
Western Ontario (Ivey)	✓	
York (Schulich)		✓
European Business Schools:		
Cambridge (Judge) [U.K.]	✓	
ESADE [Spain]	✓	
IE [Spain]	✓	
IESE [Spain]	✓	
IMD [Switzerland]	✓	
INSEAD [France]	✓	
London Business School [U.K.]	✓	
Oxford (Said) [U.K.]	✓	
Rotterdam SOM (Erasmus) [Netherlands]	✓	
Australian Business Schools:		
Australian Graduate School of Mgmt (AGSM)		✓
Melbourne Business School (MBS)		✓

EXHIBIT 9.4   INTERVIEW POLICIES AT THE WORLD'S LEADING BUSINESS SCHOOLS   (Page 3 of 3)

	Interview is required	Interview is not required
Asia-Pacific Business Schools:		
Asian Institute of Mgmt (AIM) [Philippines]	✓	
CEIBS [PRC]	✓	
Chinese University of Hong Kong (CUHK) [PRC]	✓	
Chulalongkorn University (Sasin) [Thailand]	✓	
HKU of Science and Technology (HKUST) [PRC]	✓	
Indian Institute of Management (IIMA) [India]	✓	
Indian School of Business (ISB) [India]	✓	
International University of Japan (lUJ) [Japan]	✓	
Nanyang Technological Univ. (NTU) [Singapore]	✓	
National Univ. of Singapore (NUS) [Singapore]	✓	
Latin and South American Business Schools:		
EAPUC [Chile]	✓	
EGADE [Mexico]		✓
INCAE [Costa Rica]	✓	
South African Business Schools:		
Cape Town (UCT)	✓	
The Wits Business School		✓

Chapter 10

Packaging Your MBA Essays and Application

A product that looks good is worth something.
—Merchant's adage

American English vs. British English—Spelling and Punctuation

☞ *Tip #92:   Proofread your essay and application materials, reviewing spelling and punctuation in light of one of the two major systems—American English or British English.*

American English and British English are the two major engines behind the evolving English language. Other English-speaking countries—most notably Canada, Australia, New Zealand, India, the Philippines, and South Africa—embrace a variant of one or both of these two major systems. Although American and British English do not differ with respect to grammar per se, each system has its own peculiarities in terms of spelling and punctuation. The purpose of the following material is to provide a snapshot of these differences.

Spelling Differences

Generally, the place of your undergraduate institution will determine whether you are writing an application and adhering to spelling and punctuation conventions consistent with American or British English. For example, if you attended Cambridge University, you'll in all likelihood be spelling words according to British English (for example, "summarise," "favour," and "travelling"). If you attended Boston University, you'll be spelling words according to American English (for example, "summarize," "favor," and "traveling"). *Exhibit 10.1* contains a summary of the major spelling differences. Try not to commingle the systems. Stick to one system to achieve consistency.

The following summary encapsulates some the nuances between British and American spelling:

The British generally double the final *-l* when adding suffices that begin with a vowel, where Americans double it only on stressed syllables. This makes sense given that American English treats *-l* the same as other final consonants, whereas British English treats it as an exception. For example, whereas Americans spell *counselor, equaling, modeling, quarreled, signaling, traveled,* and *tranquility,* the British spell *counsellor, equalling, modelling, quarrelled, signalling, travelled,* and *tranquillity.*

Certain words—*compelled, excelling, propelled,* and *rebelling*—are spelled the same on both platforms, consistent with the fact that the British double the *-l* while Americans observe the stress on the second syllable. The British also use a single *-l* before suffixes beginning with a consonant, whereas Americans use a double *-l.* Thus, the British spell *enrolment, fulfilment, instalment,* and *skilful,* Americans spell *enrollment, fulfillment, installment,* and *skillful.*

Deciding which nouns and verbs end in *-ce* or *-se* is understandably confusing. In general, nouns in British English are spelled *-ce* (for example, *defence, offence, pretence)* while nouns in American English are spelled *-se* (for example, *defense, offense, pretense).* Moreover, American and British English retain the noun-verb distinction in which the noun is spelled with *-ce* and the core verb is spelled with an *-se.* Examples include: *advice* (noun), *advise* (verb), *advising* (verb) and *device* (noun), *devise* (verb), *devising* (verb).

With respect to *licence* and *practice,* the British uphold the noun-verb distinction for both words: *licence* (noun), *license* (verb), *licensing* (verb) and *practice* (noun), *practise* (verb), *practising* (verb). Americans, however, spell *license* with an *-s* across the board: *license* (noun), *license* (verb), *licensing* (verb), although *licence* is an accepted variant spelling for the noun form. Americans further spell *practice* with a *-c* on all accounts: *practice* (noun), *practice* (verb), *practicing* (verb).

Exhibit 10.1   Spelling Differences Between American English and British English

American English		British English	
-ck	check	-que	cheque
-ed	learned	-t	learnt
-er	center, meter	-re	centre, metre
-no e	judgment, acknowledgment	-e	judgement, acknowledgement
-no st	among, amid	-st	amongst, amidst
-in	inquiry	-en	enquiry
-k	disk	-c	disc
-l	traveled, traveling	-ll	travelled, travelling
-ll	enroll, fulfillment	-l	enrol, fulfilment
-m	program	-mme	programme
-o	mold, smolder	-ou	mould, smoulder
-og	catalog	-ogue	catalogue
-or	color, favor	-our	colour, favour
-s	defense, offense	-c	defence, offence
-z	summarize, organization	-s	summarise, organisation

Punctuation Differences

The following serves to highlight some of major differences in punctuation between America English and British English.

Abbreviations

American English	British English
Mr. / Mrs. / Ms.	Mr / Mrs / Ms

Americans use a period (full stop) after salutations; the British do not.

American English	British English
Nadal vs. Federer	Nadal v. Federer

Americans use "vs." for versus; the British write "v." for versus. Note that Americans also use the abbreviation v. in legal contexts. For example, Gideon v. Wainright.

Colons

American English	British English
We found the place easily: Your directions were perfect.	We found the place easily: your directions were perfect.

Americans often capitalize the first word after a colon, if what follows is a complete sentence. The British prefer not to capitalize the first word that follows the colon, even if what follows is a full sentence.

Commas

American English	British English
She likes the sun, sand, and sea.	She likes the sun, sand and sea.

Americans use a comma before the "and" or "or" when listing a series of items. The British do not use a comma before the "and" when listing a series of items.

American English	British English
In contact sports (e.g., American football and rugby) physical strength and weight are of obvious advantage.	In contact sports (e.g. American football and rugby) physical strength and weight are of obvious advantage.

The abbreviation "i.e." stands for "that is"; the abbreviation "e.g." stands for "for example." In American English, a comma always follows the second period in each abbreviation (when the abbreviation is used in context). In British English, a comma is never used after the second period in either abbreviation.

Note that under both systems, these abbreviations are constructed with two periods, one after each letter. The following variant forms are *not* correct under either system: "eg.," or "eg." or "ie.," or "ie."

Dashes

American English	British English
The University of Bologna – the oldest university in the Western World – awarded its first degree in 1088.	The University of Bologna - the oldest university in the Western World - awarded its first degree in 1088.

The British have traditionally favored the use of a hyphen where Americans have favored the use of the dash. Discussion of the two types of dashes is found in both upcoming segments: *Using Readability Tools* and *Editing Tune-ups*.

Quotation Marks

American English	British English
Some see education as a "vessel to be filled," others see it as a "fire to be lit."	Some see education as a 'vessel to be filled', others see it as a 'fire to be lit'.

Americans use double quotation marks. The British typically use single quotation marks.

American English	British English
Our boss said, "The customer is never wrong."	Our boss said, 'The customer is never wrong.'
Or: "The customer is never wrong," our boss said.	Or: 'The customer is never wrong,' our boss said.

Periods and commas are placed inside quotation marks in American English (almost without exception). In British English, the treatment is twofold. Punctuation goes inside quotation marks if it's part of the quote itself; if not, quotation marks go on the outside. This means that in British English periods and commas go on the outside of quotation marks in all situations not involving dialogue or direct speech. However, in situations involving direct speech, periods and commas generally go inside of quotation marks because they are deemed to be part of the dialogue itself.

NOTE ⋖ Today, the practice of using single quotation marks is not ubiquitous in the United Kingdom. A number of UK-based newspapers, publishers, and media companies now follow the practice of using double quotation marks.

Using Readability Tools

☛ *Tip #93:* *Review documents for effective use of readability tools: bolds, bullets, dashes, enumeration, headings and headlines, indentation, italics, and short sentences. Look to apply edit touch-ups and check for grammatical gremlins (diction).*

Bolds

Bolds may be used to emphasize key words or phrases or aid in dividing an essay into parts. Bolding the occasional key word causes words to jump out at the reader, making the job of reading your writing easier. Underlining or capitalizing does basically the same job as bolding. Underlining is a carryover from the days of the typewriters when bolding was not an option. With the advent of word processing, bolding and italics have taken over. Be careful not to overuse bolding. You will not only dull the effect but also risk patronizing the reader. Moreover, remember an unwritten rule of publishing: Never use bolds, full caps, and underlining at the same time.

Bullets

Bullets are effective tools when paraphrasing information. They are excellent for presenting information in short phrases when formal sentences are not required. Bullets are de rigueur for use in PowerPoint® presentations or flyers. In business school presentations, bullets (either square or circular) are commonly used in résumés or employment records and/or when presenting extracurricular activities. Bullets are not, however, recommended for use in the body of your essays. It is not considered good practice in formal writing to use hyphens (-) or asterisks (*) in place of bullets.

Résumé Excerpt

*PROFESSIONAL EXPERIENCE*_____

BANK OF AMERICA, Hartord, Connecticut   20xx–present
Associate and Financial Analyst

- Analyzed branch performance and devised new strategies to improve regional market share.
- Formulated a two-year marketing plan for two branches.
- Developed new commission system and assisted in implementation.
- Devised tax saving strategies and advised principal clients on investment portfolio compositions.

Dashes

Dashes can be used to vary the rhythm of a sentence, and to present ideas with a bit of flair. The use of the dash is considered more dramatic compared with the comma.

Dartmouth College, the world's oldest business school program, awarded its first MBA degree in 1900.
or
Dartmouth College – the world's oldest business school program – awarded its first MBA degree in 1900.

194

Enumeration

Enumerations involve the numbering of points. Listing items by number is more formal but very useful for ordering data. Note that the words "first," "second," and "third" may also function in a similar manner.

Essay excerpt
Given time constraints, I see three potential scenarios that would overcome such an impasse. I would play a different role in each scenario to facilitate timely competition. The three scenarios are:

i)   We have the same solution.
ii)   We have different solutions.
iii) We have no solution at all.

Essay excerpt
I feel that my greatest long-term contributions working in this field will be measured by: (1) my ability to find ways to define and quantify, in "dollars and cents" terms, the benefits of ethics and corporate citizenship, and (2) my ability to sell corporations on the proactive benefits of these programs as a means to market the company, products and employees.

Headings and Headlines

Headings and headlines may be especially useful in writing essays for business school, as both devices help the reader obtain information very quickly. Headings and headlines are similar devices; the difference lies in their length and purpose. Headings are usually a word or two in length; headlines are usually several words in length, and may even be a line or two in length. The purpose of headings is to divide information under sections. The primary purpose of headlines is to summarize or paraphrase information, especially to capture the reader's attention. As an example, consider a short article about buying diamonds, centered on the four C's. Predictable headings would include "Color," "Clarity," "Cut," and "Carat Weight." The same article might instead employ the following headlines: "Less color, more desirable," "Fewer inclusions, greater value," "Better cut, better sparkle," and "More carats, more the merrier."

Headlines are used in the "Disney" essay written by Shannon (pages 50–52). Through the use of the six caption headings—Is your watch accurate?... The dial of creativity... The gears of teamwork... The strap of humanity... The hands of direction... The case of leadership... The complete watch—we gain a hint of what is being discussed in each section. For more on headlines, refer to Tip #49 in *Chapter 4* (page 88).

Indentation

Two basic formats may be followed when laying out a written document: "block-paragraph" format and "indented-paragraph" format. The block-paragraph format typifies the layout of the modern business letter. Each paragraph is followed by a single line space (one blank line). Paragraphs are blocked, meaning that every line aligns with the left-hand margin with no indentation. Often, paragraphs are fully justified, which means there are no "ragged edges" on the right-hand side of any paragraph.

The indented-paragraph format is the layout followed in a novel. The first line of each paragraph is indented and there is no line space used between paragraphs within a given section. Note, however, that the first line of opening paragraphs, those that begin a new section, are not indented (they are left justified).

This book employs both layout formats. The basic text follows the block-paragraph format while the sample essays included in *Chapters 3, 4,* and *5* follow the indented-story format. For the purposes of writing business school essays, the most commonly followed format for online business school essays is the block-paragraph format.

Italics

Italics, like bolds, serve similar purposes. Think of using italics to highlight certain key words, especially those of contrast or illustration. For example, words of illustration commonly include: first, second, and third. Two obvious words of contrast include "no" and "not." Be careful of overusing italics, because they are tiring on the eye and will make the page look unduly busy.

> I grew up understanding work as the act of filling a position, *not* as a career that should be strategized and planned.

Short Sentences

There is power in short sentences and you should concentrate on using a few of these in your essays. Short sentences catch the eye and stand as if "bare naked" in front of the reader.

> I like beer. Beer explains more about me than anything in the world. Who am I? I am the beer man – at least that is what many of my close friends call me.

One tip that has some merit is the "topic sentence, one-line rule." Topic sentences are effectively the first sentence of each paragraph you write. The practice of trying to keep most of your topic sentences to a single typed line in length will make it easier for the reader to grasp the main ideas in each of your paragraphs.

Avoiding Two Common Admissions Blunders

☞ *Tip #94:   Avoid two common bloopers: Forgetting to switch school names in your applications and implying that practice is the only way to "learn" about business.*

Forgetting to Switch School Names

Every year admissions officers receive application essays which read wonderfully except that they contain the names of the wrong business school. For example, a person completing a London Business School application states, "This is why I want to apply to INSEAD." Obviously, this is not going to do wonders for your application chances. This may strike you as an oversight that you would never commit yourself. However, when pressured by deadlines, and when cutting and pasting parts of one application to fit another, it becomes a lingering possibility.

Saying You Cannot Learn Business from Books

If you write in your application essays that businesspeople don't learn from books, or that entrepreneurship cannot be taught, you should stop and think about what you are saying. The admissions reviewers will likely want to respond by asking why you want to go to business school. Of course, any mature, seasoned businessperson would surely recognize that effective and efficient business practices best combine theory and practice. And this is hardly different from any other practical endeavor. No sane person would try to build a large home without a blueprint. What's a blueprint? It's the theory. And it's an integral part of the solution. Period.

If you say you cannot learn from books (notwithstanding the fact that books are not the only tool one can learn from in business school), you are belittling the role of business schools, business school administrators, and business school professors. Any business professor would acknowledge that theory is important in making optimum decisions and avoiding fundamental mistakes. Saying that books or theories don't "count" is a blooper from the admissions side of the equation.

Tips for Writing Smart

☞ *Tip #95: Avoid MBA speak.*

MBA speak is easier to illustrate than to describe. It refers to a style of writing that has a business focus, but is full of jargon and generalities. Our goal is to keep MBA speak out of our writing. When it does appear, we must edit out the jargon and turn generalities into specifics.

> I quickly learned IT best practices and took charge developing the new operating model, building the governance framework and modeling resource capacity. Our team proactively involved the partner and the client in our activities, and I contributed by ensuring the CIO and his team addressed critical action items. We built on each others ideas and leveraged individual strengths. Through collaborative teamwork, we were able to complete the project and ultimately change the client's perception.

Encountering MBA speak causes us to reread the same sentences over because the words don't stick. Our mind is hearing the words, but we are unable to grab hold of them. Conquering MBA speak requires attacking the jargon and vague terms. In the previous passage, we ask, What does "governance framework" or "modeling resource capacity" or "critical action items" really mean? If they are precise technical terms, we could place short definitions in brackets right next to each of them as they are introduced. Vague terms include "best practices," "proactively involved," "leveraging individual strengths," "collaborative teamwork," and "client's perception." We want to replace these words with words that better describe the situation. For instance, what are the exact strengths of each team member, how is teamwork collaborative, and what were those aspects of the client's perception that were changed.

☞ *Tip #96: Favor politically correct writing.*

The masculine generic refers to the sole use of the pronoun "he" or "him" when referring to situations involving both genders. Avoid using "he" when referring to both "he or she"; likewise avoid using "him" when referring to both "him or her." Avoiding the masculine generic and maintaining gender-neutral language signals to the reader that you are sensitive in acknowledging both sexes. The simple fact is that greater than 50 percent of admissions personnel are female. Thus, it is not only politically correct, but also politically astute to avoid using the masculine generic.

Consider the way the following sentences read from a female perspective:

Original: Today's chief executive must be extremely well rounded. He must not only be corporate and civic minded, but also be internationally focused and entrepreneurially spirited.

There are essentially two ways to "fix" this:

- Either write "he" or "she" (or "him" or "her"):

Today's chief executive must be extremely well rounded. <u>He</u> or <u>she</u> must not only be corporate and civic minded, but also be internationally focused and entrepreneurially spirited.

- Or put the sentence in the plural using "they" or "them":

Today's chief executives must be extremely well rounded. <u>They</u> must not only be corporate and civic minded, but also be internationally focused and entrepreneurially spirited.

☞ *Tip #97:* *Think in terms of a top-down, expository writing style. Be able to summarize any essay in just one sentence.*

MBA essay writing is expository writing. The primary purpose of expository writing is to inform or persuade, not to entertain. Writing that exists to inform or explain should follow a top-down writing style, also known as the "inverted pyramid approach." This means that we conclude at or near the top and then proceed to supply details. If the reverse occurs, inefficiency will result, because the reader will not be able to figure out the main point of our writing until the end, and details, therefore, will be much harder to remember. Perhaps the best example of the top-down approach in action is the newspaper. Newspaper writers know that if a story is too long and needs to be cut, the editor will start at the bottom and work up. Simply put, this is where the least critical information is. Contrast this with the world of entertainment (movies and TV shows), or the creative world of fiction, where we enjoy and expect surprise endings. We would never want to go to a movie and be told at the very beginning what the whole movie was about. This is not the case in the world of expository writing, of which MBA essay writing is a subset. Don't play "I've got a secret" and leave the reader guessing.

Favor the top-down approach to writing:

Most Important☺

Next Most Important

Next Most Important

Least Important

Avoid the bottom-up approach to writing:

Least Important

Next Most Important

Next Most Important

Most Important☹

☞ *Tip #98: Focus your writing. Try not to discuss too many things at one time.*

Try not to discuss too many ideas at one time. Remember that it's better to do "a lot with a little" than "a little with a lot." As a fairly reliable generalization, it is true that most MBA applicants are prone to make a similar mistake with essay content. They try to cover too many topics in a given essay, sacrificing depth of writing. Given the fact that essays have length limits, discussing too many things will inevitably lead to superficiality.

Consider the following analogy that centers on storytelling. You have just spent a year traveling around the world. You arrive back to tell a bunch of your friends all about your epic journey (over beers!). You know it's impossible to explain everything about the vast terrain you've traveled in a three hour chat-fest. So you naturally focus in on one of the most memorable, quintessential, intriguing, unexpected parts of the journey—the day you went to the market in Morocco. You build your first travel story about your trip to Morocco and everything else flows from that nexus.

The technique of focusing conversation is the same in speaking, or storytelling, as it is in writing. A laundry list of places traveled, coupled with a chronology of the means of transportation used to get from place to place is hardly interesting. It is the detail and the cohesiveness of the message that moves us as listeners or readers. Just as a great storyteller knows how to build a story around a key person, place, thing, or idea, so too does the good writer know how to narrow the focus to engender interest. This is where the seasoned writer is separated from the amateur. The seasoned writer knows of the impossible task at hand that lies in trying to cover "everything" in one page, so he or she focuses instead on one aspect of the topic at hand, and in taking a stand, a memorable writing piece is created.

☞ *Tip #99: Cherish the "for example" technique.*

The following sentences were taken from application essays written by prospective business school students. Each statement made by the candidate is matched by a response that likely exists in the mind of the reviewer immediately after reading the sentence. One of the best tips to use to avoid vagueness in your writing and help ensure that you lend adequate support for the points you are making involves placing "for example" immediately after what you write, and proceeding to add support. As a practical matter, it is up to the writer to decide whether to leave "for example" in your essay or edit it out, particularly if you are looking for more seamless connections between ideas and support points.

Candidate	Growing up in both the East and West, I have experienced both Asian and Western points of view.
Reviewer	Do you mind telling me what these Asian and Western points of view are?
Candidate	I am an energetic, loyal, creative, diligent, honest, strict, humorous, responsible, flexible, and ambitious person.
Reviewer	Do you care to develop your discussion by choosing two or three of these traits and supporting each with concrete examples?
Candidate	Although ABC Company did not flourish, I still consider my effort a success because I was able to identify strengths and weaknesses in my overall business skills.
Reviewer	What were the strengths and weaknesses you were able to identify?

Candidate	Not only did I develop important operational skills in running a business, but I experienced and witnessed the challenges that entrepreneurs face on a daily basis.
Reviewer	What were these challenges?
Candidate	I believe teamwork, along with leadership, is the key to business success because no one person can do everything or possesses the know-how and temperament to solve every problem.
Reviewer	Wonderful, but I sure hope you're going to tell me more about how know-how and temperament are key factors in the successful execution of teamwork and/or leadership.
Candidate	Sleeping in cheap hostels and on Eurorail trains, I got a much better picture of life in Europe than tourists do from the windows of a moving bus.
Reviewer	Prove it!

The following pairings address vagueness in writing. The "original" statement is vague while the "better" example incorporates detailed support.

Original	Sometimes I wish I could entertain broader points of view, especially those that directly attack my value system. It is important to hold to one's convictions and not be unduly persuaded by others.
Better	Sometimes I wish I could entertain broader points of view especially those that directly attack my value system. For example, during one of our community college fundraising brainstorming sessions, a member of the committee suggested organizing a rave party and donating profits to the school. Although I could see that an event like this would generate a sizable profit, I vetoed the idea based on two considerations: the first was its association with a rave party, which has strong drug-related connotations, and the second, the inappropriateness of not informing the donors of our purpose.
Original	My college education in Florida provided me with an incredible chance to develop myself. I pursued a rich choice of academic, athletic, professional, and social activities. At different times during my undergraduate education, I was a member of the Varsity Debate Team, Varsity Tennis Team, and a member of both a well-known professional business fraternity and a social fraternity.
Better	My college education in Florida provided me with an incredible chance to develop myself. I pursued a rich choice of academic, athletic, professional, and social activities. At different times during my undergraduate education, I was a member of the Varsity Debate Team, Varsity Tennis Team, and a member of both a well-known professional business fraternity and a social fraternity. Using just a few words to summarize what each experience taught me: from debate, I learned to be organized and think ahead; from tennis, I learned to be persistent and not give up; and from my business and social fraternities, I learned to work in groups, work with rules, and value personality.

Original

I grew up in a Maine farm family that was ethnically Scottish, but really your everyday New England household. I am thankful now for a stable, happy childhood. My parents gave me the best education and upbringing they could. They taught me to be caring and respectful of people and the environment. They taught me honesty, humility, and the silliness of pretense.

Better

I grew up in a Maine farm family that was ethnically Scottish, but really your everyday New England household. I am thankful now for a stable, happy childhood. My parents gave me the best education and upbringing they could. They took me to museums, libraries, and swimming and ballet lessons. They taught me to be caring and respectful of people and the environment. Often they taught by example. When I was four or five, my elder brothers and I accidentally lit a field on fire. Wind caught the flames, which quickly engulfed the field and came dangerously close to our house and barn. After the fire was put out, my parents felt our guilt and remorse and never mentioned it. We learned the mercy of compassion and forgiveness in addition to the foolishness of playing with matches in dry fields on windy days. My mother taught me honesty in a different way: When we stole balloons she made us return them and individually admit our guilt, apologize, and offer to pay from our birthday money (we didn't get allowances). The humility of facing that storekeeper, whose sweet disposition and insistence that we keep the balloons made my guilt worse, has stayed with me until this day.

Original

In the international publishing arena, Asia and Africa are the biggest future international market for English books, if population is used as a measure. English is arguably the most influential language in the world, based on the number of people who speak English and on its expanding international usage in business and travel.

Better

In the international publishing arena, Asia and Africa are the biggest future international market for English books, if population is used as a measure. English is arguably the most influential language in the world, based on the number of people who speak English and on its expanding international usage in business and travel. How "big" are Asia and Africa? In terms of population, three quarters of the world's people currently live in on these two continents – from the Middle East to South Africa to India to China. This population statistic is quite amazing. If we wanted to statistically sample four persons from all the world's people, here is what would likely happen. The first would be from China, the second from India, the third from Africa or from somewhere else in Asia – perhaps the Middle East, Indonesia, Japan, or eastern Russia. The last of the four persons would have to be chosen from all of North America, South America, Europe, and Australia!

Original

I was brought up out of context – an English girl in a British colony. I went through 13 years of international school and my primary school hailed students from 28 nationalities.

Better

I was brought up out of context – an English girl in a British colony. I went through 13 years of international school and my primary school hailed students from 28 nationalities. I remember when my fourth-year teacher had the brainchild of holding an "International Day". Everyone wore a traditional or national costume and brought a dish of traditional cuisine. There is no real national costume for England, so I was dressed as an English Rose, and brought Yorkshire Parkin, a sweet ginger cake as my dish.

Original   As an undergraduate, I chose to attend Oxford. Established in the 1200s, it is England's oldest university, where many ancient traditions are still alive.

Better   As an undergraduate, I chose to attend Oxford. Established in the 1200s, it is England's oldest university, where many ancient traditions are still alive. An example of one of these traditions includes the verbal promise that every undergraduate must make upon formal admission to the university. This promise includes not bringing sheep into the library for fear of damaging the books!

☞ *Tip #100:* *Your essays and other application materials are ready when they "stand still." Let the "final draft" of your essays (in print or digital format) sit for at least a couple of days. When you can no longer make substantial changes to them, your essays and application package are ready to be submitted.*

Your essays are almost certainly the last things you'll be working on to complete your application. Notwithstanding a pending deadline, you really can't finalize your essays if you're still making changes to them. If you find yourself picking up your essays, reading through them, and still registering lots of changes, then your essays are not sitting still. Even though it's frustrating to make additional changes, the good news is that you're making your writing better and better. Soon you'll find that you can't really make a major change, only little tweaks. At this point, your essays are ready.

MBA essay writing and application preparation does fall squarely within the domain of expository writing. In order to provide further explanation of Tip #100, the following excerpt is taken from *The Little Red Writing Book,* a book dedicated to helping individuals build basic expository writing skills.

Wait until your writing stands still before you call it finished.
Rare is the writer who can sit down and knock out a perfect writing draft without corrections. Most proficient writers take at least three drafts to finish short writing works. For example, you may be writing a cover letter to accompany your updated résumé. First, you write to get your ideas down on paper. Second, you edit through what you have written, add detail, make connections, and make corrections. Third, you wait 24 hours and reread, making minor changes. The longer the work, the more times this process is repeated for individual sections. The number of drafts required for an entire work depends on the length of the work and its complexity. A two-line office memo is likely to be done in a single draft because it is short and simple. A one-page poem might take a dozen drafts because it is longer and more difficult.

When is it really finished?
Making changes to your writing is annoying and grueling. But eventually, with changes made, you will likely be satisfied with what you have written and not want to add or delete anything. This is the point at which your writing is finished—your writing is "standing still."

The word "finished," when referring to writing, should really be enclosed in quotation marks because writing is never actually finished. With respect to writing done for everyday purposes, completion is an end in itself. However, for more permanent writing works such as novels, writing can be continued because it can always be improved. Even published books can be reworked and re-edited. Weeks, months, and years after a book is published, an author will inevitably contemplate changes.

Appreciate the process.

Writing is a creative process. You discover things as you force yourself to write. What is especially satisfying is turning junk writing into something worthwhile. When you put together a lengthy piece, such as a personal essay or business report, you will naturally begin by writing some areas well. Other areas you'll not be satisfied with, and those must be reworked. Let's call the parts you like "flowers" and the parts you dislike "dirt." As you focus your efforts on the "dirt," you begin to make improvements and, sometimes to your surprise, these areas become as good as or better than one or more "flowered" areas. This is extremely gratifying. You are inspired. You gain energy. You now try to improve other "dirt" areas until there are none left. Later, you go back to an original flowered area and make it even better, thus raising it up one notch from anything done before. The writing process is a never-ending process of flowers and dirt.

Most people hate reworking their writing. It is human nature. The pressure and agony of writing is one reason alcohol has been humorously dubbed "the occupational hazard of professional writers." It is not writing per se, but the rewriting and redrafting process of writing that can drive a person to drink. Worse is the reality of knowing that even before you begin to write—no matter how well you write—your writing will require revision. Fortunately, for most students and business professionals, the everyday writing process is not filled with the same emotional highs and lows as it is for a person making a living from writing.

It is a great feeling taking a look at something you wrote a long time ago, be it an old college essay, business report, personal letter, or poem, and say to yourself: "Wow, this is funny. Some of this stuff blows me away! How did I come up with it?" There is no absolute answer. Skill, luck, boldness, and naiveté are key ingredients in the writing process.

Appendixes

If you don't like your ranking, just wait five minutes until another one comes round the corner.
      —Dean of leading American business school

APPENDIX I – SUMMARY OF MBA ADMISSIONS STRATEGIES 1 TO 100

Chapter 1 – What are Schools Really Looking For?

☞ Tip #1:   Plan your attack and chart your progress.

☞ Tip #2:   Try to submit applications to all schools in a single round. If not, submit applications to "lesser" schools first.

☞ Tip #3:   Consider the need to retake the GMAT, but "protect" yourself against a lower score.

☞ Tip #4:   Decide on your career goal before asking any recommender for a recommendation and/or before undertaking any interview session.

☞ Tip #5:   If you're undecided about your career direction, a good rule of thumb is to formulate a career goal that is primarily an extension of your current career path.

☞ Tip #6:   Write a response to the optional or "blank question."

☞ Tip #7:   Build your application around a theme and think of yourself as a unique brand.

☞ Tip #8:   Reality check—boil down the whole MBA process.

☞ Tip #9:   Remember your target audience.

☞ Tip #10: In a waitlist situation, write a strategic follow-up letter to support your candidacy.

Chapter 3 – Writing The Classic MBA Essays

☞ Tip #11: Make an outline for your "who are you?" essay.

☞ Tip #12: Decide on the best writing approach for your "who are you?" essay.

☞ Tip #13: Choose between two time-tested ways to begin a "who are you?" essay—write a short introduction that engenders interest or, alternatively, begin with a summary or lead sentence.

☞ Tip #14: Break your discussion into three or four major parts.

☞ Tip #15: Choose specific, concrete examples to support what you say.

☞ Tip #16: Consider the use of quotes and anecdotes.

☞ Tip #17: Consider the appropriate use of readability tools to ensure reader friendliness.

☞ Tip #18: Make an outline for your "career goals" essay.

☞ Tip #19: Ensure that this essay contains a clear statement of your career goals and make mention of your goals in the first paragraph of your essay or, alternatively, in the first sentence of the second paragraph.

☞ Tip #20: Create goal statements.

☞ Tip #21: Create vision statements.

☞ Tip #22: Clarify your career path.

☞ Tip #23: Summarize key elements or your background—professional, educational, cultural/international, and personal experience—in the body of your "career goals" essay.

☞ Tip #24: Choose examples that are both specific and relevant.

☞ Tip #25: Test your "career goals" essay by viewing it as an argument in disguise.

☞ Tip #26: Reflect upon those classic traits that define a businessperson: purposefulness, practicality, resourcefulness, and the desire to see the commercial impact of plans and ideas.

☞ Tip #27: Mention (or imply) that an MBA is a missing link between where you are now and where you will be in the near future. You may choose to mention your proposed MBA major, in addition to your career goals, as a way to draw a link.

☞ Tip #28: Discuss academic reasons for wanting to do an MBA, including the need to gain additional knowledge and business theory en route to securing greater professional opportunities.

☞ Tip #29: Cite the need to obtain cross-functional skills. A common example is a person who has expertise in finance and who wants to study marketing (or vice-versa).

☞ Tip #30: Evaluate other reasons for wanting an MBA, including but not limited to the following: switching industries, signaling that you are ready for career-advancement opportunities, pursuing work in a different geographic region, securing a hedge against job uncertainty, obtaining an important credential, gaining future contacts, and making new friends.

☞ Tip #31: Mention that a school has a talented, diverse student body, high-caliber faculty, and/or top-notch facilities, and/or strong alumni networks.

☞ Tip #32: Cite positive comments made by current students, alumni, or industry experts that you believe capture the essence of what attracts you to a given school.

☞ Tip #33: Cite specific courses that you would like to take and/or mention the names of one or two professors whose courses you would like to enroll in.

☞ Tip #34: Mention wanting to do some independent research and cite a proposed research topic.

☞ Tip #35: Evaluate other reasons for wanting to attend a particular school, including academic specialties, joint-degree programs, exchange programs, special leadership programs, teaching methods, class size, and geographic location.

☞ Tip #36: If enrolled in a two-year program, mention what you would like to do with your summer internship opportunity.

☞ Tip #37:   Cite extracurricular organizations you may want to join while attending a given business school.

☞ Tip #38:   Think in terms of how you might contribute to the school as an alumnus or alumna.

☞ Tip #39:   Find out as much first-hand knowledge as you can about the school. For example, visit the campus, sit in on a class, talk to alumni, contact student group leaders, or engage social media.

☞ Tip #40:   Research your prospective schools. Use the various search engines—Google, Bing, Yahoo, Ask, AOL, etc.—to obtain relevant and current information. Even travel guidebooks—Lonely Planet, Fodor's, Frommer's, Insight Guides, etc.—can be useful to glean information about the city and the environment in which your chosen business school is located. Also, refer to *Appendix II: GMAT & MBA Informational Websites* for a list of dedicated websites, including chatrooms and MBA podcasts.

Chapter 4 – Writing The *Other* MBA Essays

☞ Tip #41:   Do not define your background too narrowly. Your background envelops professional and personal experiences and educational and cultural backgrounds.

☞ Tip #42:   Find your "diversity trigger."

☞ Tip #43:   Use a workable structure and signpost your discussion.

☞ Tip #44:   Be honest. Don't try to outguess the admissions committee.

☞ Tip #45:   Summarize any discussion of personal or professional weaknesses by showing how each is a strength in disguise or, at least, what you have learned as a result of struggling with your weaknesses.

☞ Tip #46:   Consider a "creative" approach in describing your strengths and weaknesses.

☞ Tip #47:   Decide on the "mix" and order of your accomplishments.

☞ Tip #48:   Ensure that your accomplishments have a "wow!" factor. Imagine yourself as a critical reader asking, "Is this accomplishment difficult?…Why is this impressive?"

☞ Tip #49:   Consider using "headlines" to summarize and highlight your accomplishment(s).

☞ Tip #50:   Do not define "leadership" too narrowly.

☞ Tip #51:   When writing team-building essays (or referencing team building within leadership or accomplishment essays), focus on those interactions among team members that require individuals to develop rapport, nurture trust, and maintain accountability.

☞ Tip #52:   Signpost your difficult situation so the reader can more easily figure out what it is. Don't wait until the end of the essay to summarize the event or situation.

☞ Tip #53:   Consider using quotes from people as a way to help the reader understand what you and/or other people actually felt.

☞ Tip #54:   In terms of describing your difficult situation and addressing what you have learned from it. A good weighting is to spend two-thirds describing and one-third writing what you've learned.

☞ Tip #55:   Consider scenario analysis.

☞ Tip #56:   Signpost your discussion using enumeration.

☞ Tip #57:   Reveal as much of your character and personal and professional strengths as possible—motivations, spiritual enlightenment, emotional balance, intellectual fervor, latent potential, insights, likes and dislikes. These essay questions invite (and expect) you to get "fancy" and take chances.

☞ Tip #58:   Make sure you directly answer the question at hand. Often, it's best to do this in the opening sentence of the essay.

Chapter 5 – Writing Optional Essays

☞ Tip #59:   Readability is of paramount importance. Try to keep each entry to the equivalent of a single page (approximately 500–600 words). You must make every effort to help the committee get through your optional questions. Think of the reviewer as skimming through your additional information.

☞ Tip #60:   View the optional area as having four possible uses. Determine which of these four uses or combination thereof will best serve you.

☞ Tip #61:   Consider using any "signature" essay as an optional essay.

Chapter 6 – Résumé and Employment Record

☞ Tip #62:   Use corporate profiles, especially if your company or organization is not well known.

☞ Tip #63:   Choose a professional format for your résumé.

☞ Tip #64:   Use bullet points to start each line of your résumé, when highlighting a description of your work experience (i.e., responsibilities and/or accomplishments). Compared with previous jobs held, use an equal or greater number of bullet points when listing your most recent job experience.

☞ Tip #65:   Use verbs and consistent verb tenses to begin each bullet point.

☞ Tip #66:   Quantify your work-related accomplishments with number-based modifiers.

☞ Tip #67:   Add "employment summaries" to explain what you found important or significant about each of your job experiences.

☞ Tip #68: Review "employment themes" as the basis of writing meaningful employment summaries.

☞ Tip #69: Anticipate strengths and weaknesses in your employment record.

Chapter 7 – Letters of Recommendation

☞ Tip #70: Decide as early as possible who your recommenders will be and prepare to "recruit" them.

☞ Tip #71: Send your résumé or employment record, along with a personal letter, to each recommender.

☞ Tip #72: Update your résumé and/or employment record and complete summaries on what you feel you have learned or what you feel is significant about your experiences. Think of your experience as divided between hard skills (quantitative skills) and soft skills (qualitative skills).

☞ Tip #73: Communicate to your recommenders where you feel your career is heading.

☞ Tip #74: If your recommender insists that you draft your own letter (or draft answers to individual recommendation questions), then ask a friend to draft the letter based on the input you have received from your recommender. Your recommender will still have to vouch for what is written in the letter.

☞ Tip #75: Think detail. Your goal is to get the recommender to write in a specific and concrete manner, typically highlighting one or two major work accomplishments, one or two distinguishing personal traits, or one or two strengths or weaknesses.

☞ Tip #76: Welcome any opportunity to involve yourself in this process. If recommenders allow you to view your recommendations before they are submitted, check to see that each letter contains sufficient supporting detail, and that all letters work as a unit to address your background in a meaningful and varied way.

☞ Tip #77: Send thank-you notes or e-mails to your recommenders.

Chapter 8 – Extracurricular Presentations

☞ Tip #78: Mention why you feel an extracurricular entry is significant.

☞ Tip #79: Present hobbies and interests in lieu of extracurricular activities.

Chapter 9 – Interviews

☞ Tip #80: Review the school's website and/or any multimedia promotional materials.

☞ Tip #81: If you know who any of your interviewers will be, learn as much as you can about them.

☞ Tip #82: Practice with mock interview questions.

☞ Tip #83: Be able to "defend" every line of your résumé (or employment record) in the event that an interviewer asks about details of a previous job or project.

☞ Tip #84: Articulate your career goals and your career vision.

☞ Tip #85: Be prepared to define and/or contrast the terms "leadership" and "management."

☞ Tip #86: Be able to articulate the advantages and disadvantages of the case-study method versus the lecture method.

☞ Tip #87: Relax and be yourself.

☞ Tip #88: Answer questions in a succinct manner. Don't waffle.

☞ Tip #89: Remember: For interview purposes, every school is your ideal school.

☞ Tip #90: Have questions for the interviewer.

☞ Tip #91: Send a thank-you note or e-mail.

Chapter 10 – Packaging Your MBA Essays and Application

☞ Tip #92: Proofread your essay and application materials, reviewing spelling and punctuation in light of one of the major systems—American English or British English.

☞ Tip #93: Review documents for effective use of readability tools: bolds, bullets, dashes, enumeration, headings and headlines, indentation, italics, and short sentences. Look to apply edit touchups and check for grammatical gremlins (diction).

☞ Tip #94: Avoid two common bloopers: Forgetting to switch school names in your applications and implying that practice is the only way to "learn" about business.

☞ Tip #95: Avoid MBA speak.

☞ Tip #96: Favor politically correct writing.

☞ Tip #97: Think in terms of a top-down, expository writing style. Be able to summarize any essay in just one sentence.

☞ Tip #98: Focus your writing. Try not to discuss too many things at one time.

☞ Tip #99: Cherish the "for example" technique.

☞ Tip #100: Your essays and other application materials are ready when they "stand still." Let the "final draft" of your essays (in print or digital format) sit for at least a couple of days. When you can no longer make any substantial changes to them, your essays and application are ready to be submitted.

APPENDIX II – GMAT & MBA INFORMATIONAL WEBSITES

Registering for the GMAT Exam

GMAC
- www.gmac.com

The GMAC (Graduate Management Admission Council) is responsible for administering the GMAT exam. The GMAT (Computer Adaptive Test) is offered on demand. For more information or to sign up online, go to gmac.com or mba.com. If you wish to call and talk with a GMAT representative, contact customer service:

Tel: (866) 505-6559 (Toll-free in the US or Canada)
Tel: (703) 668-9605
E-mail: customercare@gmail.com

MBA Fairs & Forums

Annual MBA fairs and forums are organized by the following two companies. To determine the dates, cities, and venues applicable to you, check their websites:

World MBA Tour
- www.topmba.com

The World MBA Tour is sponsored by QS and headquartered in London, England.

The MBA Tour
- www.thembatour.com

The MBA Tour is headquartered in Lexington, Massachusetts, USA.

MBA Social Networks

The following two organizations are dedicated to providing information about the GMAT exam and the MBA admissions process and have a substantial number of visitors each month.

Beat the GMAT
- www.beatthegmat.com

MBA Club
- www.mbaclub.com

GMAT Courses

The following is a non-exhaustive listing (in alphabetical order by URL) of companies specializing in on-site and/or online GMAT courses.

- www.2020prep.com [2020 Prep]

- www.800score.com [800 Score]

- www.bestgmatprep.com [GMAT 20/20]

- www.dominatethegmat.com [Dominate the GMAT]

- www.gmatninja.com [GMAT Ninja]

- www.gmatprepster.com [GMAT Prepster]

- www.gmat-zone.com [GMAT Zone]

- www.jamboreeindia.com [Jamboree]

- www.kaplan.com [Kaplan Educational Centers]

- www.latutors123.com [LA Tutors 123]

- www.magoosh.com [Magoosh]

- www.manhattaneliteprep.com [Manhattan Elite Prep]

- www.manhattanreview.com [Manhattan Review]

- www.mba-center.net [MBA Center]

- www.mbahouse.com [MBA House]

- www.mlic.net [MLIC]

- www.neworiental.org [New Oriental]

- www.oxfordseminars.ca [Oxford Seminars]

- www.perfectgmat.com [Shawn Berry GMAT Preparation]

- www.powerscore.com [Power Score]

- www.prep.com [Richardson Prep Center]

- www.primegmatprep.com [Prime GMAT Prep]

- www.princetonreview.com [The Princeton Review (TPR)]

- www.stratusprep.com [Stratus Prep]

- www.testmasters.net [TestMasters]

- www.veritasprep.com [Veritas Test Prep]

Other GMAT & MBA Websites

The following is a sampling of websites (in alphabetical order by website URL) that are dedicated to providing information about the GMAT exam and/or MBA admissions.

- www.accepted.com [Accepted]

- www.admissionsconsultants.com [Admissions Consultants]

- www.admitadvantage.com [Admit Advantage]

- www.amerasiaconsulting.com [Amerasia Consulting]

- www.aringo.com [Aringo MBA Admissions Consulting]

- www.cgsm.org [The Consortium for Graduate Study in Management]

- www.clearadmit.com [Clear Admit]

- www.essayedge.com [Essay Edge]

- www.expartus.com [Expartus]

- www.foreignmba.com [Foreign MBA]

- www.gmac.com [Graduate Management Admission Council]

- www.gmat-mba-prep.com [GMAT MBA Prep]

- www.gmattutor.com [GMAT Tutor]

- www.gradschoolroadmap.com [Grad School Road Map]

- www.ivyleagueadmission.com [Ivy League Admission]

- www.mbaadmit.com [MBA Admit]

- www.mbaexchange.com [The MBA Exchange]

- www.mbamission.com [MBA Mission]

- www.mbapodcaster.com [MBA Podcaster]

- www.mbaprepschool.com [MBA Prep School]

- www.mbastrategies.com [MBA Strategies]

- www.poetsandquants.com [Poets & Quants]

- www.squareoneprep.com [SquareOnePrep]

- www.shineadmissions.com [Shine MBA Admissions Consulting]

- www.stacyblackman.com [Stacy Blackman]

- www.thegmatcoach.com [The GMAT Coach]

Information on Business School Rankings

The following provides information about business school rankings. A number of major magazines and newspapers release annual or biannual rankings.

Title: The Best B-Schools (U.S. Schools)
Source: BusinessWeek
- www.businessweek.com

The *BusinessWeek* ranking comes out every two years (even years) in the fall.

Title: America's Best Graduate Business Schools
Source: U.S. News & World Report
- www.usnews.com

The *U.S. News & World Report* ranking comes out every year in the spring.

Title: The Top 100 Full-Time International MBA Programmes
Source: Financial Times
- www.ft.com

The *Financial Times* ranking comes out every year in the month of January.

Title: Top Full-Time International MBA Programmes
Source: The Economist
- http://www.economist.com/

The *Economist* ranking comes out in the fall of each year.

Title: Best US Business Schools
Source: Forbes
- www.forbes.com

The *Forbes* ranking comes out every year in the month of August.

Latin America Business School Rankings
Source: America Economia
- www.americaeconomia.com

The *America Economia* posts rankings on its website for Latin American business schools.

Australian Business School Rankings
Source: Australian Education Network
- www.australianuniversities.com.au

The Australian Education Network posts rankings on its website for Australian business schools.

APPENDIX III – CONTACT INFORMATION FOR THE WORLD'S LEADING BUSINESS SCHOOLS

Business schools are listed in alphabetical order within each of the following regions—U.S., Canada, Europe, Australia, Asia Pacific, Latin America, South America, and South Africa. The schools included in this appendix are compiled based on ranking information contained in various magazines and newspapers including, but not limited to, *BusinessWeek, US News & World Report,* and the *Financial Times.*

U.S. BUSINESS SCHOOLS:

Berkeley, University of California at – Haas School of Business
Berkeley, California
Tel: (510) 642-1405
- www.haas.berkeley.edu

Carnegie Mellon University – Tepper School of Business
Pittsburgh, Pennsylvania
Tel: (412) 268-2268
- www.tepper.cmu.edu

Chicago, University of – Booth School of Business
Chicago, Illinois
Tel: (773) 702-7743
- www.chicagobooth.edu

Columbia University – Columbia Business School
New York, NY
Tel: (212) 854-5553
- www.gsb.columbia.edu

Cornell University – Johnson Graduate School of Management
Ithaca, New York
Tel: (800) 847-2082 (U.S./Canada)
Tel: (607) 255-4526
- www.johnson.cornell.edu

Dartmouth College – Tuck School of Business
Hanover, New Hampshire
Tel: (603) 646-8825
- www.tuck.dartmouth.edu

Duke University – Fuqua School of Business
Durham, North Carolina
Tel: (919) 660-7705
- www.fuqua.duke.edu

Harvard Business School
Boston, Massachusetts
Tel: (617) 495-6128
- **www.hbs.edu**

Massachusetts Institute of Technology – MIT Sloan School of Management
Cambridge, Massachusetts
Tel: (617) 253-2659
- **http://mitsloan.mit.edu**

Michigan, University of – Ross School of Business
Ann Arbor, Michigan
Tel: (734) 763-5796
- **www.bus.umich.edu**

New York University – Stern School of Business
New York, New York
Tel: (212) 998-0100
- **www.stern.nyu.edu**

North Carolina at Chapel Hill, University of – Kenan-Flagler Business School
Chapel Hill, North Carolina
Tel: (919) 962-3236
- **www.kenan-flagler.unc.edu**

Northwestern University – Kellogg School of Management
Evanston, Illinois
Tel: (847) 491-3308
- **www.kellogg.northwestern.edu**

Pennsylvania, University of – Wharton School
Philadelphia, Pennsylvania
Tel: (215) 898-6183
- **www.wharton.upenn.edu**

Stanford University – Stanford Graduate School of Business
Stanford, California
Tel: (650) 723-2766
- **www.gsb.stanford.edu**

Texas at Austin, University of – McCombs School of Business
Austin, Texas
Tel: (512) 471-5893
- **www.mccombs.utexas.edu**

University of California at Los Angeles, Anderson School of Management
Los Angeles, California
Tel: (310) 825-6944
- **www.anderson.ucla.edu**

Virginia, University of – Darden Graduate School of Business Administration
Charlottesville, Virginia
Tel: (434) 924-3900
- **www.darden.virginia.edu**

Yale University – Yale School of Management
New Haven, Connecticut
Tel: (203) 432-5932
- **www.mba.yale.edu**

CANADIAN BUSINESS SCHOOLS:

McGill University – Desautels Faculty of Management
Montreal, Quebec
Tel: (514) 398-8811
- **www.mcgill.ca/desautels**

Queen's University – Queen's School of Business
Kingston, Ontario
Tel: (613) 533-2302
- **www.queensmba.com**

Toronto, University of – Rotman School of Management
Toronto, Ontario
Tel: (416) 978-3499
- **www.rotman.utoronto.ca**

Western Ontario, University of – Richard Ivey School of Business
London, Ontario
Tel: (519) 661-3212
- **www.ivey.uwo.ca**

York University – Schulich School of Business
Toronto, Ontario
Tel: (416) 736-5060
- **www.schulich.yorku.ca**

EUROPEAN BUSINESS SCHOOLS:

Cambridge, University of – Judge Business School
Cambridge, United Kingdom
Tel: 44 (0) 1223 339700
- **www.jbs.cam.ac.uk**

ESADE Business School
Barcelona, Spain
Tel: (34) 932 806 162
- **www.esade.edu**

IE Business School
Madrid, Spain
Tel: 34 915 689 600
- **www.ie.edu**

IESE Business School – University of Navarra
Barcelona, Spain
Tel: (34) 93 253 4200
- **www.iese.edu**

IMD
Lausanne, Switzerland
Tel: 41 (0) 21 618 0111
- **www.imd.ch**

INSEAD
Fountainebleau, France
Tel: 33 (0) 1 60 72 40 05
- **www.insead.edu**

London Business School
London, United Kingdom
Tel: 44 (0) 20 7000 7000
- **www.london.edu**

Oxford, University of – Said Business School
Oxford, United Kingdom
Tel: 44 (0) 1865 278804
- **www.sbs.ox.ac.uk**

Rotterdam School of Management
Rotterdam, The Netherlands
Tel: 31 10 408 22 22
- **www.rsm.nl**

AUSTRALIAN BUSINESS SCHOOLS:

Australian Graduate School of Management (AGSM)
Sydney NSW, Australia
Tel: 61 2 9931 9490
- **www.agsm.edu.au**

Melbourne Business School
Carlton, Victoria, Australia
Tel: 61 3 9349 8400
- **www.mbs.edu**

ASIA-PACIFIC BUSINESS SCHOOLS:

Asian Institute of Management (AIM)
Makati City, Philippines
Tel: (632) 8924011 to5
- **www.aim.edu**

CEIBS
Pudong, Shanghai, PRC
Tel: 86 21 2890 5555
- **www.ceibs.edu**

(The) Chinese University of Hong Kong (CUMBA)
Shatin, New Territories, Hong Kong, PRC
Tel: (852) 2609-7783
- **www.cuhk.edu.hk**

Chulalongkorn University – Sasin Graduate Institute of Business Administration
Bangkok, Thailand
Tel: 66 2 (0) 2218-3856-7
- **www.sasin.edu**

(The) Hong Kong University of Science and Technology – HKUST Business School
Clear Water Bay, Kowloon, Hong Kong, PRC
Tel: (852) 2358-7539
- **www.mba.ust.hk**

Indian Institute of Management Ahmedabad (IIMA)
Ahmedabad, India
Tel: 91 79 2630 8357
- **www.iimahd.ernet.in**

Indian School of Business (ISB)
Hyderabad, India
Tel: 91 40 2318 7474
- **www.isb.edu**

International University of Japan – Graduate School of International Management (GSIM)
Niigata, Japan
Tel: 81 (0) 25-779-1106
- **gsim.iuj.ac.jp**

Nanyang Technological University – Nanyang Business School (NTU)
Singapore
Tel: (65) 67911744
- **www.ntu.edu.sg**

National University of Singapore – NUS Business School
Singapore
Tel: (65) 6516-2068
■ **www.bschool.nus.edu.sg**

LATIN AMERICAN & SOUTH AMERICAN BUSINESS SCHOOLS:

UC Management School
Santiago, Chile
Tel: 56-2 2354-2238
■ **www.mbauc.cl**

EGADE – TEC de Monterrey
Garcia, NL, Mexico
Tel: 52 81 8625 6030
■ **www.egade.itesm.mx**

INCAE Business School
Alajuela, Costa Rica
Tel: 506 2433 9908
■ **www.incae.ac.cr**

SOUTH AFRICAN BUSINESS SCHOOLS:

Cape Town, University of – UCT Graduate School of Business
Cape Town, South Africa
Tel: 27 (0) 21-406 1338/9
■ **www.gsb.uct.ac.za**

Wits Business School
Johannesburg, South Africa
Tel: 27 11 717-3600
■ **www.wbs.ac.za**

APPENDIX IV – EVALUATING YOUR MBA PROGRAMS

The following categories may be useful when evaluating the MBA schools/programs of your choice. You may want to assign ratings of 1 to 5, with 1 being the highest score and 5 being the lowest score.

Major categories	School A	School B	School C	School D	School E
Ranking or reputation					
Curriculum and academic specialties					
Teaching method and class size					
Location and living environment					
Job placement and employment opportunities					
Alumni and networks					
Financial cost					
Total Score					

APPENDIX V — FLOWCHARTING THE MBA ADMISSIONS PROCESS

The following flowchart typifies the workings of the admissions process at many leading business schools. It assumes that interviews are required and that a select group of candidates are invited to interview after an initial review of their application files.

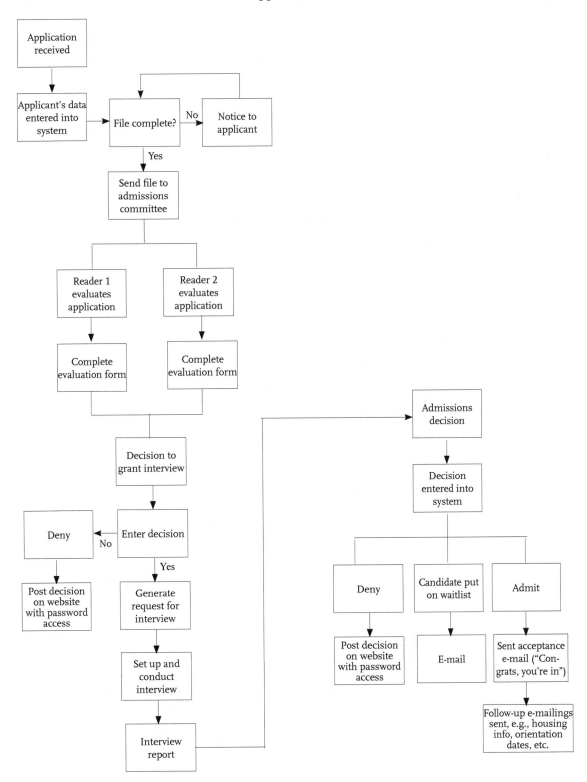

Form A: The following chart is useful for keeping track of the application deadlines of the schools your are applying to.

Business Schools	Rank	App down-loaded	Fin. aid. info	1st round	Reply	2nd round	Reply	3rd round	Reply	Deposit req'd by

Form B: The following chart is useful for keeping track of those items necessary to complete your application: transcripts, GMAT scores, letters of recommendation, application essays, and interviews.

Business Schools	Transcripts sent	GMAT taken	GMAT sent	1st recom.	Rec'd (or sent)	2nd recom.	Rec'd (or sent)	3rd recom.	Rec'd (or sent)	Essays written	Interviews scheduled	Thank you sent

APPENDIX VII – HOW TO GET THE MOST OUT OF YOUR BUSINESS SCHOOL EXPERIENCE

Computer Skills

There are three computer application skills that a prospective MBA student needs prior to attending business school. These include word-processing, spreadsheet, and graphic capabilities. The vast majority of candidates possess proficiency with MS Word® (word-processing application), but many are rusty with respect to the other two capabilities. Mastering the basics of a spreadsheet application is a must, and Microsoft Excel® is the de facto standard. For example, given the actual and projected hypothetical profit scenario below, a prospective student should be able to type these figures onto an Excel spreadsheet and create a basic line graph, or a pie chart, or bar chart, showing revenues, expenses, and profits.

Periods Revenues Expenses	1 875 500	2 1,050 550	3 1,260 605	4 1,512 665	5 1,814 732
Profits ('000)	375	500	655	847	1082

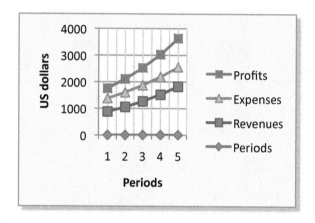 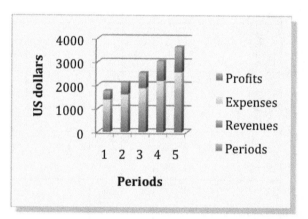

Mastering the basics of a graphic application, such as Microsoft PowerPoint®, is very helpful. You may need to do a slide presentation and/or need to include clip art in your reports. Proficiency with a more advanced graphics program such as Photoshop or Illustrator is a plus, but not a necessity. A great way to bring yourself up to speed with any computer application program is by tutoring using online videos. Lynda.com is an excellent company that can be joined with a nominal, monthly pay-as-you-go fee.

Quantitative Skills

The ability to familiarize yourself with key concepts covered in the core first-year courses can greatly assist you in getting a jump and not falling behind in your coursework during the first-year of business school. Most first-year courses include coverage of five or six basic skills areas. Four of these courses are quantitative in nature and include accounting, economics, finance, and statistics; two other core course, namely marketing and management & organizational behavior, are qualitative in nature. A splendid book that gives you insight into all major areas in overview fashion is *The 10-Day MBA*, 3rd ed., Silbiger, 2005, ISBN 978-0060799-07-6. Also, Khan Academy (khanacademy.org) is worth checking out for short videos on basic academic skill-building areas.

Books in the *Barron's Business Review Series* are highly recommended if you can stomach a more in-depth review. These excellent books cover each of the previously mentioned skill areas:

➢ *Accounting* – Eisen, 5th ed., 2007, ISBN 978-0-764135-47-7
➢ *Economics* – Wessels, 4th ed., 2006, ISBN 978-0-764134-19-7
➢ *Finance* – Groppelli and Nikbakht, 5th ed., 2006, ISBN 978-0-764134-20-3
➢ *Business Statistics* – Downing and Clark, 4th ed., 2003, ISBN 978-0764119-83-5
➢ *Marketing* – Sandhusen, 4th ed., 2008, ISBN 978-0-764139-32-1
➢ *Management* – Montana and Charnov, 4th ed., 2008, ISBN 978-0-764139-31-4

Barron's also publishes another series called *Barron's Business Library Series,* which provides in-depth coverage of more specific topics such as purchasing, human resources, publicity, and public relations, but books in this series are more useful as supplementary reading while on the job rather than for preparation prior to attending business school. For more information in locating these books, try www.barons.com.

Writing and Speaking Skills

Business school is not a haven for the vocally timid. Class participation in a given course may constitute 50 percent of your final grade. Your fellow classmates will compete with you for "air time." Professors may randomly call on you, especially if you are not contributing to in-class discussion. It is hard to hide behind the large name card placed conspicuously in front of you. Not only must you have courage, but you must also have clear thoughts. You should endeavor to come across as confident and coherent. Therefore, before starting business school make sure you can stand before a room of say 30 to 50 people and give a speech without trembling. Two organizations that specialize in building personal effectiveness through improved public speaking are Dale Carnegie (www.dalecarnegie.com) and Toastmasters International (www.toastmasters.org). If applicable, plan to take a Dale Carnegie public speaking course before attending business school, or join Toastmasters, even if it is only for a few months before attending business school.

Perhaps the best all-round tip for ease in presenting information involves using enumerations. Take your topic, break it into three to five points. For example, "The purpose of this report, essay, or speech is to summarize several reasons why Plan ABC makes sense. First…, second…, third…, moreover…, lastly…"

People and Networking Skills

It has been said that there are three reasons why a person goes to business school: the knowledge, the credentials, and the contacts. Many of your classmates will achieve substantial positions in business within 10 to 15 years from the time of leaving business school. Your ability to make friends and keep in touch will pay rich dividends—tangible and intangible. Certain classmates will remain your best friends, but remembering personal information about many others will not be easy.

Because of the strange, interconnected nature of life and business, you may have future need to contact several of your business school classmates, despite having totally different career paths and personal outlooks at the time of business school. Your ability to remember personal details will help cement future ties. Any former classmate will be flattered if you remember things so long afterward, and they will certainly believe that you are a sharp individual to be able to do so. To this end, consider using the notes feature of your e-mail program to maintain updated notes on each person's hobbies, alma maters, hometowns, birthdays, names of siblings, children, or parents, and any other information you deem interesting or relevant.

Job Search Skills

In reality, a lot of people go to business school not knowing what they really want to do with their careers (even if they claim to know so in their applications). However, the better you know what you want to do with your career, the more you can get out of your business school experience. For example, if you're pretty certain that you want to work in venture capital, you have the advantage of joining relevant clubs, meeting other classmates with similar interests, securing relevant internships, tailoring academic course offerings, and doing independent research in this area. Make a point to find out what you really want to do; keep at it. Ask classmates who may have already worked in your desired field. They will give you an insider's view, complementary but different from the one that you will read about in recruitment brochures, or from the viewpoint that a recruiter will present in a less than completely candid sales pitch.

One worthwhile and often overlooked resource within any career services office is personality testing. Most tests are offered free of charge through the career services centers of major business schools. For example, the Myers-Briggs Type Indicator test (MBTI) is well known. This test comes complete with a written narrative based on the results of your test. With the help of a trained career services administrator, the results of a number of other such tests can indicate whether you are made for work in the world of banking or consultancy, public relations, or government.

Controlling Stress

Most stress in business school is precipitated by heavy workloads, especially during the first year. Here organization and prioritization is key. One source of stress is not finding time to do things you enjoy, be they sports, hobbies, outside reading, etc. Putting time into your courses and endless group meetings will leave you with little time for yourself. Get creative. Given that there are some 100 waking hours in a week, carve out some time for yourself without feeling guilty. If you don't, things can become a treadmill. You will most certainly feel guilty not keeping in touch with many of your friends. Tell your friends at the outset not to expect long e-mail replies. But do plan on making a semi-annual newsletter, to be sent out in December and June of each year.

Falling behind in coursework is another major source of stress. Although everyone must set his or her own schedule, a good tip is to make a systematic review of your notes every Saturday morning. This will combat cramming. Another tip, used by a number of the very best students, entails making a course summary. Pretend that you are going to either teach the course next time or give your outline to another student. Your ability to try to summarize the course contents will force you to come to grips with major topics. Many students end up doing this anyway when making their own cheat sheets for cracking case-study problems. But this same principle can be applied to coursework. There is also a lot of satisfaction, confidence, and ownership gained from knowing that you completed a set of ten-page course summaries for each of your courses. Put it in your own handwriting to make it personal.

Be Positive

Concentrate on picking good people for your study groups. Group work may constitute 50 percent of your total study time and 50 percent of your grade in some courses. You want to get off to a good start. Do more than your fair share of work and be cheerful and you will get a reputation as a good person to work with.

A great way to keep your attitude in check is to pen a "gratitude journal." Each day, write down just a few things that you are grateful for or appreciative of. This process acts as a fountain of positive energy and helps to "reset our perspective." It's a reminder of how lucky we are.

ON A PERSONAL NOTE

Ruminations of a veteran GMAT test-prep instructor and MBA admissions coach.

It is perhaps strange to address the questions "Should I pursue an MBA?...Is an MBA worth it?" at any place other than the beginning of the book. However, for those who insist on going to a top business school, these questions have already been answered or are a mere afterthought. Although the answer to this question is a personal one, I believe there are many "incomplete" ways to analyze the question, so much so, that I have chosen to write a short response to address it.

The most incomplete answer comes from analyzing the question only from a quantitative perspective. This involves evaluating the cost of a business program including tuition, books, housing, food, and other living and incidental expenses, and adding to this the opportunity cost of forgone wages (including two years' salary and benefits), and comparing all of this to the increase in salary you expect to receive post-MBA. The flaw in this approach is that it is terribly difficult to project the expected revenue to be received in your future working years. For example, a single idea gained during your MBA program could be, for you, a million-dollar idea; another idea could save you hundreds of thousands of dollars when making an important future business or personal decision.

The biggest flaw, of course, is that such an approach ignores qualitative considerations. These considerations include an increased feeling of self-confidence, sense of accomplishment, and personal fulfillment gained from completing your graduate education. Other qualitative reasons include making new friends, gaining new contacts, pursuing an enriching academic experience, bolstering problem-solving skills, honing personal skills, and improving your ability to think and reason. As one MBA graduate remarked, "It's two years of learning to think outside the box."

A common deficiency in thinking about an MBA purely in quantitative terms is the inability to account for the "people factor." When facing a business or personal problem or opportunity, there is a certain strength in knowing you can email, call, or simply remember the personas, characteristics, and idiosyncrasies of one or more business school classmates. What would they do in this situation? In the words of another business school graduate, "I never feel isolated because I have a reservoir to draw upon."

There is some truth to the brash remark: "If you have to ask whether it is worth doing an MBA, you're not the right person to do one." However, one way to answer the questions "Should I pursue an MBA/Is an MBA worth it?" is to view the MBA in the broader light of all graduate degrees, in which the MBA is neither greater nor lesser than any other graduate degree. Here, the belief is, "A person should pursue an advanced education credential, be it business, law, medicine, engineering, international relations, or the sciences because obtaining an advanced education credential is a great way to finish one's formal education." Stated from an opposite angle, "Pursue an MBA unless you have a good reason not to." Some good reasons for not doing so would include: (1) "I have a great job and to give it up to go to business school means risking not getting it back again," (2) "I have my own growing business and to leave to go to business school would entail the risk of losing it, even if placed in the hands of a capable manager while I am at business school," and (3) "I have a family and leaving to go to business school would cause too much disruption and strain."

Perhaps the acid test for the questions "Should I do an MBA/Is an MBA worth it?" arises when asking business school graduates whether they would make the same decision again. Interestingly, a number of law school graduates answer no to the question of whether they would pursue a law degree (or a legal career) if they had to do things over. However, extremely rare is the MBA graduate who says, "Boy, that was a dumb decision, I wouldn't do that again." Along the way you may meet a few arguably cynical MBA students or graduates who will tell you that an MBA is just a two-year job search. But even these graduates—throwing all other possible positive qualitative and quantitative factors to the wind—will answer yes to the question at hand, if for no other reason than the "credential factor."

Praise for *Getting into Business School : 100 Proven Admissions Strategies to Get You Accepted at the MBA Program of Your Choice*

"A wonderful tool which can help you fully understand the process, and make a difference."

Linda B. Meehan, former Assistant Dean and Executive Director of Admissions and Financial Aid Columbia Business School

"Other MBA application books provide 'guidance,' but Royal's manual gives you hands-on, usable knowledge to really get the job done right. It removes the intentional mystery and confusion of this very important first step to getting one of the most valuable professional degrees."

Steve Silbiger, Author of *The Ten-Day MBA: A Step-By Step Guide to Mastering The Skills Taught in America's Top Business Schools;* Darden Business School graduate, University of Virginia

"A great book for students looking for help in applying to MBA programs. I've referred instructors to material contained in several books over the years, including Kaplan's, The Princeton Review's, and others. *Getting into Business School* (and its prepublication print editions) is the only book that was consistently used by teachers and praised by students. A typical comment from our students was: 'Can I keep it?'"

David E. Cleland
Former International Vice President for both Kaplan Educational Centers and The Princeton Review

"Applying to a top business school is hard work. My first application package took me around 40 hours to complete. It gets easier after that but the most important thing is to develop the ability to constantly boil everything down, especially when writing the application essays. Brandon's approach helps you combine who you are and what you've done with where you're going in order to present a complete and distinguished picture of yourself."

Jeremy Cheung
Graduate, Harvard Business School

"It is said, 'You cannot judge a book by its cover'; however, people still tend to do so. This is also true when it comes to reading MBA applications. The reader relies heavily on what the applicant reveals in writing. Admissions committee members will read your application like a book, so why not make it the best one possible? You only have one shot at making a good first impression. The best-read applications are those with hours of well-thought-out planning and preparation behind them. Brandon Royal's book, *Getting into Business School,* will be instrumental in assisting you to get it right the first time."

Joann Pitteloud, former MBA Director of Admissions
IMD/Switzerland

"Every candidate has gone to university, has at least a couple of years of work experience, and has a certain amount of life experience. One part of the application process involves simply restating your academic, professional, and personal accomplishments. Another part is about how to interpret these experiences in a meaningful way. This is the trickier but more interesting and rewarding part of applying to business school. Read this book and gain insights into how other candidates have done it."

Brian Li, GM of Wealth Management, Bank of East Asia
Stanford Business School graduate

"Mr. Royal clearly knows how to combine academic expectations with real-world competence. Even if the applicant went no further in his or her application, the advice on how to assemble and present appropriate information is a life skill well worth acquiring. Anyone considering an MBA at some point in their careers would be well advised to use this book; not only will it improve their application chances, it provides a model of effective communication that is worth emulating."

Dr. Ailsa Stewart-Smith, Director of Executive MBA
University of Cape Town, South Africa

"This book is a fantastic resource for any person applying to business schools. Brandon's publication helped me to organize my application and refine my strategy to enhance my chances of being admitted to a top-choice business school. I would recommend this book to be read and reread before and during the application process."

Jesse Friedlander, JP Morgan, Equity Research
MA/MBA graduate, SAIS/Wharton

"Getting into a top MBA program is more competitive than ever. Show your leadership skills early and get this book."

Tom Fischgrund, Author, *The Insider's Guide to the Top Ten Business Schools*; former Senior Marketing Manager, Coca-Cola Company; Harvard Business School graduate

"There are no guarantees when it comes to MBA admissions. However, as in the business world, effective communicators always come out ahead. Successful applicants know how to turn even a generic B-school application into a showcase of their own talents and accomplishments. Mr. Royal's publication is valuable in that it shows applicants how to do just that."

Yukiko Asada, Director of Admissions, Graduate School of International Management
International University of Japan

"Brandon Royal's excellent, comprehensive and easy-to-use guidebook is one of the few resources which addresses the needs of candidates applying to business school in Europe and Asia."

Mary Clark, former Director of Marketing and Admissions
Global Executive MBA, IESE Business School

INDEX

Page numbers in *italics* indicate exhibits.

ABOUT THE AUTHOR

Brandon Royal (CPA, MBA) is an award-winning educational author and a graduate of the University of Chicago's Booth School of Business. This book represents, in part, his distilled experience gained from having developed and taught MBA Admissions Courses for Kaplan Educational Centers in Hong Kong and from having conducted hundreds of hours of individual tutoring sessions that helped scores of applicants build superior applications and achieve acceptance at the world's leading business schools.

To contact the author:
E-mail: contact@brandonroyal.com
Website: www.brandonroyal.com

Nonfiction Books by Brandon Royal

The Little Blue Reasoning Book:
  50 Powerful Principles for Clear and Effective Thinking

The Little Red Writing Book:
  20 Powerful Principles for Clear and Effective Writing

The Little Gold Grammar Book:
  40 Powerful Rules for Clear and Correct Writing

The Little Red Writing Book Deluxe Edition
  Two Winning Books in One, Writing plus Grammar

The Little Green Math Book:
  30 Powerful Principles for Building Math and Numeracy Skills

The Little Purple Probability Book:
  Master the Thinking Skills to Succeed in Basic Probability

Getting into Business School:
  100 Proven Admissions Strategies to Get You Accepted at the MBA Program of Your Choice

Ace the GMAT:
  Master the GMAT in 40 Days

Ace the GMAT Math:
  Master GMAT Math in 20 Days (eBook only)

Ace the GMAT Verbal:
  Master GMAT Verbal in 20 Days (eBook only)

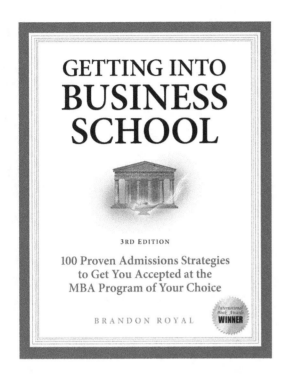

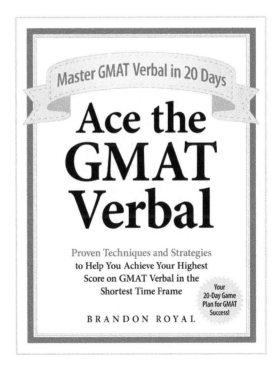

CPSIA information can be obtained
at www.ICGtesting.com
Printed in the USA
BVHW010141271218
536315BV00029B/708/P

9 781897 393802